PRAEGER LIBRARY OF U.S. GOVERNMENT DEPARTMENTS
AND AGENCIES

The United States Air Force

PRAEGER LIBRARY OF U.S. GOVERNMENT DEPARTMENTS
AND AGENCIES

Consulting Editors

ERNEST S. GRIFFITH

Former Dean and Professor Emeritus, International Service School, American University; Former Director, Legislative Reference Service, Library of Congress; Author, *The American System of Government* and *The American Government in Action*

HUGH LANGDON ELSBREE

Former Chairman, Department of Political Science, Dartmouth College; Former Managing Editor, *American Political Science Review*; Former Director, Legislative Reference Service, Library of Congress

The
United States
Air Force

Monro MacCloskey

BRIGADIER GENERAL, USAF (RET.)

FREDERICK A. PRAEGER, *Publishers*

New York · Washington · London

FREDERICK A. PRAEGER, PUBLISHERS
111 Fourth Avenue, New York, N.Y. 10003, U.S.A.
77–79 Charlotte Street, London W.1, England

Published in the United States of America in 1967
by Frederick A. Praeger, Inc., Publishers

Library of Congress Catalog Card Number: 67-20488

Printed in the United States of America

Acknowledgments

I wish to thank here the many Air Force people who have, through the provision of research materials, helped me with the preparation of the book.

In particular, I wish to express my appreciation to Lieutenant Colonel Walter S. Vancleave, USAF, for his chapter on current Air Force doctrinal thinking, prepared especially for this book, and to Dr. Robert F. Futrell, Professor of Military History, Aerospace Studies Institute, Air University, for his chapter on the Air Forces in World War II. The writings of J. S. Butz, Jr., Technical Editor of *Air Force/Space Digest,* on future aerospace technological developments were of great value to me in the preparation of the chapter on the aerospace outlook.

Special thanks are due my wife, Betty, and Miss Jacqueline Davis for their labors in the production of the manuscript, and William Leavitt, Senior Editor for Science and Education, *Air Force/Space Digest,* for his assistance with the final draft.

In the writing of a book on so vast a subject as the U.S. Air Force, there is, unavoidably, especially in an era of rapid change, the chance of occasional factual error. I have made every effort to ensure the accuracy of historical and other statements but assume responsibility for any errors of fact that may appear.

MONRO MACCLOSKEY

Washington, D.C.

v

Preface

The United States Air Force has come a long way since the gas-balloon days when it was an insignificant section of the Army. Air Force career people have seen aerospace power transform many traditional military concepts. During its brief history, aviation has developed into a major force for Free World security, economic strength, and technological progress.

The USAF today organizes, trains, and equips units to support national policy at any required level of operation. This incredibly complex job is accomplished through the teamwork of Headquarters USAF, the sixteen major Air Force Commands, and the four separate USAF operating agencies.

In 1966, the Air Force had a strength of more than 800,000 officers, enlisted men, and cadets, with which to provide the nation's primary capabilities to maintain general aerospace supremacy and deter aggression, to defend the United States against aerospace attack, control vital aerospace areas, and conduct strategic aerospace warfare against selected targets if deterrence fails. The Air Force also provides the primary capabilities to furnish close combat support for the ground forces; furnish logistical support including airlift, support, and resupply of airborne operations; perform aerial photography and tactical reconnaissance missions; meet the major space requirements of the Department of Defense; and provide research, development, testing, and engineering of satellites, boosters, space probes, and associated systems necessary to support specific projects and programs arising under basic agreements between the Department of Defense and the National Aeronautics and Space Administration. In addition, it trains forces to interdict enemy sea power through air operations, conduct antisubmarine warfare and protect shipping, and conduct aerial mine-laying operations.

Many members of the Air Force are inclined to shut their eyes to their own military tradition, perhaps because it is such a short one in terms of years. But the Air Force heritage of achievement is great. Thousands of members of the nation's military aerospace force can look back to experience in World War II, when the Army Air Forces provided the major strike, air defense, air transport, air reconnaissance, and close air support for the Allied forces. Those years of AAF specialization led to the establishment, in 1947, of the United States Air Force as a separate service with prime responsibility for offensive and defensive air operations for the United States.

Later, in Korea, the tremendous effectiveness of the USAF in many other roles was overshadowed, at the time, by dramatic air victories over the Communist MiG's. The official histories tell a story more impressive than the headlines of that period, not only of gaining and maintaining air superiority to protect U.S. surface forces, but of vast numbers of enemy soldiers and their equipment destroyed from the air.

Today, with public attention focused on Southeast Asia, we can lose sight of the fact that the Soviet Union's formidable strategic aerospace force of bombers and missiles and its strategic submarine force remain the primary threat to the United States and its Allies. The most critical responsibility of the USAF is the prevention of nuclear war, and the only practical means is through the counter-threat of superior strategic forces. Thus, Air Force strategic deterrence continues to be the cornerstone of our national defense.

> —*Brigadier General* MONRO MACCLOSKEY
> *USAF* (*Ret.*)

Washington, D.C.

Contents

List of Charts

A section of photographs follows page 52.

I

Origin and Development of Air Power, 1861-1939

The Civil War

It began with balloons.

The use of ungainly gas bags for military purposes in the early period of the Civil War marked the beginning of military aviation in the United States. Balloons already had a military history. The French had used them as early as the French Revolution. The first military air organization, the French Aerostatic Corps, was created in 1794. The interest of the French dated from October 15, 1783, when Jean de Rozier made the first successful flight in a hot-air balloon. Following this significant ascension, Benjamin Franklin wrote, on November 21, that balloons could be used by military forces for several purposes "such as elevating an engineer to take a view of an enemy's army, works, etc., conveying intelligence into or out of a besieged town, giving signals to distant places, or the like." The French army apparently shared Franklin's views. Their military balloons were used primarily for reconnaissance.

By the time the Civil War began, balloons and aeronauts had become known and accepted in America, and it was no surprise that the best known balloonists, including New Englander James Allen, John Wise of Pennsylvania, John La Mountain, and Thaddeus S. C. Lowe, volunteered their services.

On April 19, 1861, just four days after President Lincoln made his first call for troops, Allen and a balloonist friend, Dr. William

H. Helme, a dentist, offered their services, which were accepted. Both were members of the Rhode Island 1st Regiment. They arrived in Washington with two balloons and, on June 9, after inflating one balloon from a Washington gas main, made the Army's first captive balloon ascent.

Allen intended to use his balloons to observe Confederate troops reportedly moving on Washington from the west. In preparation for the Manassas campaign, General Irwin McDowell had ordered Allen to the front to report on Confederate troop movements. Unfortunately, the fabric of one balloon ruptured so badly, as it was being inflated at a gas plant in Alexandria, that it could not be repaired. The second balloon was destroyed when it was blown into a telegraph pole while being towed to a launching site in Falls Church, Virginia.

Discouraged by the loss of his balloons, Allen left the Army. However, he resumed military duty in March, 1862, and later became head of the Balloon Corps—a post he held until the Corps was dissolved in June, 1863.

John Wise, who had responded to the President's call for volunteers, was contacted on June 12, 1861, by Major Hartman Bache, acting chief of the Topographic Engineers. Wise was asked for an estimate of the cost and time needed to furnish a 20,000-cubic-foot capacity balloon constructed of raw silk. Wise estimated a cost of $850 and two weeks' delivery time. The construction of the balloon was ordered, and, on July 1, 1861, Wise was inducted into the federal service as a military balloonist.

Arriving in Washington on July 17, Wise was instructed to inflate the Army's first balloon and report to General McDowell's headquarters prepared to make observations by daybreak of July 20 at the battle of Manassas. It was not until early on the morning of the 21st, however, that the balloon was inflated. The ground crew walked the balloon up Pennsylvania Avenue to Georgetown, up the Chesapeake and Ohio Canal and across the Potomac River to Fairfax Road, where the group met Major Albert J. Myer, Chief Signal Officer. Myer was responsible for conducting the balloon party to the front.

Already one day late and impatient to reach the battle area, Myer ordered the balloon to be tied to a supply wagon. As soon as it was safely fastened, he directed the driver to whip his horse into a gallop. Lurching from side to side, the balloon was badly torn and deflated. Tragic as the mishap seemed at the time, if the launching site had been reached as planned, the balloon and ground party would probably have been captured by the Confederates.

Returning immediately to Washington, Wise repaired his balloon. On July 24, he made several ascensions from Arlington, Virginia, in the course of which he was able to observe and report Confederate field artillery guns being placed in position and Confederate scouting parties probing Union Army positions. General McDowell, encouraged by this valuable information, ordered Wise to a position at Ball's Crossroads (now McLean), Virginia. As the inflated balloon was being towed down narrow winding roads to the new location, it was blown against telegraph wires, which cut the tow ropes. The balloon floated off toward Confederate lines. To prevent its capture, it was shot down by Union troops near the site of the Custis-Lee Mansion in Arlington National Cemetery. The Army blamed Wise for the misfortunes of his balloon and terminated his services as a military balloonist.

John La Mountain volunteered his services, two balloons, and a portable gas generator to the Union Army in May, 1861. Offered an assignment as an aerial observer at Fortress Monroe, he accepted and thus became the only free-lance balloonist in the war. His first ascent near Fortress Monroe on July 25 was restricted to low altitude, because of high winds, and was of no military value. On August 3, his launching site was transferred to the Army transport *Fanny,* anchored off Hampton Roads. Following several ascents, he reported new Confederate artillery emplacements with guns apparently sighted on Fortress Monroe and on ships in the Norfolk area.

In early October, La Mountain, with his new, large balloon named the *Saratoga,* was transferred to the Army of the Potomac and attached to Brigadier General W. B. Franklin's headquarters at Cloud's Mill. There he began his free flights over Confederate lines. Taking advantage of the prevailing east wind at low altitude, he would drift over the rebel forces to the west, make his observations, jettison some of his ballast in order to ascend to higher altitudes, and pick up the westerly winds at altitudes that would carry him back over the Union lines. He would then release gas to descend. This strategy, and the resulting reconnaissance, were both successful.

On November 16, a high wind blew the *Saratoga* off its mooring, and it drifted across Confederate lines, where it was lost. La Mountain was unable to obtain another balloon and was discharged on February 19, 1862.

Thaddeus S. C. Lowe was the most successful of the civilian balloonists with the Union Army. On June 18, 1861, using his balloon *Enterprise* near Washington, he transmitted the first telegraphic message from a balloon to a station on the ground—to President Lincoln in the White House. In September, 1861, Lowe became head of the Balloon Corps of the Army of the Potomac—the Army's first air arm.

Lowe was also the first aeronaut to direct artillery fire from a balloon. On September 24, he telegraphed the errors in range and deflection of Union artillery fire to the battery commanders several miles away. His subsequent request for additional balloons, ground equipment, and aeronauts was approved, and, by January 1, 1862, the Balloon Corps had seven balloons and the aeronauts to man them. As the new equipment became available, Lowe expanded his operations by setting up a number of observation stations along the Potomac River. To service these stations, and because it was easier to make ascensions from water than from land, an eight-year-old Navy coal barge, the U.S.S. *George Washington Parke Custis,* was assigned to the Balloon Corps in November, 1861. Thus, a coal barge became the first "aircraft carrier" in history.

During its eighteen months of existence, the Balloon Corps was under the jurisdiction of three branches of the Army: the Topographic Engineers, the Quartermaster Corps, and the Corps of Engineers. The Topographic Engineers exercised administrative control over the military aeronauts beginning with the first Allen ascent on June 19, 1861. The Quartermaster Corps took over administrative control on March 31, 1862, holding it until April 7, 1863, when the Corps of Engineers took over.

One of the first acts of the Chief Engineer of the Army of the Potomac was to reduce Lowe's pay from $10 to $6 per day. Lowe protested and then resigned, leaving the service on May 7, 1863. The Balloon Corps was disbanded in June, 1863, twenty-three months before the end of the war. For the next thirty years, there was no aeronautical organization in the U.S. Army.

In evaluating the accomplishments of the Balloon Corps, it should be noted that the success or failure of its operations was largely dependent on the attitude of the Union Army generals who exercised operational control over the aeronauts. For example, in the West, Generals Thomas W. Sherman and John Pope never permitted their aeronauts, John H. Steiner and John Starkweather, to operate. General John Sedgwick, who commanded a corps during the Chancellorsville campaign, reported that Lowe's observations had furnished full and frequent reports of enemy movements, which could not have been obtained by any other method. Generals McClellan and Porter also believed in the value of balloons, but they were replaced by officers who were not interested in aerial operations.

During the Civil War, balloons demonstrated their value in making reconnaissance, reporting the location and movement of hostile ground forces, conducting artillery fire against enemy targets, and communicating to the ground by telegraph. These were the roles and missions of balloons in the Army's first attempt to utilize airspace in the conduct of warfare. Had Lowe been given the full support and backing of the Army, considerable progress might have been made in military aeronautics.

The Spanish-American War Period

In the years between the Civil War and the Spanish-American War, the U.S. Army was largely employed as a frontier force for protection against the Indians. Because of the mobility of the hostile tribes, there was little use for balloons during the Indian engagements. Thus, despite the fact that, in 1884, France, Germany, Spain, Italy, England, and Russia had established balloon corps as branches of their armies, there were no balloon operations in the United States between 1863 and 1890.

But Brigadier General Adolphus V. Greely, Chief Signal Officer of the Army from 1887 to 1906, had not forgotten the use of balloons during the Civil War. He was impressed, too, by their use in European armies. On October 1, 1890, when Congress charged the Signal Corps with collecting and transmitting information for the Army, General Greely interpreted this responsibility to include aerial navigation and aeronautics and, in the following year, he sent Lieutenant William A. Glassford to France for a year to study balloon developments and to purchase one balloon for the United States.

In the meantime, Greely had asked for money to organize a balloon corps and had gotten funds. In 1892, a balloon section was established in the Signal Corps. The Army's single balloon, which Glassford had brought back from France, was displayed at the World's Fair in Chicago in 1893. It created a sensation. During many ascensions at the Fair, Glassford used a telephone for communication between a balloon and the ground for the first time in history.

In 1896, the Army's one balloon ruptured while being inflated. Glassford ordered a replacement immediately. It was made of silk by Sergeant William Ivy and his wife.

When the Spanish-American War started, the new balloon was shipped to New York, then to Tampa on May 31, 1898, under the direction of Lieutenant Colonel Joseph E. Maxfield. At Tampa, Maxfield received instructions that one of his two balloon companies was to proceed immediately to Santiago, Cuba, although, at that point, he did not have any soldiers under his command and his equipment and one balloon were still in freight cars in various parts of the Tampa railroad yard. When Maxfield sailed for Cuba, his command consisted of three officers, twenty-four enlisted men, and but a portion of his equipment.

Although the troops arrived in Santiago on June 22, the balloon company was not permitted to disembark until June 28. When the equipment was finally taken ashore, Maxfield found that there was no hydrogen generator and no acid or iron filings, so the balloon could be inflated only once. The tropical summer heat had softened the varnish of the balloon. Torn panels had to be repaired by Sergeant Ivy. And the balloon detachment was made up of soldiers who had never seen an ascension, let alone handled a balloon.

Despite equipment shortages and inexperienced ground handling crew, three flights were made on June 30. Observations confirming the presence of the Spanish fleet in Santiago harbor were reported to General William R. Shafter, the commander of the American expedition. Lieutenant Colonel George M. Derby, chief engineer for General Shafter, had been placed in command of the balloon company over Lieutenant Colonel Maxfield. After one ascension the following day during the Battle of San Juan Hill, Derby ordered the balloon forward to a position about 650 yards from the trenches of the Spanish infantry. Maxfield advised against being so close to the enemy lines, but the balloon was moved forward over his objections, and a second ascension took place that day.

Despite the heavy infantry ground fire, Maxfield and Derby were able to locate a trail up the hill by which the U.S. forces could advance in two columns instead of one. The observers also directed artillery fire from El Pozo Hill against the enemy-occupied trenches on San Juan Hill. These two feats helped the successful U.S. capture of San Juan Hill. But the balloon was so badly punctured by Spanish ground fire that it could not be repaired. Its loss ended ballooning in the Spanish-American War. Although a second balloon company equipped with two new balloons was organized in Tampa, the war ended before it could be deployed to Cuba.

Dirigibles

For several years before and after the Spanish-American War, the Signal Corps had advocated the purchase of a dirigible. These airships were of both the rigid type, in which the shape of the gas container was maintained by a rigid structure inside, and the non-rigid type, in which internal gas pressure maintained the shape of the gas container. The gas envelopes were cylindrical in shape, driven by one or more propellers attached to a cabin hung under the bag and powered by gasoline engines. The new dirigibles were steerable.

Although France, Germany, Italy, Russia, and England had assigned dirigibles to their armed services, the Signal Corps was unable to get money for airships. In European armies, it was believed that dirigibles would be useful not only for reconnaissance, as the balloon had been, but also for the air transportation of high-ranking government officials, and, in the view of a few very imaginative planners, for strategic bombing purposes.

Brigadier General James Allen, the Chief Signal Officer who replaced Greely, was so favorably impressed with the flying demonstration of Thomas Scott Baldwin's dirigible at the St. Louis air show in October, 1907, that he applied to the War Department Board of Ordnance and Fortification for an allotment of $25,000 "or so much thereof as may be necessary" to purchase an experimental nonrigid dirigible balloon. The request was approved and the 20,000-cubic-foot-gas-capacity dirigible was delivered at Fort Myer, Virginia, on July 20, 1908. This was the only dirigible purchased by the Army until World War I.

Airplanes

Meanwhile, the concept of the airplane, which would revolutionize war, was developing in the United States and abroad.

Efforts to construct a successful heavier-than-air flying machine had been carried on by many inventors during the nineteenth century. Experiments were conducted by Percy S. Pilcher of Great Britain, Otto Lilienthal of Germany, and Octave Chanute and John Montgomery of the United States. They all built and learned to fly gliders. Others, including Sir Henry Maxim of Great Britain, Alphonse Penaud of France, and Samuel P. Langley of the United States, tried to build engine-powered planes.

Dr. Samuel Pierpont Langley was a scientist who began his experiments in aerodynamics in 1885. He was the Secretary of the Smithsonian Institution from 1887 to 1906, during which period he received gifts and federal grants to continue his experiments. On May 6, 1896, one of his steam-powered model airplanes (No. 5) flew a half mile over the Potomac River, and on November 28, 1896, his model plane No. 6 flew three-quarters of a mile along the river.

On April 29, 1898, a board of Army and Navy officers reported on Langley's models and recommended that he be given $50,000 to continue his experiments. The recommendation was approved, and Langley was asked to build a full-size test airplane. The inventor designed and constructed a tandem monoplane 62 feet long with a 48-foot span, called "Aerodrome A." The first trial flight was made on October 7, 1903, and the second on December 8. Both flights failed because the launching apparatus did not function properly.

Langley did no further work on the plane, which was put in the Smithsonian. However, in 1914, it was flown by Glenn Curtiss after a number of structural changes had been made.

Wilbur and Orville Wright, who had been experimenting with gliders before building a powered airplane, began their glider operations at Kitty Hawk, North Carolina, in September, 1900. After building and flying three gliders, they began construction of the first Wright airplane in 1902. It was a biplane 21 feet long, 8 feet high, and with a wing span of 40⅓ feet. No suitable engine was available from American manufacturers, so the Wright brothers designed and built their own four-cylinder engine, which developed about twelve horsepower.

On December 17, 1903, Orville Wright made the first successful powered airplane flight at Kitty Hawk, covering a distance of 120 feet in twelve seconds, and the air age opened.

Aviation Developments Under the Aeronautical Division

In the United States, the revolutionary implications of the powered heavier-than-air flying machine were not understood. The efforts of the Wrights to interest the U.S. Government in their airplane were unsuccessful.

Foreign governments were, however, interested in the Wright airplane. In 1904, British representatives asked the Wrights about the purchase of their plane. A little later, representatives of the French Government made inquiries of the Wrights about acquiring the plane. The Wrights, however, preferred that the United States have the first opportunity to use the plane and they offered it to the U.S. Army twice in 1905. The proposal was referred to the Army Board of Ordnance and Fortification, which was responsible for investigating new weapons. Remembering the $50,000 award to Dr.

Langley in 1898, and perhaps skeptical that such a plane existed, the Board would not establish any performance requirements or take any action until an airplane was demonstrated which would fly and carry an operator.

On May 22, 1906, the U.S. Patent Office issued a patent on the Wright plane (No. 821393). That same year, the Aero Club of America published a bulletin on the Wrights' flights of 1904–5. This was brought to the attention of President Theodore Roosevelt, who instructed Secretary of War Taft to investigate. Correspondence between the Board of Ordnance and Fortification and the Wrights began in May, 1907. After numerous conferences, the Board was convinced of the Wrights' reliability, and, on December 23, 1907, specifications calling for bids on a heavier-than-air machine were issued. These specifications called for a machine that could carry two persons with a combined weight of 350 pounds, carry enough fuel for a flight of 125 miles, have a speed of 40 miles per hour, and be able to take off and land in a field without requiring a specially prepared area.

Twenty-one proposals were received, but, on the closing date, February 1, 1908, only three bids complied with the specifications. The Wright bid of $25,000 was one of those accepted, but their plane was the only one delivered and accepted. Delivery of the Wright plane was made at Fort Myer, Virginia, on August 20, 1908.

The new plane was a modification of the 1905 model. It was a pusher type with the thirty-horsepower engine and propeller mounted behind the pilot and passenger. The plane was mounted on skids like the previous models and was launched from a starting track. Less than a thousand spectators witnessed the first flight on September 3. But later on, Orville Wright drew large crowds when he flew. Lieutenant (later General) Frank Lahm became the first Army officer to ride as a passenger on September 9.

Tragedy marred the final preliminary flight on September 17. Lieutenant Thomas E. Selfridge, who had been associated with Alexander Graham Bell in aeronautical experiments, had been given permission to ride as a passenger with Orville Wright that afternoon. The plane crashed from an altitude of about 125 feet when a propeller and rudder wire broke. Selfridge was killed—the first American officer to lose his life in the air. Selfridge Air Force Base, Michigan, was named in his honor. Orville Wright's extensive injuries put him in the hospital for two months.

In the official acceptance test on July 27, 1909, Lahm again flew as passenger-observer on a flight lasting one hour, twelve minutes, and forty seconds, which not only fulfilled the contract requirements but also established an unofficial world record for a two-man flight.

The final trial—a speed test—was flown on July 30, 1909, with Lieutenant (later General) Benjamin D. Foulois as official observer. The plane achieved an average speed of 42½ miles per hour, and won a $5,000 bonus for the Wrights. The plane was formally accepted on August 2, 1909.

Meanwhile, ballooning was on the wane. For several years after the Spanish-American War, little ballooning was done in the Army. Officers and men were not available for the duty and compressed hydrogen was impossible to obtain. Although theoretical and practical instruction in ballooning had been started at Fort Myer in September, 1902, and had been extended to include the service schools at Fort Leavenworth, Kansas, in August, 1906, there was hardly any equipment to work with.

It was ballooning as a sport that rekindled official War Department interest in the gas-bags. Two U.S. Army officers, Captain Charles de Forest Chandler and Lieutenant Lahm, used their military leaves to study ballooning. Chandler and Major Samuel Reber officially represented the army in 1906 in a free balloon ascent in Massachusetts sponsored by the Aero Club. In the same year, Lahm won the first International Balloon Race in France. Lahm and Major Henry B. Hersey piloted the balloon *United States* from Paris to Fylingsdale, England, to win the Gordon Bennett trophy.

Impressed by the developments in the lighter-than-air and heavier-than-air fields of aviation, the Army took some first steps to build an air arm. On August 1, 1907, Brigadier General James Allen, Chief Signal Officer of the Army, signed Office Memorandum No. 6, which stated: "An Aeronautical Division of this office is hereby established, to take effect this date." It specified that "This division will have charge of all matters pertaining to military ballooning, air machines, and all kindred subjects."

The establishment of the Aeronautical Division marks the birth of the present-day United States Air Force.

Captain Chandler was detailed in charge of the new division, and Corporal Edward Ward and Private Joseph E. Barrett, both in the Signal Corps, were assigned to the division. Private Barrett apparently was not air-minded. He deserted shortly thereafter, reducing the Army's new air arm to a strength of one officer and one enlisted man.

While awaiting delivery of the first heavier-than-air flying machine, the Signal Corps rejuvenated its experiments in balloon photography begun in 1893. Successful experiments in radio communications were also conducted by installing receivers in balloons.

Meanwhile, although the first army airplane had been accepted, the Wrights still had to train two officers as pilots. Lahm and Foulois were chosen, but Foulois was sent as the official delegate to the International Congress of Aeronautics at Nancy, France, and was replaced by Lieutenant Frederic E. Humphreys. The two pilots soloed on October 26, 1909, at College Park, Maryland. Foulois returned in late October and was given three instruction flights. The next month, Lahm and Humphreys cracked up the plane in making a low turn. They both returned to their respective services afterward, leaving the Aeronautical Division with one damaged airplane, one partially trained pilot, and a number of enlisted mechanics.

Foulois received correspondence-course instruction in flying from the Wrights and, under the guidance of one of their instructors, soloed on March 2. Until 1911, the Army air arm consisted of one pilot and one plane.

Before 1911, no funds had ever been appropriated by Congress specifically for aeronautics. The Signal Corps had used funds appropriated for maintenance of military telephone and telegraph facilities to keep flying. In March, 1911, Congress appropriated $125,000 for Army aeronautics. Twenty-five thousand dollars was made available immediately, and the Aeronautical Division ordered five new planes. The appropriation enabled the Signal Corps to establish its flying training school at College Park to train aviators.

Experiments were also conducted in aerial photography and map making and in radio telegraphy. Particularly worthy of note was the testing of the bombsight and the Lewis machine gun, which were to become standard equipment on Allied planes during World War I. The College Park school began to send some of its young officers to aircraft manufacturing plants for shop and flying instruction. Quite by accident, the school also pioneered night flying. Captain Chandler, who had flown to Annapolis, Maryland, to see the Army-Navy baseball game on June 1, 1912, had engine trouble, which delayed his departure after the game. On his return flight to the school, he encountered turbulence, further delaying his arrival. By following the signal lights along the B&O Railroad, he reached the airfield. Resourceful mechanics threw gasoline and oil on the field and ignited it, enabling him to make a safe landing. That very same day, young Lieutenant H. H. Arnold, who was to become the famous "Hap" and Chief of the Army Air Forces in World War II, established a new Army airplane altitude record of 6,450 feet.

By November, 1912, the school had eight airplanes on hand, eight hangars, fourteen flying officers, thirty-nine enlisted men, and one civilian mechanic. One of the planes, a Burgess, was the Army's first tractor plane, with the propeller mounted in front of the plane. During the same month, artillery fire was directed from an airplane for the first time. Airplanes were used to locate targets, give the range and azimuth from the battery, and give the necessary corrections to lay the fire on the target. Radio telegraphy was the most successful method of communicating with the artillery batteries.

Until the middle of 1911, there were no prescribed tests for qualification as an Army pilot, so the regulations of the Federation Aeronautique Internationale (FAI) were adopted, and all Army pilots were required to pass the FAI test to be rated. The Aero Club of America was the only U.S. representative for the FAI. The following year, it was decided that a more exacting test was required. A new rating, "Military Aviator," was announced in War Department Bulletin No. 2, dated February 23, 1912. Later that year, Army pilots who were rated Military Aviators were made eligible to receive the FAI rating as Expert Aviator without further tests.

By November, 1912, winter weather was so bad that flying was impossible at College Park. The Army accepted the invitation of Glenn Curtiss and sent the Curtiss pilots and mechanics to his school at San Diego, California. The Wright pilots and mechanics went to Augusta, Georgia. San Diego eventually became the Army's first permanent aviation school. The College Park school was closed on November 18, 1912.

Despite its head start in aeronautics as the result of the Wrights' invention and development, the United States soon fell behind European nations in military aviation. In the six years after the purchase of the Wright plane, only twenty-four heavier-than-air machines were bought by the U.S. Government, although France, Germany, and the British Royal Flying Corps could each boast of 100 serviceable planes. The United States, bordered by friendly nations on the north and south and oceans to the east and west, felt secure from hostile forces and did not enter the military aviation competition.

Military aeronautics was expensive. The commercial value of the airplane was yet to be proved and, while the value of the airplane in military operations was beginning to be accepted, the cost was not. The Signal Corps found it extremely difficult to obtain funds from Congress for its aeronautical activities. The public had lost interest in aviation, too. Ballooning was no longer popular and flying machines were considered too hazardous. Because of the danger in flying, it was also hard for the Signal Corps to retain trained pilots on flying duty. The fatality rate among the early pilots was high—twelve out of the first forty-eight.

There was no well-defined official statement of the status of the air arm and its roles and missions in the Army. When on May 16, 1913, a bill, H.R. 5304, was introduced that provided for removing aviation from the Signal Corps and establishing it as a separate organization, Captain (later General) Billy Mitchell, Foulois, and others, as well as the War Department, opposed the idea. The only officer favoring the bill was a pilot, Captain Paul W. Beck, who had drafted it.

Army Aviation Under the Aviation Section

Statutory recognition for Army aviation was finally achieved on July 18, 1914, when a new H.R. 5304 was enacted. The bill created in the Signal Corps an Aviation Section having a strength of sixty officers and 260 enlisted men in addition to those already authorized. The Act created the grades of Junior Military Aviator, Military Aviator, and Aviation Mechanic, provided flying pay, and restricted aviation students to unmarried lieutenants under thirty years of age.

Under the Act, the Aviation Section was "charged with the duty of operating or supervising the operation of all military aircraft, including balloons and aeroplanes, all appliances pertaining to said craft, and signaling apparatus of any kind when installed on said craft; also with the duty of training officers and enlisted men in matters pertaining to military aviation."

Thus, U.S. Army aviation was established for the first time on a permanent basis—just ten days before World War I began.

World War I

At the beginning of the war, Germany had 180 airplanes, France 136, Belgium 24, and England either 48 or 63 (historical sources disagree). German airplanes had complete freedom of the air in the early days. Flying back and forth across Allied lines, they located targets for their artillery and observed and reported lightly held points of the Allied lines for penetration by German forces. They were also used to map Allied defenses. Except for enemy small-arms ground fire, they flew at will.

The French, too, quickly appreciated the military value of the airplane and, by the fall of 1914, were using planes for reconnaissance purposes to good advantage.

At first, there was a kind of gallantry in air warfare. When German and Allied planes flew past each other in the early days of the war, the pilots waved. Before long, however, they were shooting at one another with pistols, and observers in the rear cockpits were firing with rifles. The French improved on this air-to-air gunnery by mounting machine guns in front of the pilot so that, by aiming his airplane, he could fire on his adversary. The machine guns were synchronized with the engine to allow firing between the blades of the propeller. The next step was the development of tactics for aerial combat. The battle for control of airspace had begun.

In August, 1914, bombing from airplanes was conducted by dropping bombs and hand grenades without the use of a bombsight. That month, German planes bombed Paris, and three Zeppelins bombed Allied territory. It was not until early 1915 that the German Zeppelins began to bomb London.

It is interesting to note that bombing by the warring nations coincided with the tests of the Riley Scott bombsight and dropping mechanism being conducted by the United States at the North Island, San Diego, school. The official tests, carried out from August 17 to 24, 1914, used thirty dummy and live explosive bombs, numerous grenades and one 3-inch standard artillery shell. The dummies were dropped from 1,000 and 2,000 feet, live bombs from 2,000 feet, on a 100-foot bull's-eye target. Accuracy and detonation and fragmentation results were excellent. It was concluded that bombing instruction would be given at the school. Unfortunately, however, the Chief Signal Officer, Brigadier General George P. Scriven, was convinced that the airplane's mission was primarily reconnaissance. Consequently, no bombsights were purchased, and none were on hand when the United States entered the war three years later.

It was also during August, 1914, that President Wilson issued a proclamation prohibiting U.S. citizens from participating in the war or transporting contraband for a belligerent. Since the proclamation did not bar the manufacture and sale of U.S. arms and munitions within this country, many American aircraft and engine manufacturers were able to supply European countries, with the exception of Germany. Some expansion of the American factories resulted, and aircraft manufacturers gained experience in building planes and engines. But the foreign business created a problem for the Army Aviation Section. It had trouble getting aircraft from factories already working to capacity on foreign orders.

Military Aviation in Mexico in 1916

The Army's 1st Aero Squadron was the only American tactical air organization to be field-tested before the United States entered World War I. On March 9, 1916, the Mexican bandit chief, Pancho Villa, raided Columbus, New Mexico, with a band of several hundred followers, killing seventeen American citizens. He was chased across the border, but escaped. Brigadier General John J. Pershing was ordered to organize a force of 15,000 troops to enter Mexico and capture Villa. The command became known as "Pershing's Punitive Expedition."

The 1st Aero Squadron under Foulois was ordered to join Pershing's command. It arrived in Columbus on March 15 with ten pilots, eighty-four enlisted men, and eight Curtiss airplanes. The unit's pitiful state of operational readiness was quickly apparent. Four days later, the squadron flew to an advanced operating base at Casas Grandes, Mexico. Due to poor navigation equipment, inaccurate maps, incompetent and inadequate maintenance and maintenance equipment, high winds, and old airplanes, the squadron became spread out all over the area before the day was over. One plane was forced to return to Columbus, one cracked up in a forced landing at night, and the remaining six made forced landings because of darkness. It took a week to reassemble the squadron.

Later experience proved that the underpowered JN-3's could not attain sufficient altitude to clear the 12,000-foot mountains, nor withstand the storms and turbulence in the areas where Villa's troops were reported to be in hiding.

Apparently, the original intention was to use the 1st Aero Squadron for observation of advance parties of the Expedition as well as of Villa's forces, for aerial photography, and for carrying mail and dispatches. Since the planes were equipped with machine guns, strafing of enemy ground troops was also planned. A bombsight and bombs had also been requested. It is not known whether the mission contemplated the direction of artillery fire. As a result of the operation, it soon became apparent that the squadron's capabilities were limited to carrying mail and dispatches for short flights in good weather.

The exciting life of the pilots of the 1st Aero Squadron was not confined to the cockpit. On April 7, 1916, two planes carrying Foulois and Herbert A. Dargue, and Townsend F. Dodd and Joseph E. Carberry, took off from San Geronimo for Chihuahua City, Mexico, with duplicate dispatches to be delivered to Marion H. Letcher, the U.S. consul. It was agreed that the planes would land one to the north of the city and one to the south. Foulois got out of the plane as soon as it landed but, before starting into town, he instructed Dargue to join the other plane. As Dargue took off, his plane was struck by bullets fired by Mexican mounted *rurales*. Foulois, hearing the firing, ran back to the field and stopped the shooting but was promptly arrested and hustled off to jail.

In the meantime, Dodd had delivered his duplicate dispatch to the consul. Dargue and Carberry, who were guarding their planes, were surrounded by a hostile mob, which burned cigarette holes in the wings, slashed the fabric with knives, and even removed nuts and bolts from the planes. Carberry got his engine started, took off, and flew to an American smelter about six miles away. Dargue started up his engine and took off in a shower of stones. But the top section of the plane's fuselage flew off, damaging the stabilizer, and Dargue had to make an emergency landing immediately. He was able to hold off the crowd until the Mexican guards arrived. The airplane was repaired later that day.

After several hours in jail, Foulois was able to contact the colonel who served as chief of staff under General Eulallo Gutierrez, the military governor of Chihuahua. The colonel took him to General Gutierrez, who ordered his release. Carberry returned at dawn the next morning, and in the early morning the planes left Chihuahua to avoid another encounter with a hostile crowd.

On April 20, the squadron was ordered to return to Columbus to take delivery of its new planes. Of the eight planes taken into Mexico the preceding month, only two were still in service, and they were both considered unsafe for further field use. They were flown to Columbus, condemned, and destroyed. The new planes, Curtiss N-8's and R-2's, were turned over to the squadron but, while the Advisory and Inspection Board found them satisfactory, the pilots found many reasons why they were not.

For all practical purposes, air operations in Mexico ended in the late summer. From March 15 to August 15, 1916, the 1st Aero Squadron flew 540 missions for a total of 346 hours, covering 19,533 miles.

In contrast with the great military potential being demonstrated by aviation in the European conflict, the operations of the 1st Aero Squadron in Mexico were a fiasco. The shortcomings of U.S. Army aviation were appalling. Early in the European war, aircraft were fulfilling a number of roles and missions: strategic and tactical reconnaissance and the prevention of reconnaissance by the enemy's aircraft, direction and control of artillery fire, destruction of enemy forces and matériel by explosive and incendiary missiles and other means, and transportation of high-ranking officials. Three types of planes were being used to perform these missions—reconnaissance, pursuit, and combat.

The most important of the three was the reconnaissance plane carrying a pilot and observer. Its function was to obtain information on enemy operations and to direct and correct the fire of field artillery batteries. The pursuit plane was a fast, highly maneuverable single-seater. It was the pursuit pilot's job to climb above enemy planes, then dive down on them, preferably out of the sun, to prevent reconnaissance of his troops and to rid the air of hostile planes. The combat plane, the largest of the three, was equipped with two or three light automatic machine guns and sometimes a heavier rapid-fire gun. Its function was to convoy and protect reconnaissance airplanes and drive off hostile planes. Both the combat and reconnaissance planes could carry bombs.

The U.S. Aviation Section considered that it already had a satisfactory type of reconnaissance plane and was experimenting with planes of the other two types. But there were none available when the United States entered the war in 1917.

The Air Service During World War I

The organization of military aeronautics in the U.S. Army was totally inadequate for fighting a war on a large scale. The Aviation Section had 131 officers, practically all pilots or student pilots, and 1,087 enlisted men. By European standards, its 200–300 aircraft were little better than trainers. It did have one fully organized unit, the 1st Aero Squadron, which left Columbus for Europe on August 5, 1917, under the command of Major Ralph Royce. Airfields, instructors, training curricula, and experience were badly needed.

On May 26, 1917, French Premier Alexandre Ribot cabled the United States Government asking that it send to the French front by June 30, 1918, a flying corps of 4,500 planes, 5,000 pilots, and 50,000 mechanics. This was a far larger air force than France had been able to build in three years of war and was far out of proportion to the ratio of ground troops to air troops planned for the American Expeditionary Force.

Congress passed the Aviation Act of July 24, 1917, and now armed with adequate funds, but lacking in wartime experience and knowledge of military aviation requirements, the Army turned to England and France for guidance in its air building. A U.S. mission was sent to Europe in June under Colonel Raynal C. Bolling. The Bolling group recommended that the United States discontinue the development and construction of American-designed pursuit planes and concentrate on the production of trainers, the English-designed de Havilland-4, a two-place reconnaissance bomber, and the newly developed Liberty engine. They also recommended that pursuit planes be bought from France and England.

A vast training program was initiated in which ground school was conducted at colleges and universities and basic flight training given on newly constructed airfields. To take advantage of the combat experience of Allied pilots, advanced flying training was carried on overseas.

The aircraft procurement program got off to a slow start. An aircraft industry could not be built overnight. There was great delay in communications between the factories and the combat zone, and there was neither centralization nor quality control at the factories. On March 15, 1918, the first U.S.–built DH-4, with a Liberty engine, was shipped from Hoboken. It was test-flown in France on May 17, 1918.

The delay in the production of aircraft resulted in the passage of the Overman Act of May 20, 1918, which removed Army aviation from the Signal Corps. Major General William L. Kenly, a pilot, was designated the Director of Military Aeronautics and was responsible for training and operations. The organization became officially recognized as the Air Service, U.S. Army. Control over production of airplanes, engines, and aircraft equipment was vested in the Army's Bureau of Aircraft Production. Since both components reported separately to the Secretary of War, there was no direct coordination between the using and procuring agencies. This problem was temporarily solved by the appointment of John D. Ryan as Director of Air Service, with jurisdiction, as Second Assistant Secretary of War, over both components—a management technique that had been proving successful in England.

Aircraft production increased rapidly under the new setup. It is estimated that, by the time of the armistice on November 11, 1918, U.S. factories had built approximately 7,800 trainers, 3,500 combat aircraft, mostly DH-4's, and had purchased about 5,000 aircraft overseas. DH-4's were coming off American assembly lines at a rate of 260 per week.

Major Billy Mitchell, the man who was, in a very real sense, the major prophet of U.S. air power, was one of five U.S. Army aviators in Europe on April 6, 1917, when we entered the war. He was an air observer in Spain at the time, had learned to fly in 1916, and, as a major, had served as chief of the Aviation Section, Signal Corps. After the U.S. declaration of war, Mitchell was authorized to visit the front as an observer.

During the next few months, he visited airfields, depots, headquarters, and tactical air units and made several flights over the front lines. Until the arrival of General Pershing in June, Mitchell was a free agent and studied intensely the doctrines and logistical and administrative foundations of air power. He was a firm believer that the only real defense against aircraft are other aircraft. After surviving a night raid by German planes, he also acquired a great respect for the material and psychological effects of bombing.

Mitchell was tremendously impressed by the philosophy of the employment of air power expressed by Major General Hugh M. Trenchard, Marshal of the Royal Air Force, whom he visited in May. Trenchard considered the airplane a primarily offensive weapon and strongly advocated strategic bombardment and unified air command. On his own initiative and with French help, Mitchell prepared and submitted to the War Department a plan for the organization of the AEF air force. This was followed by reports covering all details of the air war. He is also said to have been largely responsible for French Premier Ribot's cable to the United States.

Mitchell joined Pershing's staff in June as aviation officer, and was appointed to a board of officers to recommend the organization and composition of the Air Service, AEF. The board recommended a strategic force of thirty bombardment groups and thirty fighter groups and another force, the size of which would be determined by the strength of the ground forces to which it was attached. Pershing approved the board's recommendations only for the air support units. Later programs included pursuit and bombardment squadrons, but authority was never granted to organize a U.S. strategic bombardment force.

In September, 1917, Mitchell became Air Commander, Zone of the Advance; in August, 1918, Chief of Air Service, First Army; and in October, Chief of Air Service, Army Group, with the rank of brigadier general.

The majority of the American pilots and mechanics who arrived at the front for combat duty in 1917 and early 1918 had been trained overseas. Without combat planes of their own, they could acquire no combat experience unless they served as replacements in Allied air units. This policy was adopted as an interim measure. Trained Americans were then grouped into squadrons for use on the French and British fronts until the American armies were on the front and the airmen could be assigned to U.S. forces.

In preparation for the eventual transfer of a sector of the front to the Americans, the Allied command directed that American units should be concentrated in the Toul sector. It was here that pilots of the famous "Hat-in-the-Ring" squadron won their first individual victories by shooting down two German planes. As the build-up of squadrons took place, they were organized into groups—and groups into wings.

In June, American army and air units were moved close to the salient the Germans had driven into the French lines at Chateau-

Thierry. The American First Pursuit Group and First Corps Observation Group, augmented by some French units, were combined to form the 1st Brigade under Mitchell. The Germans had numerical superiority as well as higher performance planes. As a result, the 1st Brigade was hard pressed to protect observation planes on missions behind enemy lines, and the pursuit pilots were often outmatched.

After five weeks, the Germans were stopped and hurled back, and, while the 1st Brigade accomplished its primary mission of supplying intelligence to the armed forces, the effort had cost many lives and aircraft. During the same campaign, American pursuit aircraft participated in an attack on the German supply base at Fere-en-Tardenois. Although the mission was costly, it forced the Germans to use their pursuit planes to protect the supply base, thus weakening their strength over the front.

In September, 1918, the First Army was given its first objective—the elimination of the St. Mihiel salient, which had been sticking into the French lines for four years. In the preceding month, all American air units on the French front were placed under Mitchell's command. Augmented by French squadrons and working with the RAF's nine bombardment squadrons, Mitchell's forces had numerical superiority for the first time.

The Allied attack began on September 12, but for two days bad weather kept most of the planes on the ground. On September 14 and 15, Mitchell's planes were in operation. About 500 pursuit and observation planes flew in support of ground forces. The others were organized into two air brigades, which alternately attacked the right and left flanks of the St. Mihiel salient and struck targets behind the German lines, strafing columns of ground forces and bombing supply and communications facilities. Losses were heavy on both sides but, with Allied planes on the offensive, most of the air action occurred behind German lines. The results were excellent, and Allied ground forces were soon advancing almost all along the front.

That was the largest air engagement in the war. Altogether, 1,481 Allied aircraft were employed, of which 609 were from American squadrons. While preparations for so large a battle could not be entirely concealed, a degree of tactical surprise was achieved. Great credit was due Mitchell and his staff, who planned and executed the entire air operation.

Air power was used next during the Meuse-Argonne campaign, which began September 26. For this air operation, Mitchell had a force of 800 aircraft, of which about 600 were American. His strategy was to follow the same tactics that had been successful at St. Mihiel: tactical surprise and concentration of forces. Pursuit patrols flying at two altitudes defended the front by breaking up German air attacks on the ground forces. Since the Germans had numerical air superiority and employed large formations, Mitchell organized the balance of his offensive force into pursuit and bomber groups. These groups attacked enemy airdromes, communications and supply installations, and troop concentrations.

The largest of these strikes occurred on October 9, when 200 Allied bombers, escorted by about 150 three-place aircraft, flying in two waves, attacked and disrupted a concentration of German army reserve forces assembling for a counterattack. More than thirty tons of bombs were dropped in this single operation. Subsequent operations over a twenty-four-hour period brought the total to about sixty-nine tons—probably the greatest bombardment strike of the Air Service during the war.

The observation squadrons were more successful in spotting enemy artillery, directing field artillery fire, and performing visual reconnaissance than in the previous campaign. Twenty-three balloon squadrons which were at the front on Armistice Day also played a valuable role in this kind of mission.

As the war proceeded, a command structure for Allied strategic bombing of Germany evolved. Major General Trenchard had been designated commander of the RAF's Independent Force (of bombers) when the latter was organized on June 6, 1918. Trenchard was made directly responsible to the British Air Ministry, and strategic bombardment with targets in Germany was assigned to him. In October, the Inter-Allied Independent Air Force was constituted with Trenchard in command under the Supreme Command of Marshal Ferdinand Foch. The U.S. Air Service was to have been a participant, but the war came to an end before the organization got started.

The Air Service Between the Wars

During the war, some U.S. air crews were trained by the British to fly the large Handley-Paige night bomber, but the U.S. Air Service was never equipped with them. The postwar history of the Air Service might have been quite different had it obtained World War I experience in strategic bombardment in addition to its ground support missions. But even without strategic bombing experience, many pilots returned to the United States with the profound conviction that air power would be the primary weapon in future wars. Many believed that the airplane was a unique weapon of destruction with such potential that an air force should be established as an independent arm and that, until the Air Service achieved autonomy, it could not prepare its concept of operations or develop the needed aircraft.

Many plans were suggested for the organization of air power during 1919–20, but most studies endorsed preconceived notions. Pershing's Dickman Board and the War Department's Menoher Board opposed any change in the control of aviation. An important exception was Secretary of War Newton D. Baker's Cromwell Mission, composed of men with broad experience in aviation, which, after a fact-finding tour in Europe, unequivocally endorsed a separate department for air.

Air stayed with the Army. Secretary Baker supported the recommendations of the War Department, which became effective in the Army Reorganization Act of 1920. The Act made the Air Service a combatant arm of the Army with an authorized strength of 1,516 officers, 16,000 enlisted men, and 2,500 flying cadets—out of a total of 280,000 men for the entire Army. The office of the Second Assistant Secretary of War was abolished. Regulations were published providing for commanders of tactical units to be flyers, allowed flying pay up to fifty per cent of base pay, and assigning the rank of major general for the Chief of the Air Service. The Assistant Chief was to be a brigadier general. The Air Service was also given control of its research and development, procurement of aircraft and related items of equipment, and its personnel and training functions. The War Department insisted that the tactical squadrons operate under control of the Army commanders as integral elements of divisions and corps.

Leading the fight for full recognition of air power was General Billy Mitchell. He was Assistant Chief of Air Service from 1920 to 1925 and an irritant to the War Department General Staff. But to the Army flyers, he was a hero. In 1919, he began an intensive campaign to court public opinion and win support for independent air power. He gave press interviews, made speeches, wrote articles and books—all on the subject of air power.

His boldest attacks were directed against the Navy. Mitchell insisted that an airplane could sink any surface ship by bombs or torpedoes. His requests for a suitable vessel for a test were refused by the Navy until Congressional interest forced the Navy to acquiesce. In July, 1921, aircraft from Mitchell's 1st Provisional Air Brigade based at Langley Field attacked and sank three captured German ships—a destroyer, the cruiser *Frankfort,* and the heavily compartmented battleship *Ostfriesland*—off the mouth of the Chesapeake Bay. A joint board deprecated the effectiveness of the aerial bombing, but Mitchell clinched the validity of his claims by sinking obsolete battleships, the *Alabama* in September, 1921, and the *Virginia* and *New Jersey* in September, 1923, in tests off Cape Hatteras.

On September 5, 1925, Mitchell used the disaster of the Navy's dirigible *Shenandoah* to issue a press statement in which he charged the high command of the Army and Navy with "incompetency, criminal negligence, and almost treasonable administration of the National Defense." He was ordered to Washington to stand trial before a general court-martial. The trial, lasting from October 25 to December 17, allowed him to advertise his views on air power before the American public. But he was found guilty on charges under the omnibus 96th Article of War and suspended from duty for five years. Shortly thereafter, he resigned from the Army to continue his crusade.

The controversy of the Mitchell era helped stimulate Government interest in what to do about the Air Service. There were several studies. The Lassiter Board, composed of a group of general staff officers, recommended to the Secretary of War in 1923 a ten-year expansion program and the creation of an offensive striking force of pursuit and bombardment units to operate under control of an Army general headquarters (GHQ) in time of war. The Lambert Committee of the House of Representatives, appointed in 1924, examined the entire area of military aeronautics. After hearing 150 witnesses, the Committee made its report in December, 1925, and proposed a single Department of Defense with equal representation for ground, naval, and air forces. But another committee, appointed by President Calvin Coolidge in September, and headed by Dwight D. Morrow, also published its findings the same month. It opposed the idea of a separate air force and a Department of Defense. It did recommend that the Air Service be redesignated the Air Corps, that it should have representatives on the General Staff, and that an Assistant Secretary of War for aviation matters be appointed.

The Air Corps Act of July 2, 1926, changed the air arm's name from Air Service to Air Corps, created the office of Assistant Secretary of War to help foster military aeronautics, established an air section in each General Staff division for a three-year period, and authorized a five-year program to bring the Air Corps strength up to 1,518 officers, 2,500 flying cadets, 16,000 enlisted men, and 1,800 serviceable aircraft. However, funds were not made available to accomplish the expansion. The Air Corps remained a combatant branch of the Army—but with much less prestige than the others.

By 1933, many Air Corps officers felt it was hopeless to fight for an independent air arm separate from the Army and Navy. They elected to adopt as a temporary solution the creation of a GHQ air force. Studies prepared by the Air Corps and the War Department were reviewed by a board headed by Major General Hugh A. Drum, Army Deputy Chief of Staff. The board's report endorsed the idea of a GHQ air force of 1,800 aircraft and recommended it be used for both tactical and strategic operations, including strikes against major installations in hostile territory.

The reorganization went into effect on March 1, 1935. The Commanding General, GHQ Air Force, Langley Field, Virginia, was responsible for the organization, training, and operation of the force, reporting to the Chief of Staff in peacetime and the commander of the field forces in wartime. All Air Corps tactical units distributed through the nine corps areas were assigned to the GHQ Air Force. The Chief of the Air Corps retained responsibility for individual training, supply, and procurement functions. Administrative control of the air bases remained a responsibility of the various corps area commanders.

The divided authority between the Air Corps and the corps area commanders and between the two elements within the Air Corps was the fundamental cause of the discord and administrative difficulties that soon arose. For example, the combat effectiveness of the Air Corps was the responsibility of the Commanding General GHQ Air Force, yet he had no voice in the individual training and indoctrination of air crews nor in the development and procurement of equipment. These functions were exercised by the Chief of Air Corps. Both of these agencies were on the same command level and reported separately to the Chief of Staff, U.S. Army. With the CG, GHQ Air Force, favoring separation of the arm from the Army and the Chief of Air Corps strongly opposed, it was normal for the officers assigned to each agency to push the divergent views of their chiefs, with resulting disunity.

Recommendations submitted by both commands failed to produce a solution. One improvement made in May, 1936, exempted GHQ Air Force bases from control by corps area commanders except for court-martial jurisdiction. A consolidation was finally effected on March 1, 1939, when the GHQ Air Force was assigned to the Chief of Air Corps by War Department directive. While the new command set-up proved to be short-lived, it coincided with a vast Air Corps expansion program stimulated by threats of war from overseas.

In the summer and fall of 1938, during the crisis over Czechoslovakia, Hitler and his Luftwaffe demonstrated the significance of air power in power politics. President Roosevelt recognized the importance of the Luftwaffe and concluded that only American industry could provide the tremendous aircraft production likely to be needed soon by the European nations who would have to oppose Hitler.

On January 12, 1939, in a message to Congress, President Roosevelt noted that the increased speed, range, and capacity of airplanes abroad had changed our requirements for defense aviation, and he urged that $300 million be appropriated for the purchase of Army aircraft. The President described the existing force of approximately 1,700 tactical and training planes, 1,600 Air Corps officers, and 18,000 enlisted men as "utterly inadequate."

Congress passed the necessary legislation on April 3. It authorized the procurement of 3,251 aircraft and approved a total Air Corps strength of 3,203 officers, 45,000 enlisted men, and 5,500 airplanes.

Meanwhile, the endless analyses of roles and missions of the Army air arm had continued during the 1930's. Little foresight had been shown. For example, in its report of September 26, 1934, entitled "Doctrines for the Employment of the GHQ Air Force," the Joint Board of the Army and Navy had accepted the substance of earlier studies discounting the value of air power and failed to define clearly the Air Corps responsibilities in national defense.

But there was some small progress. In a revision of Joint Action of the Army and Navy, published on September 11, 1935, the Air Corps mission was better defined. It provided that the Air Corps would operate as an arm of the mobile army both in the conduct of operations over the land in support of land operations and in the conduct of air operations over the sea in direct defense of the coast, and that, under some conditions, it would conduct air operations in support of or in lieu of naval operations. While the delineation of responsibilities was somewhat vague, it provided further justification for the Air Corps requirement of a long-range bomber.

In his message to Congress on January 4, 1939, President Roosevelt pledged U.S. protection of the Western Hemisphere. Hemisphere defense concepts were changing rapidly. An Air Corps board had already completed a study of "The Air Corps Mission under the Monroe Doctrine." In March, 1939, the air doctrines propounded by the board were re-examined and restated, emphasizing the primary mission of defense against air attacks by the destruction of enemy aviation at its bases.

War in Europe began at dawn on the morning of September 1, 1939. On the same day, General George C. Marshall became Chief of Staff, U.S. Army. In reviewing the board's report on hemisphere defense, General Marshall concluded that it established a specific mission for the Air Corps for the first time.

In June, 1940, the Air Corps listed its roles and missions in the Western Hemisphere in order of priority. They were to prevent the establishment of hostile air bases in the Americas; to defeat hostile air forces lodged in the hemisphere by attacking their bases; to defeat hostile air forces by aerial combat; to prevent the landing of expeditionary forces by attacking transports and supply ships; to cooperate with the mobile army in ground operations; and to operate in support of or in lieu of U.S. Navy forces against hostile fleets. This concept of air power employment exerted a tremendous influence over Air Corps planning during the 1939–41 period.

II

Prelude to Global War

When World War II began in September, 1939, the United States declared its neutrality. American policy was to remain out of the war, if possible, and to keep the totalitarian forces out of the Western Hemisphere. This second objective required an extension and a quickening of our rearmament program. We needed carrier-based aircraft, long-range bombers, and new strategic bases.

The policy of neutrality and static defense was short-lived. Soon the United States identified the defense of the Western Hemisphere with the survival of the Allies. Allied success would prevent an Axis invasion of this hemisphere. By supporting the Allies, the United States would gain the time necessary for building up its own defenses. Our neutrality restrictions were relaxed and our armament manufacturing and industrial facilities began a vast expansion program. Lend-lease aid to Great Britain began in 1941, and we were on our way to becoming the "arsenal of democracy."

The air war in Europe stimulated Air Corps expansion. The vital role of the Luftwaffe in German offensive operations and the success of the RAF in the Battle of Britain spurred the United States to put greater emphasis on strengthening its air power. The Air Corps expansion during 1939–41 became a race to overtake the Axis air forces, which had been on a war footing for several years.

Legislation enacted by Congress following the Presidential message of January 12, 1939, had already authorized Air Corps expansion to a total strength of 5,500 aircraft, 3,203 officers, and 45,000 enlisted men. To utilize these increases, the Air Corps prepared a plan for 24 tactical groups to be combat-ready by June,

1941. In May, 1940, the Air Corps planned a 41-group program. Two months later, this was expanded to a 54-group program, which would provide 4,000 tactical airplanes, 16,800 officers, 15,000 aviation cadets, and 187,000 enlisted men.

The fall of Poland, the airborne invasions of Norway, Denmark, Holland, and Belgium, the British defeat at Dunkirk, and the collapse of France spurred further expansion plans by the air arm. In the fall of 1941, the Air Corps planned an 84-group program for June 30, 1942, with a strength of 400,000 officers and men and 7,800 combat aircraft. By December 7, 1941, 70 tactical groups, including 14 heavy bombardment, 9 medium bombardment, 5 light bombardment, 25 pursuit, 11 observation, and 6 transport groups had been activated. But few were equipped with suitable aircraft and many were only at cadre strength.

Aircraft manufacturers were finding it extremely hard to keep up with the constantly repeated upward revisions of production goals. In 1939, contracts were being awarded to the aircraft industry on a one-shift basis, but, as skill and experience increased, the plants went into three-shift production schedules. In May, 1940, President Roosevelt called for an annual production of 50,000 planes—an increase from approximately 2,000 aircraft a year to more than 4,000 a month. Between July, 1940, and December, 1941, 22,077 military aircraft were built, of which the Air Corps received 9,932, the U.S. Navy, 4,034, and Great Britain, 6,756.

The need for flying personnel and technicians for the expanding Air Corps increased rapidly. Entrance requirements for applicants for flying training were relaxed. Air National Guard and Reserve units were inducted into Federal service. Pilot training objectives jumped from 300 annually in 1939 to 30,000 a year in 1941. Primary flight training was given at forty-one civilian schools; advanced flying training was conducted at the Air Corps schools at Randolph, Brooks, and Kelly Fields. To meet the huge expansion, twenty-eight more training bases were authorized, most of which were completed in 1941.

By early 1941, the air defense of the United States had become a pressing concern. In March, the Air Corps was given the responsibility for air defense, and four numbered air forces were created: the 1st and 2d in the northeast and northwest parts of the United States, the 3d and 4th in the southwest and southeast. On April 12, 1941, each of the four was directed by the War Department to organize a bomber command and an interceptor command to meet the need for offensive and defensive task forces. The bomber commands were to serve as support commands of the field army responsible for ground defenses of the region. Interceptor commands were to be responsible for air defense squadrons, anti-aircraft batteries, and aircraft warning units.

Other organizational changes occurred in 1941. The Air Corps established the Technical Training Command to direct schools for ground crews and technicians. The Air Corps Maintenance Command was charged with supply and maintenance, and the Matériel Division made responsible for procurement, research, and development. The Air Corps Ferrying Command was created to fly aircraft overseas for delivery to the RAF. Flying training was eventually focused in the newly established Flying Training Command created in 1942.

Command began to be centralized. Back in 1939, the GHQ Air Force had been assigned to the Chief of Air Corps to ensure better coordination and centralized control. This relationship ended on November 19, 1940, when the GHQ Air Force was removed from the jurisdiction of the Chief of Air Corps and was given a separate status under the Commander, Army Field Forces. At the same time, Major General H. H. Arnold, who was Chief of Air Corps, was appointed Acting Deputy Chief of Staff with responsibilities that presumably included the coordination of these two Army aviation agencies.

Within a few months, it was apparent that this new arrangement was unsatisfactory, and, in March, Secretary of War Henry L. Stimson directed that the Army's air arm be placed under a single commander. The pattern was followed on the civilian side. In April, Robert A. Lovett was appointed to fill the long-vacant post of Assistant Secretary of War for Air. On June 20, 1941, the Army Air Forces (AAF) was created to coordinate and direct the activities of the Air Force Combat Command (formerly GHQ Air Force) and the Air Corps. General Arnold, who retained his position as Deputy

Chief of Staff, was directly responsible to the Army Chief of Staff and charged with establishing policies and plans for all aspects of aviation affairs. He was also authorized a staff, known as the A-Staff, to carry out his functions. The new Chief of Air Corps, Major General George H. Bret, and the Commanding General of the Air Force Combat Command, Lieutenant General Delow C. Emmons, were responsible to General Arnold for service and combat functions, respectively.

Expansion of the air arm was rooted in the national concern for hemispheric defense. Until 1940, the United States had confined the overseas assignment of troops to Hawaii, Panama, and the Philippines. But the German successes in Europe, the coordinated military and political actions, and the surprise, speed, and power of their military attacks sharpened our anxiety for our own security. Studies were prepared in great detail of the possible routes for a German invasion of the Western Hemisphere and the steps the United States could take to prevent such attacks. The presence of German airplanes in Latin America was already raising questions about the security of the Panama Canal.

One of the most significant actions taken in hemisphere defense was announced by President Roosevelt on September 3, 1940— the exchange of U.S. destroyers for British bases. Under this arrangement, Britain received fifty old but urgently needed destroyers and, in return, gave the United States ninety-nine-year leases on eight bases in British possessions in the Western Hemisphere. As a result, AAF reconnaissance aircraft were operating from Gander, Newfoundland, and in the Caribbean by late 1941.

Early in 1941, before the United States formally entered the war, the first of a series of secret conferences began between U.S. and British staff planners. They explored methods to defeat the Axis powers and planned for the employment of forces.

The Allied planners based their offensive strategy on the assumption that, with Germany the leading and most powerful member of the Axis, the decisive war theater would be the Atlantic and European areas. Long-range plans for offensive action against the Axis included such measures as economic pressure by blockade, sustained air offensives against German military power supplemented by air offensives against other regions under enemy control that contributed to that power, early elimination of Italy, raids and minor offensives against the Continent, support of all neutrals and belligerents who opposed the Axis, build-up of forces for a land offensive against Germany, and capture of positions from which the offensive could be launched.

The roles and missions of the air units were described in general terms. The policy of the Allied air forces would be to achieve as quickly as possible a superiority of air strength over the enemy, particularly in long-range striking forces.

The final report of the planners, entitled "United States–British Staff Conversations" (short title ABC-1), was submitted on March 27, 1941. Tentative agreements reached therein were not politically binding. It was agreed that, if the United States entered the war, the recommendations for joint action would require the approval of the U.S. and British governments and their chiefs of staff. But the U.S. Chiefs of Staff approved ABC-1 in its essentials and used it as a basis for operational and logistic planning. After Pearl Harbor, the over-all ABC-1 strategy was adopted, and the coordinated British-American endeavors were essentially those contained in the planners' report. Thus, ABC-1 was one of the important military documents of World War II.

The Army Air Forces Establishment

One of the reasons for the creation of the Army Air Forces on June 20, 1941, had been to eliminate internal friction between the combat and service agencies. Unfortunately, this result was not achieved, and the Air Force struggle for recognition continued. As Chief of the Army Air Forces, General Arnold's responsibilities included, among others, control of all aerial operations of the Air Force Combat Command (formerly GHQ Air Force), except for units assigned or attached to task forces, overseas garrisons, or other commands, and for plans for the air defense of the country under direction of the Chief of Staff. Certainly the authority given to the Chief of the Army Air Forces was the greatest single step toward autonomy so far, but it soon conflicted with the mission of General Headquarters (GHQ) of the Army.

On July 6, 1941, the Army GHQ mission had been enlarged to include the planning and command of operations. This directive and the regulation establishing the Army Air Forces overlapped in the areas of operational planning and control. To settle the issues raised by the conflict, a board was convened on August 14, to recommend a major reorganization of the War Department. By the time its changes were put into effect, the United States had been at war for several months.

As a result of the board's study, GHQ was inactivated, and three autonomous and coequal commands were established in 1942 under the Chief of Staff, U.S. Army: Army Air Forces, Army Ground Forces, and Services of Supply (redesignated in 1943 as the Army Service Forces). The Operations Division of the War Department General Staff became responsible for the planning and operations of all theaters and the four defense commands.

The Commanding General, AAF, now became a member of the Joint Chiefs of Staff and the Combined Chiefs of Staff—the top command of the land, sea, and air forces of the United States and Great Britain. The Office of the Chief of Air Corps and the Air Force Combat Command, which were sources of internal friction, were also eliminated in the reorganization. This arrangement continued throughout the War.

III

Air Power in World War II

BY ROBERT F. FUTRELL

NOTE: *Dr. Futrell, the author of this chapter, is Professor of Military History at the Air University. In 1961, he wrote* The United States Air Force in Korea, 1950–1953 *(New York: Duell, Sloan, and Pearce) and was a contributor to* The Army Air Forces in World War II *(Chicago: University of Chicago Press).*

In World War II, air power became much more than a supporting agency to land and sea battles. From the beginning of the conflict on September 1, 1939 to its conclusion on September 2, 1945, all of the belligerent nations made a tremendous use of military aircraft, although none of them chose to employ a pure air power strategy. In each nation, national leaders organized and employed air capabilities in the manner that reflected their national objectives and basic concepts of war.

The experience of the United States in mobilizing for air warfare reveals the great importance attached to air operations. For several years, U.S. aviation production became the largest single industry in the history of the world. In the five years 1941–45, U.S. aircraft and parts producers turned out a product valued at $45 billion. In the peak year of 1944, the United States produced 96,318 aircraft with a value of over $16 billion. More than 1,200,000 persons were employed in the aircraft and parts industry during this year. At its peak strength, the U.S. Army Air Forces included 269 combat groups and 79,908 aircraft. The U.S. Navy ultimately possessed 28 large attack aircraft carriers and 71 smaller escort carriers and 41,272 planes.

The United States followed a balanced-force concept (ground, sea, and air forces) and a surface strategy. As a result, General Henry H. ("Hap") Arnold, Commanding General, U.S. Army Air Forces, was compelled to conclude: "The enemy was beaten through the forceful application and complete coordination of land, sea and air power. No one service carried the war exclusively: all shared equally."

In looking back at World War II, General Arnold believed that many fundamental lessons could be learned about the employment of air power, but he thought that all of the lessons drawn by the victorious Allies would need to be viewed against the fact that, at many times, the Allies had won victories by very narrow margins, frequently because of enemy blunders. Thus, if Hitler had correctly understood air power, Nazi Germany might well have triumphed in Europe. Arnold demanded that all studies of World War II assess the reasons for the enemy's failures as well as the causes of Allied success. This work of studying and documenting the air power lessons was begun within the Army Air Forces as early as 1944. In the summer of that year, Arnold established an AAF Evaluation Board in each combat theater to study and report on how air power was being used. The major evaluation, however, was initiated at the direction of President Franklin D. Roosevelt, who ordered a civilian and military evaluation project that resulted in the preparation and publishing of 208 reports on the strategic air war against Germany and 108 on the war against Japan. Late in 1944, General Arnold also asked one of the nation's leading aeronautical scientists, Dr. Theodore von Kármán, to assemble a task group and study the role of scientific research and development in relation to air power. The report of this scientific study committee, entitled *Toward New Horizons,* was published in December, 1945. Utilizing these exhaustive evaluations and his own experience as wartime commander of the Army Air Forces, General Arnold prepared a final report on the war that was published in November, 1945. Supplemented by comments on the same subjects by other knowledgeable leaders, his report provides a convenient summary of the air power lessons of World War II.

In the course of drawing up the doctrinal blueprints for the em-

ployment of air forces in combat, the Air Corps Tactical School
had taught, during the 1930's, that the air power of a nation was
"its capacity to conduct air operations" and that air power was
"measured by the immediate ability of a nation to engage effectively
in air warfare." Looking backward at the tremendous mobilization
effort required to field Army and Navy air forces in the global
combat, Arnold gave a much broader definition of air power:

> Air power includes a nation's ability to deliver cargo, people, destructive
> missiles and war-making potential through the air to a desired destination
> to accomplish a desired purpose. Air power is not composed alone of the
> war-making components of aviation. It is the total aviation activity—
> civilian and military, commercial and private, potential as well as existing.

As a result of lessons learned in combat, Arnold and other high-
ranking American commanders acknowledged new requirements for
unified command and control of American military forces. In
Arnold's opinion, national security demanded unity. "The greatest
lesson of this war," he reported, "has been the extent to which air,
land and sea operations can and must be coordinated by joint
planning and unified command." True of all forces, this observation
was doubly true of air power. In spite of the tremendous war production effort, aviation remained essentially scarce and quite expensive
throughout the entire war. There was never enough air capability
to meet all the separate opportunities and requirements for it. Given
proper command and control, however, air power could be an inherently flexible force—deriving this flexibility from range, speed,
and maneuverability—and could successfully perform multiple missions. Many times up until his death in 1949, Arnold continued to
remind his listeners that "actual battle experience showed that air
power is indivisible." General Hoyt S. Vandenberg, who commanded the 9th Air Force in Europe, also taught that air power was
a unity. Summing up the matter neatly, he said: "Tactical and strategic air power are part of the same ball of wax."

In the Army Air Corps during the 1930's, many planners had
believed that the establishment of friendly air superiority—or attainment of control of the air—would be essential for successful surface
operations but that a strategic bomber offensive would be able to

penetrate to vital targets deep within an enemy nation in spite of hostile defenses. After the war, American ground commanders were unanimous in stating requirements for friendly control of the air. General Omar N. Bradley noted briefly but emphatically that "the air battle must be won if a war is to be won." Recalling his service in Europe, Lieutenant General Manton S. Eddy spoke even more strongly: "There is no question in a soldier's mind that air power is as indispensable to national security as bread and water are to life. Land forces cannot fight decisively unless the air is controlled by its sister services."

The experience of the American strategic air forces in Europe in 1942 and 1943 caused many air leaders to believe that the prior establishment of friendly air superiority would be vital to a success- ful bomber offensive. Although no bomber mission was ever turned back from its target by enemy opposition, a combination of strong German fighter defenses and the conventional explosive bomb loads of the bombers (which meant that hundreds of sorties had to be flown to destroy an important target) made the bomber loss rate prohibitive in terms of damage done to the targets. On the basis of this experience, the U.S. Strategic Bombing Survey noted:

> The significance of full domination of the air over the enemy—both over its armed forces and over its sustaining economy—must be emphasized. That domination of the air was essential. Without it, attacks on the basic economy of the enemy could not have been delivered in sufficient force and with sufficient freedom to bring effective and lasting results.

The finding that strategic bombers required air superiority in order to penetrate was based upon a relationship between the vul- nerability of the bombers and the degree of destruction of a target. The first employment of nuclear weapons against the Japanese cities of Hiroshima and Nagasaki in August, 1945, cast new light upon the relationship. Major General Orvil A. Anderson, who headed the military advisory committee of the U.S. Strategic Bomb- ing Survey (Pacific), pointed out that nuclear weapon capabilities would make decisive bombing possible, even with relatively high attrition of bomber forces. In view of the quantum jump in the ability to destroy targets, a strategic air force commander might be willing to endure fairly high attrition rates. While this was a cogent argument, Arnold remained convinced of the importance of winning air superiority as the first phase of any military campaign. He stated: "The Air Force's primary mission is to knock out enemy air power—to win the air war." Time would prove Arnold right. During the late 1940's and early 1950's, air leaders would believe that they could safely ignore Soviet defenses and plan to attack targets without first attaining control of the air. In the late 1950's, when the Russians had acquired substantial stocks of nuclear weapons and formidable air defenses, the U.S. Air Force would enunciate a counterforce doctrine and define the policy as "the ability selectively and decisively to destroy enemy military forces that could otherwise destroy the United States or its Allies."

Even though the full implications of the lesson had not been completely substantiated, General Arnold considered that World War II had generally demonstrated the validity of the strategic air doctrine. This doctrine postulated that air attack on an enemy's vitals could so deplete specific industrial and economic resources—and, on occasion, the people's will to resist—as to make continued hostile resistance impossible. Arnold pointed out that the effects of strategic air attack against Germany and Japan "were like that of a cancer, producing internal decay ultimately resulting in death." Army officers were willing to accept the position that strategic bombing had assisted surface operations, but they would not agree that it could have been independently decisive. General Bradley, for example, considered that strategic bombing in Europe "was ultimately an effective deterrent to the success of the enemy on the battlefield. . . . It had a decisive effect on the ultimate ability of the Allies to defeat Germany in a shorter time, saving many, many lives and dollars."

The years of global air combat also made it apparent that there was a close relationship between science, technology, and air warfare. Tremendous new scientific developments—electronics, jet propulsion, missiles and rockets, and nuclear weapons—had dramatic impacts upon the conduct and the potential of air warfare. The scientific fundamentals of each of these developments were known to all combatants well before World War II, but their usefulness in combat depended upon national decisions to give them technological development as weapon systems. Oddly enough, early in the war, Germany had within her grasp air weapons that might have redressed her growing aerial inferiority. However, following his easy success in Poland, Hitler arrogantly refused to order a full mobilization of Germany's economic potential for war and, in 1940, severely curtailed the development of new weapons. As a result of low development priorities and Allied bombing attacks, the Germans did not begin to employ their V-1 and V-2 missiles until June–September, 1944, when the war was entering its final act. Because of indecision on priorities and Hitler's personal insistence that the plane must be used as a fighter-bomber, the outstanding Me-262 jet fighter was not placed in serial production until November, 1944, and this was too late to affect the course of the war. After examining the role of science in World War II, Dr. von Kármán observed: "Wars are fought with weapons based on fundamentals discovered during the preceding years of peace." Another lesson that might be drawn is that scientific knowledge is of little value to military purposes unless technology translates the knowledge into combat-ready weapon systems.

In the 1920's and 1930's, American military schools taught the doctrine of Clausewitz: "War is nothing else than a continuation of state policy by different means." But after the Japanese attack against Pearl Harbor on December 7, 1941, American military and political leaders tended to favor a total defeat of the Axis aggressors and to forget the close relationship that should exist between political objectives and military operations. Thinking back over his experience as a leading air commander and planner during World War II, Major General Haywood S. Hansell, Jr. observed: "My military bosses and I were consumed with one overpowering purpose: how to win the war with assurance and fewest American casualties. We had little concern for what happened afterward." Hansell went on to say that the desire to win the war quickly and with few casualties was a good but somewhat shortsighted objective. "To be sure, in the ball game we were playing," he concluded, "we had to keep our eyes on the ball. But we should have had a better feeling for where the goalposts were located, and we should have remembered that this was a continuing tournament . . . and there would be other games."

Strategic Air Warfare

"Because the last war saw the weapons of all services employed in profusion," suggested General Carl A. Spaatz, who commanded U.S. strategic air forces during World War II and became the first Chief of Staff, United States Air Force, "one may argue the exact degree of contribution made by strategic bombing to the final decision." Spaatz did not consider that independent strategic air power had received an adequate test in the global combat, since the war against Germany had been fundamentally an infantry war supported by air power, much as the war against Japan had been a naval war supported by air forces. Although the experience of World War II cannot be used to prove that a pure strategic air power policy would have succeeded, abundant evidence points to the fact that strategic air power was the margin of superiority that yielded Allied victory and Axis defeat.

When Adolf Hitler established the *Luftwaffe* as the independent equal of the German Army and Navy in 1935, he chose to develop the new Nazi air force for an essential role in a strategy that he was confident would yield victory. Hitler believed that Germany had lost World War I because trench fortifications, combined with machine guns and artillery firepower, had given defense a superiority over offense. The war had stalemated, and a broad coalition of enemies had eventually overwhelmed Germany. To avoid the mistakes of World War I, Hitler planned to develop forces to fight *blitzkrieg* ("lightning war") ground assault campaigns that would successfully overcome individual nations in a series of small and limited wars. Armored forces, with close air support, would strike so swiftly that defenses would be paralyzed. According to this strategy, the *Luftwaffe* was designed to be flying artillery. It was principally equipped with relatively short-range fighters, dive bombers, and transport planes.

In its employment against Poland, Norway, the Low Countries, and France during 1939–40, the *Luftwaffe* was a model of effectiveness, but it was an exploitative force designed to support surface operations and it failed abjectly when it was employed against Great Britain, beginning on August 8, 1940. The *Luftwaffe* commander, Hermann Goering, planned to gain air superiority over England by destroying the Royal Air Force Fighter Command and then to employ his force against coastal defenses, transportation facilities, and population centers in preparation for a combined sea and airborne invasion of south and southeastern England. Aided by newly developed radar warning and control, the RAF Fighter Command proved decidedly superior to the German dive bombers, which were inadequately armed and unable to carry heavy bomb loads. Although it was much larger in size, a series of vacillating orders by Goering helped prevent the *Luftwaffe* from achieving a decisive concentration of force against any single objective. By mid-October, 1940, it had failed to accomplish its strategic mission and had taken heavy losses; by December, there was no doubt that the RAF Fighter Command had won the Battle of Britain.

Being unable to invade Great Britain, Hitler turned his Nazi legions against the Soviet Union on June 22, 1941. At the outset of this campaign, the *Luftwaffe* decimated the Soviet Air Force, but the Germans continued to lack long-range bombers and were powerless to prevent the Russians from rebuilding their industrial strength at factories beyond the Ural mountains. At one time, Hitler had talked about building a "Urals bomber," but he had not taken the necessary action. In assessing Germany's air war record, the U.S. Strategic Bombing Survey found that the first factor in the defeat of the German Air Force was its lack of strategic air capabilities. It stated: "The German Air Force was originally designed for direct support of ground operations, and a lack of a long-range bomber force proved a grave strategic error."

Because of the threat of the *Luftwaffe*, British rearmament programs put into effect after 1936 stressed the build-up of the RAF Fighter Command and radar networks. The RAF Bomber Command was too weak to begin strategic bombing attacks until May, 1940, and it would not gain major stature until much later in the war. All these facts became known to the United States at a series of Anglo-American conferences held in Washington early in 1941. Although the United States made no decision to enter the war, the British and American staff planners nevertheless, on March 27, completed a document usually cited as "American-British Conversations No. 1," which contained a summary of strategic policies to be implemented if the United States went to war. The conferees agreed to concentrate the main war effort against Germany as the strongest of the Axis powers. The Allied offensive would include blockade, a "sustained air offensive" against German military power, early defeat of Italy, and preparation of forces for an eventual land offensive against Germany. The agreement visualized that, as rapidly as possible, the Allies would attain "superiority of air strength over that of the enemy, particularly in long-range striking forces."

Later in the summer, in response to a request by President Roosevelt for information on the over-all production requirements that would be necessary to defeat the Axis, the Air War Plans Division of the Army Air Forces completed a major document, entitled *AWPD-1, Munitions Requirements of the Army Air Forces,* on August 12, 1941. This air war plan visualized a strategic air campaign against Germany that would disrupt her electric power system, her transportation network, and her oil and petroleum resources and would undermine the morale of the German people. The air planners estimated that the economic and social life of Germany was already strained by the war against Russia, that an Allied land offensive against Germany could not be mounted for at least three years, and that, if the air offensive were successful, a land offensive might not be necessary. They asked for overriding production priorities to build a strategic air force, to include large numbers of B-29 Superfortress bombers and the development of a 4,000-mile radius-of-action bomber (the future B-36).

The U.S. Joint Board (the Army-Navy forebear of the Joint Chiefs of Staff) accepted *AWPD-1* as a statement of Army Air Forces requirements, but it would not accept the idea that a strategic air offensive against Germany could eliminate the necessity for a land campaign. The Board warned: "Naval and air power may prevent wars from being lost, and by weakening enemy strength may greatly contribute to victory. By themselves, however, naval and air forces seldom, if ever, win important wars. It should be recognized as an almost invariable rule that only land armies can finally win wars." The Joint Board statement proved to be a very apt prediction of what the United States strategy would be after the nation went to war. At meetings in Washingon beginning on December 22, 1941, the Anglo-American Arcadia Conference proved unwilling to accept overriding strategic air priorities but instead adopted a "Victory Program" calling for increases of air, ground, and naval forces in a sequence of limited schedules to be geared to successively approved operations.

An internal reorganization of the War Department moved strategic planning up to the Operations Division of the War Department General Staff, thus ending unilateral Air Force planning. The last major Air Force plan, entitled *AWPD-42, Requirements for Air Ascendancy,* issued on September 9, 1942, followed approved strategy and defined the air mission in terms of cooperation with a surface campaign. The air missions were specified to be (1) an air offensive against Germany to deplete the German air force, to destroy construction sources of German submarines, and to undermine German war-making capacity; (2) air support for a land offensive in Northwest Africa; (3) air support of land operations to retain the Middle East; (4) air support of surface operations in the Pacific and Far East to regain base areas needed for a final offensive against the Japanese homeland; and (5) defense of the Western Hemisphere, including antisubmarine operations. In support of this surface strategy, AWPD-42 defined the priority targets in Germany as being airplane assembly plants, aircraft engine plants, submarine yards, transportation, power, oil, aluminum, and rubber production facilities. There was another important change in the planning: AWPD-1 had expected that six months of intensified bombing against Germany would begin in mid-1943, but AWPD-42 recognized that this all-out air campaign could not be undertaken until late in 1944.

When President Franklin D. Roosevelt and Prime Minister Winston S. Churchill met at the Casablanca Conference on January 21, 1943, they directed the execution of an Anglo-American bomber offensive against Germany designed to secure "the progressive destruction and dislocation of the German military, industrial and economic system, and the undermining of the morale of the German people to a point where their capacity for armed resistance is fatally weakened." This air offensive, however, was to be preparatory to a surface invasion. The Casablanca directive, for example, required the strategic bombers to give first priority to attacks against German submarine bases and construction yards. Accepted as a result of Roosevelt's insistence, and without any military discussion, the Allied objective of "unconditional surrender" approved at Casablanca virtually demanded an absolute ground conquest of the German nation. Writing later of the Casablanca directive, General Laurence S. Kuter observed: "The air weapon system was assigned a supporting role to facilitate the implementation of this conventional surface strategy."

Even though the Allied combined bomber offensive against Germany was designed to prepare the way for a surface invasion of the continent, the build-up of American strategic bombers in Europe was relatively slow, and, in the end, the major weight of the strategic bomber attack followed rather than preceded the invasion of Western Europe. In January, 1943, the Army Air Forces had only twelve heavy bombardment groups deployed in theaters against Germany, and it did not attain its maximum strength of sixty-two heavy bombardment groups against Germany until May, 1944, less than a month before the invasion of Normandy on June 6, 1944. The total of first-line B-17's and B-24's deployed against Germany increased from 413 in January, 1943, to a maximum of 5,027 in March, 1945. The RAF Bomber Command's strength increased from a miscellany of 515 light, medium, and heavy bombers in January, 1943 to a total of 1,609 Halifax, Lancaster, and Mosquito bombers in April, 1945. Of the total of 2,770,540 tons of bombs dropped by AAF and RAF aircraft against Germany, only 17 per cent fell prior to January 1, 1944, and only 28 per cent prior to July 1, 1944.

As a result of the small number of available bombers and the commitment of these forces to objectives selected in terms of the planned surface campaign, the Allied strategic bomber offensive had very little appreciable effect on Germany's munitions output or national economy during 1943, and the total armaments production of Germany steadily increased until July, 1944. As a matter of fact, Germany's industry was only partly mobilized in 1942–43 and, thus, had a large cushion that could be employed to expand production after the Allied bomber attack had begun. From January to June, 1943, moreover, the strategic bombers were required to devote their principal effort to attacks against submarine bases and pens—targets that were relatively invulnerable to bombs. In June, 1943, the Combined Chiefs of Staff directed that first priority be given to attacks against German fighter forces and the industry upon which they depended. Lacking enough bombers to handle the German aircraft target system, the U.S. 8th Air Force chose to try to destroy a "long-chance objective." Back in Washington, a committee of operations analysts assembled by General Arnold recommended that antifriction ball bearings were a potential bottleneck in German war industry. The committee—composed mostly of civilian industrialists and economists—believed that the destruction of a few ball-bearing plants would tie up German aircraft production. Although about 12,000 tons of bombs were dropped on Germany's ball-bearing plants after August 17, 1943, the U.S. Strategic Bombing Survey later reported "there is no evidence that the attacks on the ball-bearing industry had any measurable effect on essential war production."

While seeking to destroy ball-bearing factories, 8th Air Force heavy bombers sustained large losses on long-range penetration missions to Schweinfurt and Regensburg on August 17 and on a return mission to Schweinfurt on October 14, 1943. The usual interpretation is that these heavy bomber losses forced reassessment of U.S. strategic bombing effort. "The fact was," concluded the official history *The Army Air Forces in World War II,* "that the 8th Air Force had for the time being lost air superiority over Germany. And it was obvious that superiority could not be regained until sufficient long-range escort became available." Actually, this interpretation missed the mark. A close reading of Air Force correspondence of the period reveals a confidence that strategic bombers, employed in force, could still perform their missions over Germany but that an early attainment of Allied control of the air would be necessary if the invasions in Normandy and southern France were to succeed in mid-1944.

"It is a conceded fact," General Arnold told the commanders of the 8th and 15th Air Forces on December 27, 1943, "that OVER-LORD and ANVIL will not be possible unless the German Air Force is destroyed. Therefore, my personal message to you—this is a MUST—is to, *'Destroy the Enemy Air Force wherever you find them, in the air, on the ground and in the factories.'* " Effective on January 1, 1944, General Spaatz was given command of the U.S. Strategic Air Forces in Europe (USSTAF), a headquarters that combined the control over the British-based 8th Air Force and the Italian-based 15th Air Force. Between October, 1943, and February, 1944, the number of heavy bombardment groups operating against Germany increased from 26 to 48, providing increased mass for the strategic attacks. P-47 and P-51 fighters were equipped with external fuel tanks and began to fly long-range cover for the heavy bombers. The Allied fighter effort benefited from a German mistake. In December, 1943, Field Marshal Goering (ignoring the basic fact of air fighting that when aircraft of roughly equal performance meet, the one which seeks to avoid combat tends to commit suicide) issued orders to *Luftwaffe* fighter pilots to avoid Allied fighters and concentrate their attack on Allied bombers. To take advantage of Goering's mistake, Allied fighters were allowed to take the offensive —to pursue and destroy enemy fighters—rather than to provide position defense to friendly bombers. With all of these developments, the Allied air superiority campaign, begun on February 20, 1944, in what came to be called the "Big Week," was nearly able to destroy the effectiveness of the *Luftwaffe* by the time of the Normandy invasion. One of the major factors in the defeat of the *Luftwaffe* was a centralization of control over Allied air units. Although the U.S. 9th Air Force had been designated as the support for American ground armies in Europe and was busily engaged in fighter-bomber training, Spaatz was able to use 9th Air Force air-craft in the air superiority campaign. "There was no difficulty," Spaatz said, "in using 9th Air Force fighters when we needed them. If we had a mission, we could always get them."

In the months that followed, USSTAF strategic bombing capabilities were employed in attacks against German V-weapon sites and in missions in support of Allied ground troops going ashore in France. Even though Spaatz was permitted to begin attacks against Germany's oil resources on May 12, 1944, it is fair to state that a massive sustained air campaign against strategic air targets in Germany did not begin until after D-Day, when Allied ground troops were safely ashore in Normandy. By December, 1944, German reserves of fuel were insufficient to sustain effective military operations. Undertaken intensively in September, 1944, the strategic air campaign against Germany's transportation was later described by the U.S. Bombing Survey as "the decisive blow that completely disorganized the German economy." Contrary to the intention of early AAF planners, the German electric power system was never a principal target. "Had electric generating plants and substations been made primary targets, . . ." the Bombing Survey stated, "the evidence indicates that their destruction would have had serious effects on Germany's war production." Under the full force of strategic bomber attack, and with war requirements multiplying more swiftly than production could handle, the economic life of Germany virtually collapsed by December, 1944. "The German experience," states the U.S. Strategic Bombing Survey, "suggests that even a first-class military power—rugged and resilient as Germany was—cannot live long under full-scale and free exploitation of air weapons over the heart of its territory."

In the Pacific, the pattern of Allied operations and commitment of forces was different from that employed in Europe, but the strategy relative to the employment of air power was essentially the same. The Japanese had viewed aviation as purely a supporting force for surface operations, and they had organized completely separate (and seldom cooperating) Army and Navy air forces. After the surprise attack at Pearl Harbor, the Japanese exercised local air and naval supremacy in the western Pacific. Because of the successful Japanese expansion, U.S. Army Air Forces planners recognized that even the very-long-range B-29's would be unable to reach the Japanese homeland until the enemy's perimeter had been reduced. "Our armed forces in the Far Eastern Theater," stated *AWPD-42*, "are not within effective striking distance of the vital sources of Japanese military policy. . . . Hence from the standpoint of air requirements, the Far Eastern operations may be divided into two phases: (1) Air operations in support of our land and sea forces to regain bases within striking distance of Japan. . . . (2) Air operations against Japan proper to destroy her war-making capacity."

At the Quadrant Conference in Quebec during August, 1943, the Anglo-American Combined Chiefs of Staff approved advances toward Japan both through the Central Pacific and along the New Guinea-Philippines axis. AAF planners favored the Central Pacific route as being likely to provide B-29 bases at the earliest date. In the autumn of 1943, U.S. joint staff planners sought to prepare an over-all plan for the defeat of Japan. The initial draft of this study stated that it had been clearly demonstrated in Europe that air forces were incapable of decisive action and that surface invasion of the Japanese home islands would be necessary to conclude the war. The best that the Air Force representative could do to get this statement changed was to secure a new statement to the effect that a preliminary air offensive against Japan would be essential to the ultimate invasion of the home islands. At the Sextant Conference in Cairo during December, 1943, Roosevelt, Churchill, and Chiang Kai-shek declared that the Allied objective would be the unconditional surrender of Japan. They authorized the beginning of B-29 attacks against Japan from bases far in the interior of China by May, 1944, and from bases in the Mariana Islands before the end of the year.

Because the B-29 wings would mount the strategic air offensive against Japan from bases located in several different theaters of operations, Arnold secured agreement permitting the 20th Air Force to be established in Washington directly under the Joint Chiefs of Staff to control the 20th Bomber Command in China and the 21st Bomber Command in the Marianas. As written by the Joint Chiefs of Staff, the mission of the 20th Air Force was: "To achieve the progressive destruction and dislocation of the Japanese military, industrial and economic systems and the undermining of the morale of the Japanese people to a point where their capacity for armed resistance is decisively weakened." Arnold's committee of operations analysts recommended that B-29 attacks be directed against Japan's merchant shipping, steel production, urban industrial areas, aircraft plants, antifriction ball-bearing factories, and electronics industries. Japan's steel industry was thought to include a "long-chance" target; the industry depended upon coke, which was produced in only a few ovens at sites in Manchuria and on Kyushu. The analysts also pointed out that Japan's urban areas housed many small factories and were very vulnerable to incendiary attack.

With the exception that the Japanese Army and Navy air forces had already suffered grave losses of experienced personnel, the early operations of the 20th Air Force's 20th Bomber Command from bases in China were not unlike early 8th Air Force operations from Great Britain. The 20th Bomber Command was a piecemeal commitment of too little capability; it was also based in a remote area, far from all industrial targets, and where logistical support was difficult to obtain. The China-based B-29's attempted to destroy the "long-chance" coke-oven targets, but they had very little success in the effort. As time passed, it was more and more obvious that the burden of the strategic air campaign against Japan would have to be flown by the 20th Air Force's 21st Bomber Command, which was prepared to go into operation as soon as bases were built in the Marianas. Construction of these new airfields began only a few days after Admiral Chester Nimitz's forces invaded Saipan on June 15, 1944, but the airfield work did not get overriding priority, since Nimitz also required new fleet bases to support surface invasions of Iwo Jima and Okinawa and the planned invasion of Japan.

During the summer of 1944, 20th Air Force target planners became skeptical of the high priority given to Japan's steel industry as a target system, and General Arnold asked the committee of operations analysts to submit a fresh target study based on alternative assumptions that Japan might be defeated solely by air attack and sea blockade or by these plus a surface invasion. Under the first alternative, the analysts recommended a general air campaign against shipping, attacks against aircraft industries, and the saturation bombing of six urban industrial areas. Under the second alternative, they recommended priority attacks against the aircraft industry, with secondary effort against urban industrial targets and shipping.

Brigadier General Adolphus W. Greely, as Chief Signal Officer of the U.S. Army, was instrumental in organizing the first balloon corps in the late nineteenth century.

Brigadier General James Allen, Chief Signal Officer (1906–13), ordered the first dirigible to be used by U.S. airmen.

Major General William L. Kenly, head of U.S. military aviation in World War I. President Wilson chose him to head the Division of Aeronautics, which was still a part of the Army Signal Corps. A short time later, the division became an independent branch of the Army.

General Henry H. ("Hap") Arnold, pioneer airman, was the commanding general of the Army Air Forces during World War II. In 1949, Congress appointed him the first general of the Air Force, five-star rank.

American World War I aviators prepare to take off in a French-built Caudron.

A one-man basket observation balloon of World War I, surrounded by Allied officers, prepares to lift off.

General William C. ("Billy") Mitchell (standing) at his court-martial in 1925.

Colonel Charles A. Lindbergh (center) during Missouri National Guard maneuvers in 1928.

The P-51, a World War II fighter plane, in flight.

A B-17 "Flying Fortress" releases its bombs over a Nazi airfield in France, March, 1944.

The "Enola Gay," the plane that dropped the first atomic bomb. over Hiroshima, Japan, in August, 1945.

President John F. Kennedy and General Curtis E. LeMay, Air Force Chief of Staff, watch an aerial demonstration on May 4, 1962.

Change-of-command ceremonies at the Air Force Academy, Colorado Springs, Colorado. In the background is the Academy chapel, offering facilities for worship to people of all faiths.

The Northrop Scorpion F-89D, a twin-jet fighter capable of speeds of more than 600 m.p.h., was one of the Air Force's fighting planes in the Korean War.

An F-4C Phantom fighter dives toward a target in North Vietnam, 1966.

The Vela satellite orbits the earth to detect nuclear blasts and collect scientific data.

The launching of a Minuteman intercontinental ballistic missile.

Discounting the possibility that Japan would surrender without invasion, the Joint Target Group in Washington recommended that emphatic priority be given to the destruction of Japan's air power and that the urban attacks and antishipping operations be delayed.

After postponements caused by bad weather and limited facilities, General Hansell sent the 21st Bomber Command on high-level attacks against Japan's aircraft-production factories beginning on November 24, 1944. Japanese fighters and anti-aircraft artillery were not very effective against the high-flying B-29's, but, in the months that followed, the precision-bombing effort did not appear to be very successful. Bad weather scattered formations, obscured targets, and reduced bombing accuracy. The long flights to Japan and the need to lift heavy bomb loads to 25,000-foot bombing altitudes strained engines and caused substantial losses of aircraft at sea. Impatient with the results of the 21st Bomber Command, Arnold moved Major General Curtis E. LeMay to its command on January 20, 1945, but neither the new commander nor the commitment of a second B-29 wing to the Marianas appeared to give much better results. Actually, Japanese aircraft production had dropped substantially because of the B-29 attacks and the high degree of confusion produced when the Japanese attempted to disperse the aircraft plants.

As late as March 6, 1945, General LeMay considered that the 21st Bomber Command had not "really accomplished a hell of a lot in bombing results." With the arrival of a third B-29 wing in the Marianas, however, Arnold issued a new target directive on February 19. It continued to place aircraft factories in first priority but moved incendiary attacks against urban industrial concentrations into a strong second priority. Although fire raids were desired and ordered by Washington, LeMay kept his own counsel on the tactics to be employed on the great Tokyo fire raid when it was mounted on the night of March 9, 1945. LeMay called for a stream of bombers from the three wings to come in low (4,900 to 9,200 feet) and drop their incendiaries on fires started by pathfinder crews. Fearing that gunners unused to night attack might shoot at each other's planes, LeMay ordered guns and gunners removed from the B-29's. The weight saved by the removal of armament and the low altitude of attack permitted the B-29's to carry exceptionally heavy loads of incendiaries. Over the target in a steady stream in the early morning hours of March 10, the B-29's sustained moderate losses as they kindled raging fires that destroyed about one-fourth of metropolitan Tokyo. General LeMay had staked his professional career on his decision to operate the bombers at low level. "This decision, combining technical acumen with boldness of execution," General Hansell later said, "was one of the classic air decisions of the war."

In March, 1945, the Japanese government began to take serious steps to end the war, but it was unwilling to accept unconditional surrender. Top-level officials in Washington knew of Japan's desire to end hostilities, but, in September, 1944, the Combined Chiefs of Staff had committed the Allies to the seizure of "objectives in the industrial heart of Japan." At Yalta in February, 1945, this surface strategy was reaffirmed, but the Soviet Union obtained territorial concessions in return for promises to join the war against Japan. In April, American soldiers and marines began bloody battles to take Okinawa, and General LeMay diverted 75 per cent of the 21st Bomber Command's capability between April 17 and May 11 to attacks against enemy airfields on Kyushu and Shikoku in support of the invasion. In the waning weeks of May and the early days of June, 1945, however, the 21st Bomber Command continued to burn Japan's principal industrial areas. When Arnold visited Guam early in June, LeMay told him that from thirty to sixty of Japan's cities and every industrial target would be destroyed by October 1. Never successful against night-flying B-29's, Japanese fighters made their last effective opposition against a daytime B-29 attack on June 5, and, thereafter, the Japanese air forces elected to save their remaining planes for *kamikaze* ("suicide") attacks against the expected Allied invasion forces. On June 20, Emperor Hirohito told his council that it would be necessary to have a plan to close the war at once, but Japan's militarists argued against unconditional surrender. These militarists clung to the expectation that Japan's ground defenses would still be able to inflict enough casualties on Allied surface invaders to win a negotiated peace.

Japan's conditional offer to surrender was accepted on August

12, 1945. The revolutionary employment of nuclear air weapons against Hiroshima and Nagasaki and the Soviet Union's declaration of war on August 8 tended to obscure the contribution of the sustained air offensive to the victory. "Without attempting to minimize the appalling and far-reaching results of the atomic bomb," General Arnold wrote, "we have good reason to believe that its actual use provided a way out for the Japanese government. The fact is that the Japanese could not have held out long, because they lost control of their air. They could not offer effective opposition to our bombardment, and so could not prevent the destruction of their cities and industries." Based upon detailed investigations within Japan, the U.S. Strategic Bombing Survey reported that "certainly prior to 31 December 1945, and in all probability prior to 1 November 1945, Japan would have surrendered even if the atomic bombs had not been dropped, even if Russia had not entered the war, and even if no invasion had been planned or contemplated."

If history is to be considered as nothing more than the exact record of accumulated experience, one must conclude that the Allied strategic air operations of World War II did not attain the goal of producing surrender with only incidental help from other forces. On the basis of the facts, one must conclude that World War II represented an Allied victory attained with coordinated air, ground, and naval forces. But the greater strategic lesson of World War II might well be that the Anglo-American heads of state and war commanders never fully grasped the revolutionary potentialities of a strategic air force offensive. Had the war leaders been willing to trust air power's capabilities as an independent force, the strategic air offensives would have been properly designed to prepare for such exploitative ground occupations as might have seemed proper. The selection of strategic target systems for an independent air campaign would have been quite different from those selected to support concurrent air and surface operations. And, as General Spaatz ultimately observed: "Had the revolutionary potentialities of the strategic air offensive been fully grasped by the men running the war, some of the fateful political concessions made to hold the Russians in the European war and to draw them into the Japanese war might never have been made."

Coordinated Air-Surface Warfare

One of the major ironies of World War II was the discovery that air units assigned or attached to surface force units, when operating against a first-class adversary on a land mass large enough to support many airfields, proved incapable of providing effective support to the surface forces. In the course of the combat, German and Allied commanders alike gained a new recognition of the unique capabilities of air forces to operate against hostile forces in being, thus decisively affecting the outcome of the surface battle.

As a result of its organization and indoctrination, the *Luftwaffe* provided outstanding support to German *blitzkrieg* offensives against Poland, Norway, the Netherlands, Belgium, and France in 1939–40. Although German airmen jealously guarded the integrity of their *Luftflotten* ("air fleets") and *Fliegerkorps* ("flying corps"), they made every effort to perform preplanned support for the ground attack. Only observation squadrons were attached to ground commands; the flying corps were centrally controlled, and, rarely remaining at a given airfield more than a few days, they shifted the mass of their dive bombers to attack critical targets anywhere on the ground front. Beginning in Poland, the *Luftwaffe* followed a pattern of attack that gave priority to the destruction of hostile aircraft and airfields, then attacked the enemy's main headquarters and communications, and very quickly shifted to massed strikes against the enemy's beaten and disorganized ground troops. *Luftwaffe* transport planes were used for advanced flying training of pilots when they were not needed for tactical operations, such as the airborne operations in Norway and Holland in 1940 and against Crete in May, 1941. Everything worked in favor of the *Luftwaffe* in the battles on the narrow fronts that characterized early operations in Western Europe.

As Hitler extended his forces into the Soviet Union in 1941 and into North Africa in 1941–42, the *Luftwaffe* initially retained its old proficiency but it gradually became hopelessly overextended. On the Russian front, the German air units were not only overextended, but tactical reverses to the German ground armies forced the air units to devote most of their efforts to the close support of ground troops, with a great reduction in the effort that could be applied to counter-air and interdiction operations. *Luftwaffe* observation squadrons attached to army commands suffered heavy losses, with the result that the air command had to repossess those squadrons beginning in February, 1942, and reorganize them into centrally controlled groups that could provide reconnaissance for both army and air purposes. In the winter of 1942–43, JU-52 air transport forces were decimated in a futile attempt to resupply besieged ground forces at Stalingrad. According to German air commanders, the major defect in the *Luftwaffe* air transport establishment was its lack of a single responsible commander, who could have ensured its effective and continued operations.

In the United States during the 1920's and 1930's, Army air leaders conceived that an air striking force would be centrally commanded and would conduct an air offensive prior to the engagement of surface forces. At the completion of the air offensive, the entire air force would support friendly ground troops. Since they were believed to be necessary for the accomplishment of the ground mission, however, Air Corps observation aircraft and balloon squadrons were attached directly to ground units.

In early campaigns in Europe, a Royal Air Force component was attached to the British Expeditionary Forces in France, and the United States followed a similar arrangement when its forces invaded North Africa. The 12th Air Force was organized in standard air defense, bombardment, air support, and air service commands, and, in January, 1943, the 12th Air Support Command was directly attached to the U.S. II Corps for support of a ground attack into Tunisia. This arrangement worked poorly. Centrally directed *Luftwaffe* units easily overwhelmed divided Allied air squadrons. On the basis of his experience in the Western Desert, General Bernard L. Montgomery, Commander of the British Eighth Army, had already perceived that the greatest asset of air power was its flexibility, and that this flexibility could be realized only when air power was centrally controlled by an air officer who would maintain a close association with the ground commander. In a small pamphlet issued in January, 1943, entitled "Some Notes on High Command in War," Montgomery declared: "Nothing could be more fatal to successful results than to dissipate the air resources into small packets placed under command of army formation commanders, with each packet working on its own plan."

As a result of the lessons of combat, General Spaatz organized a new Northwest Africa Allied Air Force in February, 1943, and gave it command over a Strategic Air Force, a Coastal Air Force, and a Tactical Air Force. In a letter to Arnold on March 7, 1943, Spaatz described requirements for a successful surface campaign. He emphasized that "the air battle must be won first. . . . Air units must be centralized and cannot be divided into small packets among several armies or corps. . . . When the battle situation requires it, all units, including medium and heavy bombardment, must support ground operations."

Back in the United States, the War Department accepted the co-equality of land and air power and endorsed the doctrine in Field Manual 100-20, *Command and Employment of Air Power,* which was published on July 21, 1943. The manual described the new tactical air force that was to be organized for cooperation with ground armies. It specified that the tactical air mission would be to gain and maintain air superiority, to isolate the battlefield by interdicting movement of hostile troops and supplies, and to provide close support to ground forces. In a companion action of the same season, the Army Air Forces inactivated the old observation squadrons and established new tactical reconnaissance groups that would be sufficiently versatile to provide needed intelligence information to the army–tactical-air-force team. The new organizations were tested in combat in Italy, and the tactical air system was intensively developed in the major air-ground campaigns in Europe after June, 1944.

In the Pacific theaters of operations, American forces accepted the same tasks of tactical air power—air superiority, interdiction, and close air support—but employed different organization. In General Douglas MacArthur's Southwest Pacific Area, where General George C. Kenney was air commander, the entire 5th Air Force supported the Sixth Army and after June, 1944, the 13th Air Force usually supported the Eighth Army. In Central Pacific Area island campaigns under Admiral Nimitz, Navy and Marine air groups based on fast aircraft carriers provided support for amphibious invasions. According to a new plan worked out after June, 1944 (when 5th Fleet fast carriers had to withdraw to fight the naval battle of the Philippine Sea, leaving ground troops ashore on Saipan without close air support), the Marines obtained authority to allocate a Marine air wing to the integral support of each Marine infantry division. This would be an expensive commitment, but it was justified by the fact that amphibious operations would be short, intense, and extremely demanding in fire support.

The Allied organization for air transport aviation closely paralleled the eventual organization of tactical air combat and reconnaissance since (as was true for all air resources) war requirements were always too large to permit planes to be parceled out among using units. Anglo-American organization of theater airlift forces placed central control of most airlift units under some form of theater troop carrier headquarters, which could employ the planes for airlift or air-assault operations. In the European theater of operations, for example, a Combined Air Transport Operations Room (CATOR) in the Supreme Headquarters, Allied Expeditionary Forces, handled the central allocation of troop carrier capabilities.

Army and AAF officers were so generally satisfied with the air-ground system that had matured in Europe that it was incorporated into War Department Field Manual 31-35, *Air-Ground Operations,* in August, 1946. Written as an assimilation of the best lessons of World War II, this manual stated:

> The forces within a theater are composed of air, ground, and naval components. Unified command is vested in the theater commander, who is directly responsible for the administration and combat operations within the theater. It is his responsibility that operational plans provide for coordination of the forces at his disposal and that such plans are energetically and effectively executed.

As World War II drew to an end, the Allied air and ground commanders gained a broadened appreciation of each other's capabilities and requirements. General Dwight D. Eisenhower stated:

> Battle experience proved that control of the air, the prerequisite to the conduct of ground operations in any given area, was gained most economically by the employment of air forces operating under a single command. This assured a maximum of flexibility, providing a command structure under which all forms of available air power could be concentrated on tactical support missions or on strategic missions, as the situation demanded—in other words, it permitted the maximum concentration of combat air power at the decisive point at the decisive time.

IV

USAF–Separate Service

Establishment of the U.S. Air Force

The practically autonomous status of the Army Air Forces during World War II was a temporary measure, promulgated by Executive order of the President under the provisions of the first War Powers Act of 1941. Six months after the end of the war, the air arm was to revert to its prewar status. But change was foreseen, and in anticipation of postwar reorganization of the defense structure, both the Army and the Navy were examining the subject in considerable detail while the war still raged.

In May, 1944, the Joint Chiefs of Staff appointed a special committee of outstanding Army and Navy officers to examine three basic systems of defense organization. After many months of travel and many interviews with outstanding military leaders, the committee recommended in March, 1945, a plan for a Department of Armed Forces to consist of three coordinate branches.

The Navy appointed its own committee in 1945, headed by Ferdinand Eberstadt, a New York banker. The Eberstadt Report recommended the organization of the military forces into three coordinate departments, War, Navy, and Air, with the Navy retaining its air fleet. The Joint Chiefs of Staff would serve to link the three departments, and a National Security Council, under the President, would coordinate the departments with civilian agencies. Secretary of the Navy Forrestal did not accept the recommendation of a separate department for air.

In January, 1945, Senator Lister Hill of Alabama introduced a bill providing for a single Department of Armed Forces. In October, 1945, Senator Edwin C. Johnson of Colorado submitted a bill for a single Department of Military Security consisting of six divisions. During 1945, six other bills for the reorganization of the defense structure were introduced but they did not obtain hearings. When the Senate Committee on Military Affairs concluded its hearings in December, 1945, and failed to submit a report, President Truman asked Congress for legislation to combine the War and Navy Departments into a single Department of National Defense along the lines of the Joint Chiefs' recommendation. In making this proposal, the President told Congress that air power had developed to a point where its responsibilities equaled those of land and naval forces and where its contribution to strategic planning was as great. Stressing the importance of parity for air power, he advocated establishment of a separate Air Force.

A subcommittee of the Senate Committee on Military Affairs immediately began working on a unification bill with Army and Navy representatives. The final draft was introduced as a bill (S. 2044) in April, 1946, and accepted by the Committee the following month. The Navy was strongly opposed to the bill as revealed at the hearings of the Senate Committee on Naval Affairs, believing that it would lose prestige and its traditional position as the first line of defense of the United States. Primarily, the Navy objected to giving a single individual, the Secretary of Common Defense, the only statutory access to the President. It also objected to the idea of the proposed Chief of Staff of Common Defense and to the possibility of losing its land-based air units to a Department of the Air Force.

In response to President Truman's request, Secretary of War Robert P. Patterson and of the Navy James V. Forrestal submitted a report at the end of May listing their points of agreement and contention. Confronted with the deeply rooted differences between the Army and the Navy, the President submitted his own unification program in early June. The Senate Committee on Military Affairs revised the Senate bill later that month, but again it was opposed by Navy backers and died by default.

President Truman continued to urge recognition of air power and proposed that a new bill be drawn up which would be approved by the next Congress. By January, 1947, when the Eightieth Congress met, the Army and Navy had agreed on a proposal for the organization of the military departments and their functions. Their proposal was approved by President Truman and the draft bill went to Congress in February, 1947, as the National Security Act of 1947. After many Congressional hearings, it was passed by Congress and became law on July 26, 1947.

The objectives of this historic Act were (1) to provide a comprehensive program for the future security of the United States; (2) to provide three military departments—the Army, the Navy (which would retain its aviation units and the Marine Corps), and the Air Force; (3) to provide for the coordination and unified direction of the services under civilian control, but not to merge them; and (4) to provide for the effective strategic direction and operation of the armed forces under unified control.

Title I of the Act established the National Security Council (NSC), the Central Intelligence Agency under NSC, and the National Security Resources Board to coordinate all national security matters.

Title II of the Act created the National Military Establishment as an executive department headed by a civilian Secretary of Defense appointed by the President. Three coordinate departments— Department of the Army, Department of the Navy, and Department of the Air Force—were established within the National Military Establishment. The law also provided that each military department would be separately organized under its own Secretary and would function under the direction, authority, and control of the Secretary of Defense.

The responsibilities of the Commanding General, Army Air Forces, were to be transferred to the Department of the Air Force. The United States Air Force (USAF) was established and the Army Air Forces were to be transferred to the USAF. The Army Air Corps and Air Force Combat Command as AAF agencies were abolished.

The composition and the mission of the United States Air Force were stated in broad terms in the Act:

In general, the United States Air Force shall include aviation forces both combat and service not otherwise assigned. It shall be organized, trained, and equipped primarily for prompt and sustained offensive and defensive air operations. The Air Force shall be responsible for the preparation of the air forces necessary for the effective prosecution of war except as otherwise assigned and in accordance with integrated joint mobilization plans, for the expansion of peacetime components of the Air Force to meet the needs of war.

After formally approving the Act on July 26, President Truman signed Executive Order No. 9877, which prescribed the roles and responsibilities of the three services. Those assigned to the USAF were as follows:

(1) to organize, train, and equip air forces for (a) air operations including joint operations, (b) gaining and maintaining general air supremacy, (c) establishing local air superiority where and as required, (d) the strategic air force of the United States and for strategic air reconnaissance, (e) airlift and support for airborne operations, (f) air support to land forces and naval forces, including support of occupation forces, (g) air transport for the armed forces, except as provided by the Navy in accordance with paragraph 1f of Section III;

(2) to develop weapons, tactics, techniques, organization, and equipment of Air Force combat and service elements, coordinating with the Army and Navy on all aspects of joint concern, including those which pertain to amphibious and airborne operations;

(3) to provide, as directed by proper authority, such missions and detachments for service in foreign countries as may be required to support the national policies and interests of the United States;

(4) to provide the means for coordination of air defense among all services; and

(5) to assist the Army and Navy in the accomplishment of their missions, including the provision of common services and supplies as determined by proper authority.

Secretary of the Navy Forrestal became the first Secretary of Defense. On September 18, 1947, Chief Justice Fred M. Vinson administered the oath of office to W. Stuart Symington, first Secretary of the Air Force. On September 26, General Carl A. Spaatz was sworn in as the first Chief of Staff, United States Air Force. Major General Hoyt S. Vandenberg became the Vice Chief of Staff. So began the modern era of aerospace power in which the United States Air Force, in less than twenty years, would evolve into the most powerful military force in the history of the world.

Roles and Missions of the United States Air Force

The National Security Act of 1947 provided for the most significant change in the history of the nation's military organization. Executive Order No. 9877, signed on the same day as the Act, outlined the main functions of the three services in broad terms. It was soon apparent, however, that detailed arrangements had to be worked out to make the responsibilities of each service clearer.

The changing nature of war and weaponry was one of the principal causes of disagreement among the three services, particularly between the Air Force and the Navy. The tremendous technological advances which had already occurred during World War II foreshadowed an even greater emphasis on air power in the future. The Navy contested the role of the Air Force long-range bomber and Air Force concept of land-based strategic bombing, believing that aircraft carriers and the proposed supercarriers should perform the strategic bombing mission. The Air Force contended that aircraft carriers were too vulnerable to air attack and carrier-based aircraft were incapable of performing long-range strategic bombing operations.

To settle these controversies and specify the missions of the services, Secretary of Defense Forrestal held conferences with the Joint Chiefs of Staff on March 12–14, 1948, at Key West, Florida, and on August 20–22, 1948, at Newport, Rhode Island. These meetings resulted in the assignment to the Air Force of primary responsibility for strategic air warfare, and to the Navy the responsibility for control of the seas. All services were assigned collateral functions enabling each to obtain maximum assistance from another in carrying out its missions.

Disagreement over the apportionment of funds continued to plague the services after the Key West and Newport agreements. A three-way split of defense funds was a compromise at best and did not take into account the increased costs of new weapons or the mission priorities among the services. The Air Force considered its mission had a higher priority over the Army and Navy and required a larger proportion of defense funds to accomplish it.

Technological progress, bringing new aircraft with related fire control and weapon systems that were becoming more costly, had to be considered in the Air Force appropriation requests. The rapid obsolescence of its World War II equipment necessitated a rearmament program, which had to be apportioned between the present and the future. The explosion of the first Russian atomic bomb in August, 1949, resulted in pressure on the Air Force to maintain a force-in-being to deter the Soviet Union and at the same time to re-equip units with the most advanced weapons possible. This was a hard task, in view of the heavy military-budget cuttings that followed the end of World War II. Yet, as the world conflict ended in 1945, only five years were to pass before the United States was at war again—in Korea.

With the Korean War, the defense budget shot up sharply. The Joint Chiefs of Staff approved a goal of 143 Air Force wings to be attained by June 30, 1955. In 1953, after the end of the Korean War, defense appropriations were gradually cut. In December, 1953, President Eisenhower approved the Air Force program calling for 137 wings to be achieved by June, 1957.

By 1957—the year of Sputnik—the strategic-deterrent power of the Air Force, concentrated primarily in the Strategic Air Command and its force of nuclear-armed jets, was recognized as the nation's first line of defense. Massive nuclear retaliation against Soviet aggression was official policy and the Air Force became the recipient of the largest share of defense funds.

Missiles—Airpower's New Dimension

Meanwhile, air power was reaching into space. No technological advance with the exception of the airplane itself has been as important to air power as the intercontinental ballistic missile. Carrying nuclear warheads at speeds in excess of 16,000 mph, ICBM's have militarily shrunk the world so that every nation on the planet is within minutes of devastating attack. In recent years, these great boosters have also provided the base for the space programs of both the United States and the Soviet Union. Inevitably missiles have become a major component of the military power of both the United States and Russia.

In their modern form, missiles first attained significance as a Johnny-come-lately World War II Nazi weapon. A technical team of great competence headed by General Walter von Dornberger, including many rocketry experts, among them Dr. Wernher von Braun, worked on unmanned air weapons at Peenemunde, a secret German center on the North Sea. Their first operational development was the V-1 —a pulse-jet pilotless bomber—the "buzz bomb" used against England. But the "buzz bomb," terrible as it was, was still an airplane that could be tracked and attacked. The successor to the V-1 was the V-2, the first ballistic missile of the modern era. Liquid-fueled, it traveled an arc through air and space at enormous speed and on impact wrought great destruction. It is conceivable that had the Dornberger team received the requisite support early enough from Hitler and had enough V-2's been launched against England, the war's outcome might have been changed. At least, it might have dragged on considerably longer. But Hitler, until it was too late, was unimpressed by the potential of the ballistic missile, and, meanwhile, the secret Peenemunde workshop had been uncovered by a British photo reconnaissance expert and was bombed heavily.

It was not until after the war—and well into the Cold War—that missiles, married to nuclear destructive power, came into their own as a prime factor in the international power equation on land, in the sea, and in the air. A portent of today's reality was the fact that Dornberger and his team were working on a truly intercontinental ballistic missile, to be launched against America, in the last days of World War II.

In the chaos of German collapse, Dornberger and many of his colleagues either gave themselves up to or were captured by Western forces, although some of the rocket experts were taken prisoner by the Russians and transported eastward to the Soviet Union. Dornberger, von Braun, and others were brought to the United States where they re-established themselves at American facilities. During the war, there had been no serious U.S. military interest in rocketry from the strategic point of view. Indeed, it is a great irony of military history that America's now-honored rocket pioneer, Dr. Robert Goddard, who with the backing of the Smithsonian Institution, had been working on liquid-fueled rocketry since the 1920's, was engaged in research and development of rocket-assisted airplane take-off devices toward the end of the war. He died shortly after the war without seeing the missile-space era that was soon to come.

The postwar surge toward massive disassembly of the great war machine of the United States nearly dissolved American air power. A few Americans saw the potential of missiles. At their behest, German V-2 parts were brought to the United States, and Army experts, aided by some of the members of the Peenemunde team, put together and tested some twenty-five complete rockets in the early postwar period. But most long-range planners examining the future of air power saw the jet bomber carrying nuclear weapons as the prime air weapon of the future. They believed that the jet bomber could be upgraded sharply in performance, and they also anticipated powerful unmanned air-breathing aerodynamic cruise missiles. Thus, in a sense, the V-1 "buzz bomb," increased in power and performance for intercontinental deployment, was seen as the great weapon of the future. At the same time, these people examined the German ballistic missile effort and concluded much advance was needed before ICBM's could become significant. Such personages as Dr. Vannevar Bush, who had headed wartime military research and development, thought intercontinental ballistic missiles fanciful. It was decided to concentrate on aircraft and non-ballistic air-breathing missiles.

In retrospect, what seems now a lack of foresight can be understood. The first atomic bombs and the kind available in the late 1940's and early 1950's were bulky and heavy; mating them with still primitive ballistic missiles must have seemed pretty chancy. The manned jet bomber and the aerodynamic cruise missile seemed far more practical. Out of the early USAF analyses came decisions to develop the air-breathing Navaho and Snark turbo-jet guided missiles. Navaho never reached operational status, in the face of the decision in 1954 to press forward instead with a crash program to build liquid ballistic missiles. Some Snarks were built and deployed briefly until the advent of the first American ICBM, the Atlas.

There were both technical and political elements in the decision to switch to ballistic missiles. One by one the problems of guidance, re-entry and packaging of the now paramount hydrogen bomb were solved, eliminating the main technical bar to ICBM's. On the political side, German expatriate rocket experts managed to convince the Air Force, particularly the then Assistant Secretary for Research and Development Trevor Gardner, that the Russians were pushing hard in missile development. Gardner campaigned heavily, backed by such leading scientific figures as the late Dr. John von Neumann, among others, for a commitment to a crash ICBM program. By 1954, the Administration was convinced, and a program to develop the Atlas liquid-fueled ICBM was undertaken under the direction of the Air Force's Brigadier General Bernard A. Schriever (later General and Commander of the Air Force Systems Command), headquartered in California. By 1960, the Atlas was operational, and its successor, the Titan I, was in development. The Atlas had been started in the late 1940's at what is now General Dynamics Convair, but had been canceled during the period of enthusiasm for unmanned cruise missiles. It had survived as a project only because the company itself had continued to fund the development.

While the Air Force worked on Atlas and Thor, an intermediate-range ballistic missile, the Army, under the direction of von Braun, had been working on its own IRBM, the Jupiter, at Huntsville, Alabama. Jupiter and Thor had the same basic propulsion system and performance expectations. By the time it was understood that ballistic missiles were to have an enormous impact on military weaponry, a struggle between the Air Force and Army for control of the new weapon erupted. In 1957, the Soviets had shocked the world with both an ICBM and Sputnik, and the stakes rose higher. But Neil H. McElroy, then Secretary of Defense in the Eisenhower Administration, refused to end the struggle by awarding control to either service. Actually, the fact that the Air Force, following its strategic bombing role, had worked on Atlas, an intercontinental weapon, had already determined that the ballistic missile would be primarily an Air Force weapon, except for short-range Army purposes and the special case of the Polaris missile-carrying submarines which were yet to come. Eventually, the Jupiter IRBM was transferred to the Air Force from the Army, and along with the Thor, deployed overseas. Both missiles have long since completed their operational lives, although their descendants have served as workhorses of the national space program. And to the Jupiter goes the historic honor of having boosted the first American satellite into orbit in January, 1958.

Today, all three services operate ballistic missiles designed for their battle environments. The Air Force's strategic power includes a vast array of land-based Titan II liquid-fueled and Minuteman solid-fueled intercontinental missiles, as well as a number of tactical missile weapons. The Army has an assortment of tactical missiles for battlefield use. And the Navy had both tactical missiles and its Polaris strategic missile, which is fired from nuclear submarines patrolling the oceans.

In addition, in the allied space field, the Air Force has been designated the prime military space research and development agency within the Defense Department. That action was taken in 1961 by Secretary of Defense Robert S. McNamara.

USAF Operations in the Cold War Era

At the end of World War II, Berlin was an island city in the Russian zone of Occupied Germany with East Berlin under Russian control and West Berlin under the Western Powers. Access to West Berlin was by highways through the Russian zone and three twenty-mile-wide air corridors from the British and French zones. This political monstrosity imposed not only diplomatic but also military problems of the greatest complexity and delicacy.

Early in 1948, the Russians began a series of harassing tactics designed to drive the Allies out of West Berlin. By the latter part of June, the Russians had cut off all highway, barge, and rail traffic into West Berlin. The Western powers refused to knuckle under. General Lucius D. Clay, the U.S. Military Governor, and his British and French counterparts, refused to abandon West Berlin. An historic airlift was begun on June 26. In July, the Airlift Task Force (Provisional) was formed, composed of U.S. Army, Navy, and

Air Force units. A Combined Airlift Task Force was established in October to coordinate the American and British operations.

Two-thirds of the tonnage flown in was coal, without which West Berlin could not have survived the severe winter of 1948–49. Food supplies of all kinds had second priority; oil, raw materials, and medical supplies were also airlifted. By January, 1949, sufficient food supplies were on hand to permit the food ration to be raised from 1,600 to 1,800 calories per person daily. In April, 1949, an all-time high was reached when 1,938 aircraft were engaged in transporting supplies to Berlin.

Undoubtedly impressed by the airlift performance, the Russians called off the Berlin blockade on May 12, 1949. However, until September 30, 1949, the airlift continued to build up a reserve stock of supplies as a precautionary measure. The Berlin airlift had demonstrated to U.S. citizens as well as to the Russians the ability of the USAF to provide sustained, round-the-clock mass movement of cargo by air.

Korea

Less than a year after the Berlin airlift, the USAF was engaged in fighting Communist expansion in Korea. On Sunday, June 25, 1950, Communist North Korea attacked South Korea, and under the flag of the United Nations, the U.S. led the resistance against the North Korean aggression.

Most of the support for the Communist forces in North Korea eventually came from China and Russia, but, in the early days of the war, it came from the industrial centers of North Korea. Strategic bombardment of those targets began early in August, 1950, and practically all major industrial targets had been destroyed within five weeks. The B-29 strategic bombing offensive was completed in less than two months. By September 29, the Government of South Korea returned to Seoul, and the first objective of the United Nations had been accomplished.

On November 8, the first all-jet air battle occurred over the Yalu River when USAF F-80's tangled with Russian MiG-15's. The MiG's were new, fast, swept-back jets, greatly superior to the old F-80's. During the weeks that passed until the arrival of F-84's and

F-86's in December, U.S. airmen were at a serious disadvantage. The new aircraft gave USAF air superiority. On January 23, 1951, long-range F-84's escorting B-29's into "MiG Alley" encountered twenty-five MiG-15's and destroyed three of them with no losses. And, for the first time in history, jets were escorting bombers, jets were fighting jets in aerial combat, and jets were operating in close tactical support of ground forces.

The destruction of three strategic target systems contributed greatly to North Korean interest in a cease-fire. Suiho, on the Yalu River, was one of the largest plants in the hydroelectric power generating complex in North Korea, supplying much of its power to Manchuria. Heretofore protected from attack by political considerations, it was struck on June 23, 1952, and, in three days of bombing, 90 per cent of North Korean electric power was knocked out.

The next complex consisted of seventy-eight towns and villages along the Yalu that were known to contain supply centers, repair facilities, and troop concentrations. After having dropped warning leaflets to reduce civilian casualties, the centers were destroyed by incendiary bombs in the night of July 20, 1952.

Irrigation dams were another strategic target complex. Since North Korea's rice lands required water from a controlled system of irrigation, the Koreans built reservoirs to store water for crop growing periods. The large Toksan irrigation dam had been built about twenty miles north of Pyongyang. It was attacked on May 13, 1953, by fifty-nine F-84's, and the dam broke during the night. Flood waters washed out bridges and sections of the railroad and highway between Pyongyang and Sinanju. General Mark Clark reported to the Joint Chiefs of Staff in Washington that "the breaching of the Toksan dam has been as effective as weeks of rail interdiction."

A similar strike was launched against the Chasan irrigation dam. It was attacked on May 16, 1953, by ninety F-84's, and the dam broke. Flood waters destroyed sections of the railway line and the highway between Pyongyang and Sunchon.

Despite this air onslaught, North Korea and her Chinese ally fought on, hoping for face-saving victory. They mounted two major ground offensives in early June, 1953, one against the South Korean forces and the other against the U.S. Eighth Army. Allied forces supported by the 5th Air Force and Navy Task Force 77 defeated both attempts. On July 13, the Communists attacked the U.S. IX Corps with three divisions but were again defeated. The bloody fighting finally ended on July 27, 1953, some three years after the war began.

The remarkable achievements of air power—USAF, Navy, and Marine—in Korea are not widely known and are worth reporting. U.S. Far East Air Forces flew a total of 720,980 sorties, which included 66,997 counter-air, 192,581 interdiction, 57,665 close support, 181,659 cargo, and 222,073 miscellaneous sorties (reconnaissance, air control and rescue). Between June 26, 1950 and July 31, 1953, Military Air Transport Service aircraft transported 43,196 Korean War casualties to the United States for further treatment. During the fighting in South Korea, North Korean POW's estimated that air attacks destroyed more than 70 per cent of their tanks, trucks, and artillery pieces, and inflicted 57 per cent of their casualties.

The Korean War was a limited war, but it did demonstrate the effectiveness of strategic bombing and the ability of air power to support effectively a numerically inferior ground force. Since air incursions into China were precluded by official policy based on concern that attacks on Red China itself might bring on Soviet intervention and World War III, the full power of the U.S. Air Force was not deployed. No one can say today what might have been the consequences—positive or negative—of a full-scale confrontation between the United States and China.

The political limitations on the full deployment of air power during the Korean War, the allowing of sanctuary beyond the Yalu River, and the immunity given Red China from bombardment, were argued over for years after the Korean Armistice. But veterans of the Korean War would live to see the demise of the "sanctuary" idea, when, in the Vietnamese War, Communist North Vietnam, an aggressor against the South, was struck by U.S. air power.

V

Pentagon Levels of Command—
The Air Force in DOD

The United States Air Force is a constituent part of the Department of Defense. The basic charter of the Department of Defense is the National Security Act of 1947. In the years since 1947, there have been a number of changes and reorganizations of DOD, and its role as the prime agency of U.S. military power has been further strengthened.

In the National Security Act of 1947, as amended, Congress declared:

> In enacting this legislation, it is the intent of Congress to provide a comprehensive program for the future security of the United States; to provide for the establishment of integrated policies and procedures for the departments, agencies, and functions of the Government relating to the national security; to provide a Department of Defense, including the three military departments of the Army, the Navy (including naval aviation and the United States Marine Corps), and the Air Force under the direction, authority, and control of the Secretary of Defense; to provide that each military department shall be separately organized under its own Secretary and shall function under the direction, authority, and control of the Secretary of Defense; to provide for their unified direction under civilian control of the Secretary of Defense but not to merge these departments or services; to provide for the establishment of unified or specified combatant commands, and a clear and direct line of command to such commands; to eliminate unnecessary duplication in the Department of Defense, and particularly in the field of research and engineering by vesting its over-all direction and control in the Secretary of Defense; to provide more effective, efficient, and economical administration in the Depart-

Chart 1
DEPARTMENT OF DEFENSE

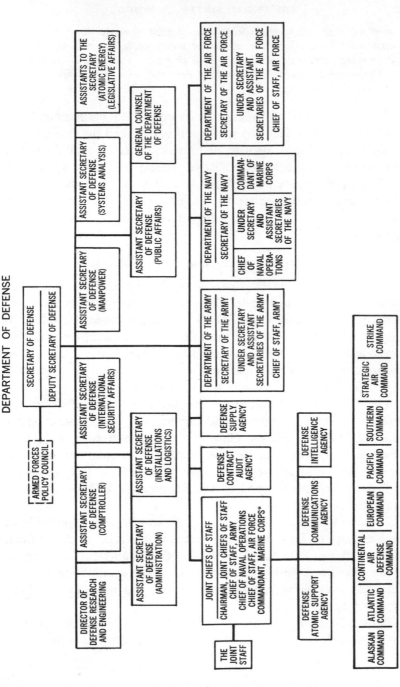

*When pertaining to Marine Corps matters

ment of Defense; to provide for the unified strategic direction of the combatant forces, for their operation under unified command, and for their integration into an efficient team of land, naval, and air forces but not to establish a single Chief of Staff over the armed forces nor an over-all armed forces general staff.

The Department of Defense is charged with maintaining and employing armed forces (1) to support and defend the Constitution of the United States against all enemies, foreign and domestic; (2) to ensure by timely and effective military action the security of the United States, its possessions, and areas vital to its interests; (3) to uphold and advance the national policies and interests of the United States; (4) and to safeguard the internal security of the United States.

Department of Defense Organizational Relationships

All functions in the Department of Defense and its component agencies are performed under the direction, authority, and control of the Secretary of Defense. The Department includes the Office of the Secretary of Defense and the Joint Chiefs of Staff, the military departments and the services within those departments, the unified and specified commands, and such other agencies as the Secretary of Defense establishes to meet specific requirements.

The Office of the Secretary of Defense includes the offices of the Director of Defense Research and Engineering, the Assistant Secretaries of Defense, and the General Counsel and such other staff offices as the Secretary of Defense establishes to assist him in carrying out his duties and responsibilities. The functions of the heads of these offices are assigned by the Secretary of Defense in accordance with existing laws.

The Joint Chiefs of Staff as a group are directly responsible to the Secretary of Defense for the functions assigned to them. Each member of the Joint Chiefs of Staff, other than the Chairman, is responsible for keeping the Secretary of his military department fully informed on matters considered or acted upon by the Joint Chiefs of Staff.

Each military department (The Department of the Navy includes naval aviation and the United States Marine Corps) is separately organized under its own secretary and functions under the direction, authority and control of the Secretary of Defense. The secretary of a military department is responsible to the Secretary of Defense for the operation of that department as well as its efficiency. Orders to the military departments are issued through the secretaries of those departments by the Secretary of Defense or under authority specifically delegated in writing by the Secretary of Defense or provided by law.

The Office of the Secretary of Defense and the Joint Chiefs of Staff, although separately organized and identified, cooperate in providing staff advice and assistance to the Secretary of Defense.

Commanders of unified and specified commands are responsible to the President and the Secretary of Defense. A unified command is a joint force of units from two or more of the military services and is usually responsible for specific military operations within a given geographical area. A specified command is an organization composed primarily of units from one military service. It operates without restriction as to geographical area. The USAF Strategic Air Command is an example of a specified command. The chain of command runs from the President to the Secretary of Defense and through the Joint Chiefs of Staff to the commanders of unified and specified commands. Orders to such commanders are issued by the President or the Secretary of Defense or by the Joint Chiefs of Staff by authority and direction of the Secretary of Defense. These commanders have full operational command over the forces assigned to them and perform such functions as are prescribed by the Unified Command Plan and other directives issued by competent authority.

It is interesting to point out that under Secretary of Defense Robert S. McNamara, the role of the service secretary changed in emphasis. Secretary McNamara saw the service secretaries as assistants to the Defense Secretary, whereas, in the past, they had traditionally served as advocates for their departments. Although this new status was clearly in line with Secretary McNamara's concept of armed forces unification, it has drawn both criticism and praise from military writers and commentators. The Secretary of Defense appeared to want the service secretaries to function as under secretaries of defense for the Army, Navy, and Air Force.

Reorganization that would create such service under secretaries by law has been discussed, but no one can say whether the Office of the Defense Secretary plans to push for such legislation or whether Congress would accept it. In any case, as service secretaries, they retain impressive responsibilities involving hundreds of thousands of people and billions of dollars.

Joint Chiefs of Staff

The Joint Chiefs of Staff came into being following a decision by President Franklin D. Roosevelt and Prime Minister Winston Churchill to establish a supreme Anglo-American military body for the strategic direction of World War II. Initially, the Joint Chiefs of Staff were the U.S. representatives on the Combined Chiefs of Staff, where they sat as colleagues and counterparts of the already existing British Chiefs of Staff Committee. They also functioned as a corporate leadership for the American military structure. On February 9, 1942, they held their first meeting as an organized body.

In March, 1942, the U.S. Joint Chiefs of Staff was composed of General George C. Marshall, Chief of Staff, U.S. Army; Admiral Ernest J. King, Commander in Chief, U.S. Fleet, and Chief of Naval Operations; and General Henry H. Arnold, Commanding General, Army Air Forces. In July, 1942, Admiral William D. Leahy was appointed to the new position of Chief of Staff to the President and was added to the Joint Chiefs of Staff as the senior and presiding member. These four able officers constituted the Joint Chiefs of Staff throughout the remainder of World War II.

The supporting organization of the Joint Chiefs of Staff included the Joint Secretariat and a number of standing committees: the Joint Staff Planners, the Joint Strategic Survey Committee, the Joint Logistics Committee, and various other committees dealing with intelligence, military transportation, munitions allocation, and communication.

During World War II, the Joint Chiefs of Staff existed informally, advising the President on military strategy, the manpower requirements of the armed forces, the requirements, production and allocation of munitions and shipping, and matters of joint Army-Navy policy. They also supervised the operations of the Office of Strategic

Services (for wartime intelligence), and the Army and Navy Staff College.

The Joint Chiefs of Staff organization continued after the war. On September 17, 1947, it was formally established as a permanent agency within the National Military Establishment and designated as "the principal military advisers to the President and the Secretary of Defense."

Since 1947, the organization has undergone seven major changes, starting with the Key West agreement of 1948 and extending to the Defense Reorganization Act of 1958. In 1949, an amendment created the office of Chairman of the Joint Chiefs of Staff, and General of the Army Omar N. Bradley became the first Chairman on August 16, 1949. In June, 1952, the Commandant of the U.S. Marine Corps was given coequal status by law as a member of the Joint Chiefs of Staff in the consideration of matters that directly concerned the Marine Corps. In June, 1953, President Eisenhower declared that the Joint Chiefs of Staff was not a command body but an advisory group responsible for formulating strategic plans.

The Defense Reorganization Act of 1958, the seventh change in the Joint Chiefs of Staff organization, included the following major points:

(1) Operational forces organized into unified and specified commands were separated from the military departments that had been executive agents and were made responsible to the Secretary of Defense through the Joint Chiefs of Staff.

(2) Operational command of all combat-ready forces was given to the unified and specified commanders. The line of authority extends from the President as Commander in Chief to the Secretary of Defense, whose orders are issued to the unified and specified commanders through the Joint Chiefs.

(3) The size of the Joint Staff of the Joint Chiefs was increased because responsibility for operational direction of unified commands had been given to the Joint Chiefs.

(4) Each service Chief of Staff was authorized to delegate major portions of his authority and duties to his vice-chief in order to be able to give his primary attention to his Joint Chiefs of Staff duties. Such duties take precedence over all other duties.

(5) The stipulation that the Chairman should have no vote in the decisions of the Joint Chiefs was deleted. The Chairman was also authorized to assign duties to the Joint Staff and to appoint its director in consultation with the Joint Chiefs and with the approval of the Secretary of Defense.

(6) The Act also specified that "the Joint Staff should not operate or be organized as an over-all armed forces general staff and shall have no executive authority, but may operate along conventional staff lines" to support the Joint Chiefs.

Organization of the Joint Chiefs of Staff

The Joint Chiefs' organization includes approximately 700 officers, 400 enlisted personnel, and 400 civilians. The authorized officer positions are divided equally among the three services. The organizational structure consists of the Joint Chiefs of Staff as a corporate body, the Joint Staff, and other agencies that assist the Joint Chiefs but are not part of the Joint Staff.

Such agencies are the office of Special Assistant for Arms Control, which provides comprehensive analyses and evaluations of U.S. policies and proposals in the field of arms control; the Joint War Games Agency, which plans, organizes, and controls war games in response to requirements of the Joint Chiefs; the Joint Command Control Requirements Group, which develops concepts and functional requirements for the establishment of a world-wide command and control system; and the National Military Command System, which encompasses the National Military Command Center in the Pentagon, the Alternate Center in Maryland, and national emergency command posts, both airborne and afloat.

The Chairman of the Joint Chiefs outranks all other officers of the armed forces but he exercises no military command over the Joint Chiefs or any of the armed forces. He is appointed by the President from officers of the regular components of the armed forces. He serves at the pleasure of the President for a two-year term but may be reappointed for one additional term.

Army, Navy, and Air Force members of the Joint Chiefs are also appointed for two-year terms and may be reappointed. The Marine Corps Commandant serves a statutory four-year term. Time limitations, however, may be waived in wartime. All appointments are subject to Senate confirmation.

The only U.S. Air Force officer who has served as Chairman of the Joint Chiefs is General Nathan F. Twining. He held the position from August 15, 1957, to September 30, 1960.

The Joint Staff performs duties prescribed by the Joint Chiefs or the Chairman. Under its director, its main task is preparing reports to aid decision-making by the Joint Chiefs. Members of the Joint Staff normally have a three-year tour of duty.

The Joint Staff directorates are organized as conventional staff lines and cover the following functional areas: J-1, Personnel; J-3, Operations; J-4, Logistics; J-5, Plans and Policy; and J-6, Communications and Electronics. Internally, J-3 and J-5 also have a geographical as well as a functional structure. Intelligence staff support for the Joint Chiefs and the Joint Staff was formerly provided by a sixth directorate, J-2, but is now furnished by the Director, Defense Intelligence Agency, an operating staff agency within the Department of Defense.

The Joint Staff also includes two special assistants to the Director of the Joint Staff: the Special Assistant for Counterinsurgency and Special Activities, who has staff responsibility for actions pertaining to counterinsurgency, cold war, and the preparation of special plans; and the Special Assistant for Military Assistance Affairs, who is charged with the preparation of plans, policies, and execution of directives and preparation of reports for the Joint Chiefs on Military Assistance Program matters.

Functions of the Joint Chiefs of Staff

Of the eighteen specific responsibilities assigned to the Joint Chiefs, the major functions are to serve as the principal military advisers to the President, the National Security Council, and the Secretary of Defense; to prepare strategic plans and provide for the strategic direction of the armed forces, including the direction of operations conducted by commanders of unified and specified commands; to prepare integrated logistic plans; to prepare integrated plans for military mobilization; to review plans, programs, and requirements; and to provide U.S. military representation on international security organizations, mutual defense boards, and other properly authorized military staffs, boards, councils, and missions.

Under the Secretary of Defense, the Joint Chiefs execute basic national security policy through their strategic planning, guidance, and operational direction to the commanders in chief of unified and specified commands, and in their directives to the service chiefs. Since, in his capacity as a member of the Joint Chiefs, each chief obtains considerable military information that is not available in service channels, he is required to keep his service secretary informed of actions taken by the Joint Chiefs.

The Joint Chiefs make recommendations to the Secretary of Defense regarding the assignment of combat forces to unified and specified commands. Forces so assigned are under the operational command of the unified commands but continue to be administered and supported by the military departments concerned. Any combat forces not assigned to unified and specified commands remain under the control of the military departments. Such forces are few in number and are confined to training, development, or specialized units.

Functions of the Military Departments

The chain of command for purposes other than the operational direction of unified and specified commands runs from the President to the Secretary of Defense to the secretaries of the military departments. The departments, under their secretaries, have the primary task of preparing forces and establishing reserves of equipment and supplies for the effective prosecution of war. They plan for the expansion of reserve components to meet the needs of war. They organize, train, and equip mobile reserve forces in readiness for emergency employment. They organize, train, and equip forces for assignment to unified or specified commands. They also prepare and submit the budgets for their departments to the Secretary of Defense, justify the budgets before Congress, and administer the funds made available for maintaining, equipping, and training the forces provided to the combat commands.

The departments conduct research and develop tactics and techniques. They develop and procure weapons, equipment, and supplies. They also provide such forces, military missions, and detachments for service in foreign countries as may be required to support the national interests of the United States. They also assist in training and equipping the military forces of other nations with which the United States has agreements. They build, man, supply, equip, and maintain bases and other installations, including lines of communication. The departments also provide departmental intelligence for use within the Department of Defense.

Functions of the Department of the Air Force

The Department of the Air Force is responsible for the preparation of the air forces necessary for the effective prosecution of war except as otherwise assigned and, in accordance with integrated mobilization plans, for the expansion of the reserve components of the Air Force to meet the needs of war. The Air Force includes aviation forces, both combat and service, not otherwise assigned.

The primary and collateral functions assigned the Air Force by the Department of Defense directive promulgated in December, 1958, clearly outline the roles and missions of the Air Force. The first of its primary functions is to organize, train, and equip Air Force forces for the conduct of prompt and sustained combat operations in the air—specifically, forces to defend the United States against air attack in accordance with established doctrines, to gain and maintain general supremacy, to defeat enemy air forces, to control vital air area, and to establish local air superiority except as otherwise assigned. The Air Force is required to organize, train, and equip Air Force forces for strategic air warfare; to develop doctrines and procedures coordinated with the other services for the unified defense of the United States against air attack; to organize and equip Air Force forces for joint amphibious and airborne operations in coordination with the other services; to provide for their training according to established doctrines; and to provide air transport for the armed forces. The Air Force must also furnish close combat and logistical air support to the Army, including airlift, support and resupply of airborne operations, aerial photography, tactical reconnaissance, and interdiction of enemy land power and communications. It is also charged with development of doctrines, procedures, and equipment for air defense from land areas, including the continental United States, in coordination with the other services.

Additional primary functions assigned to the Air Force are to formulate doctrines and procedures for the organizing, equipping, training, and employment of Air Force forces; to provide an organization capable of furnishing adequate, timely, and reliable intelligence for the Air Force; to furnish aerial photography for cartographic purposes; and, in coordination with the other services, to develop tactics, techniques, and equipment for amphibious and airborne operations.

The forces developed and trained to perform the primary functions listed above are expected to be employed to support and supplement the other services in carrying out their primary functions, whenever such participation will result in increased effectiveness and will contribute to the accomplishment of the overall military objectives.

The collateral functions assigned to the Air Force in coordination with the Army and Navy are to train forces to interdict enemy sea power through air operations, to conduct antisubmarine warfare and aerial mine-laying operations, and to protect shipping.

The Air Force has also been assigned the responsibility for certain specific tasks by the Department of Defense. It has the prime responsibility for military space research and development. It develops, procures, and mans land-based surface-to-air missile systems for air defense with ranges exceeding 100 miles. The operational employment of intermediate-ballistic missiles (500 to 1,500 miles) and the development and employment of intercontinental ballistic missiles are responsibilities of the Air Force. Also, in the combat zone, in tactical support missions, surface-to-surface missiles having a range in excess of 400 miles are usually an Air Force responsibility.

The Air Force is required to provide airlift of supplies, equipment, personnel, and combat units from exterior locations to designated bases in the combat zone. It is also responsible for the airlift of troops, supplies, and equipment in the initial and subsequent stages of airborne operation and for the air evacuation of personnel and matériel from the combat zone. Other tasks assigned to the Air Force include tactical reconnaissance, interdiction of enemy lines of communication, close combat air support of ground troops, using such weaponry as air-to-ground rockets and napalm.

Department of the Air Force Organization

OFFICE OF THE SECRETARY

The Department of the Air Force consists of the Office of the Secretary of the Air Force, the Air Staff, and the Commands. The Secretary is responsible for and has the authority to conduct all affairs of the Department of the Air Force, including the training, operation, administration, logistical support and maintenance, welfare, preparedness, and effectiveness of the Air Force, as well as research and development and such other activities as may be prescribed by the President or the Secretary of Defense as authorized by law. The Secretary of the Air Force is responsible for the operation and efficiency of the Department.

The Secretary has a personal staff to assist him in the execution of his responsibilities. Under the law there are an Under Secretary of the Air Force and three Assistant Secretaries of the Air Force in the Department. They are appointed by the President with the advice and consent of the Senate. Assistant Secretaries have been designated for Financial Management, Installation and Logistics, and Research and Development. In addition to these statutory positions, the Office includes a Special Assistant for Manpower, Personnel and Reserve Forces, a Secretariat Air Reserve Forces Policy Committee, a General Counsel, an Administrative Assistant, the Office of Legislative Liaison, the Office of Information, the Office of Space Systems, a Personnel Security Group office and a Physical and Administrative Security office. The last five offices are under the supervision of Air Force officers.

The Secretary exercises his authority through his principal civilian assistants and the Chief of Staff. He retains under his immediate supervision those activities that involve vital relationships with the Congress, the Secretary of Defense, other Government officials, and the public. In his relationships with the Air Staff, he is concerned

Chart 2
OFFICE OF THE SECRETARY OF THE AIR FORCE

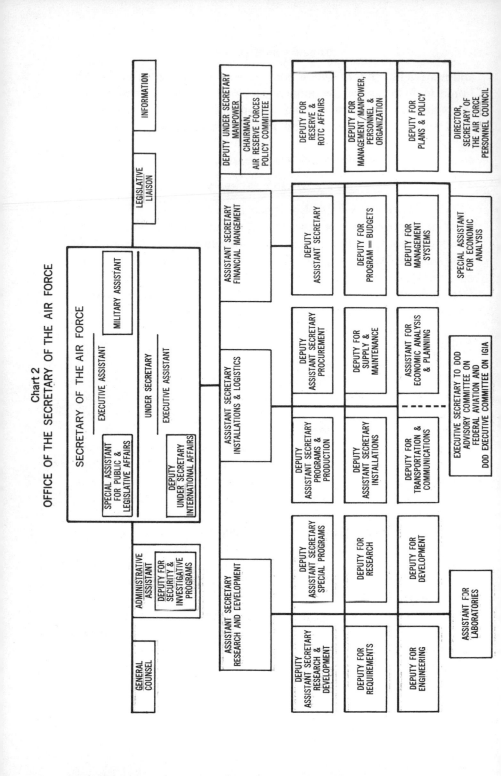

with the same matters of broad policy and plans and programs that demand the personal attention of the Chief of Staff and Vice Chief.

The Under Secretary is the chief civilian assistant and adviser to the Secretary and is kept fully informed so that he may act in his place when required. Subject to the direction of the Secretary, the Under Secretary and the other principal civilian assistants deal directly with appropriate segments of the Air Staff in such areas as manpower, financial management, and research and development.

In long-range and major problem areas, the Secretary or his assistant may provide preliminary general guidance concerning the response, plan, or program being drafted by the Air Staff. The assistants help with the presentation and interpretation of USAF proposals before the Secretary of Defense, the Congress, and the public.

THE AIR STAFF

Immediately below the Office of the Secretary is the Air Staff, which is organized into Headquarters, United States Air Force. The USAF was established within the Department of the Air Force under the provisions of Section 8062, U.S. Code 10. The Air Staff's "birth certificate" is contained in Section 8031, U.S. Code 10, which states:

> There is in the executive part of the Department of the Air Force an Air Staff consisting of: the Chief of Staff; the Vice Chief of Staff; not more than five Deputy Chiefs of Staff; other members of the Air Force assigned or detailed to the Air Staff; and civilians in the Department of the Air Force assigned or detailed to the Air Staff. The Air Staff shall be organized in such a manner, and its members shall perform such duties and have such titles, as the Secretary may prescribe.

The section also places a ceiling on the number of officers who may be assigned or detailed to permanent duty on the Air Staff and establishes a maximum length of duty tour in such assignment.

The Congress was quite explicit in prescribing the general duties of the Air Staff. Section 8032, U.S. Code 10, states:

> The Air Staff shall furnish professional assistance to the Secretary, the Under Secretary, and the Assistant Secretaries of the Air Force, and the

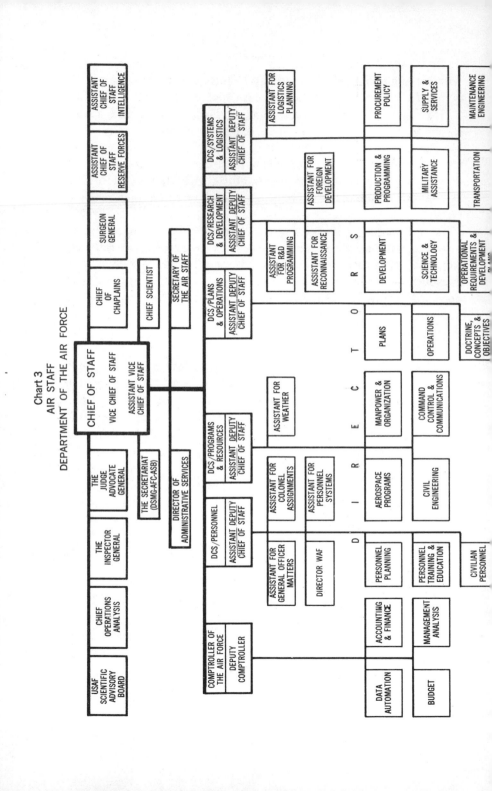

Chart 3
AIR STAFF
DEPARTMENT OF THE AIR FORCE

Chief of Staff. The Air Staff shall (1) prepare for such employment of the Air Force, and for such recruiting, organizing, supplying, equipping, training, serving, mobilizing and demobilizing of the Air Force as will assist in the execution of any power, duty, or function of the Secretary or the Chief of Staff; (2) investigate and report upon the efficiency of the Air Force and its preparation for military operations; (3) prepare detailed instructions for the execution of approved plans and supervise the execution of those plans and instructions; (4) act as agent of the Secretary and the Chief of Staff in coordinating the action of all organizations of the Department of the Air Force; and (5) perform such other duties, not otherwise assigned by law, as may be prescribed by the Secretary.

In this framework, the Air Staff establishes basic policies, programs, and priorities for the world-wide Air Force; disseminates direction, guidance, and policy interpretation as necessary to the major Air Force commands; and maintains sufficient management controls to give the Secretary of the Air Force and the Chief of Staff the information they need in managing the Air Force and in responding to the Secretary of Defense and the Congress. The Air Staff also allocates the resources (human, financial, and matériel) essential for effective support of the combat forces, and performs a continuous analysis of resource needs and expenditures. It also conducts inspection services and field surveillance adequate to identify deficiencies and, as necessary, prescribes corrective action.

The Air Staff structure is functionally organized. Each level has a clear, consistent relationship to the Chief of Staff and to the other elements of the Air Staff. It consists of the following levels and categories:

Chief of Staff, USAF, and Vice Chief of Staff (including the Assistant Vice Chief of Staff);

Special Staff Offices (Chief of Air Force Chaplains, Inspector General, Surgeon General, etc.);

Deputy Chief of Staff level;

"Assistant For" level (Assistant For Personnel Systems, Deputy Chief of Staff, Personnel, etc.);

Director level;

Division level;

Branch level; and

Section level.

The Chief of Staff is directly responsible to the Secretary of the Air Force for the efficiency and operational readiness of the Air Force. He is assisted in this task by the Vice Chief of Staff. There is no formal division of duties between the Chief and the Vice Chief; most of their tasks are interchangeable according to whatever personal arrangements the Chief makes with the Vice Chief.

In his JCS capacity and in a corporate sense, the Chief is one of the principal military advisers to the President, the National Security Council, and the Secretary of Defense. He is also the principal military adviser to the Secretary of the Air Force on activities of the Air Force. The Chief of Staff's duty as a member of the Joint Chiefs of Staff is so time-consuming that it demands his primary attention and requires that he have a special alternate. This officer, known as the "Operations Deputy for JCS matters," is the Deputy Chief of Staff, Plans and Operations.

Since the Chief's time is so largely involved with JCS matters, the demands of USAF external relations (the Congress, the public, etc.), it is the Vice Chief of Staff who runs the Air Force on a day-to-day basis.

The Assistant Vice Chief of Staff assists the Chief and Vice Chief in the discharge of their duties; makes Office of the Chief of Staff decisions and signs communications for that office; resolves differences between the Air Staff and the field, or among elements of the Air Staff; exercises general supervision over the organization and administration of the Air Staff; and assists in the review and execution of USAF plans, policies, and programs. It is his responsibility to ensure that the Air Staff operates at peak efficiency.

Although the Assistant Vice Chief of Staff has no staff, he receives assistance from the Secretary of the Air Staff for organizational planning, systems procedures, analysis, and other management matters, and from the Director of Administrative Services for staff services, support, and other administrative matters.

The doctrine and objectives that govern Special Staff elements in the Air Staff are the same as those that apply in any military headquarters. These officers are adjuncts to the Office of the Chief of Staff, independent of the basic staff structure. They report directly to the Chief of Staff. They provide advisory and support services to both the Chief and the Air Staff and assist the Chief in developing policies and supervising Air Force activities in special military fields.

There are seven Special Staff offices: Assistant Chief of Staff, Intelligence; Assistant Chief of Staff for Reserve Forces; Chief of Air Force Chaplains; Chief of Operations Analysis; Inspector General; Judge Advocate General; and Surgeon General.

Substantive Air Staff functions are delegated to the Director level. The Directors are organized by relative functions into groups under the immediate cognizance of a Deputy Chief of Staff. Not more than five Deputy Chiefs of Staff are authorized by law. Currently, they are: Deputy Chief of Staff, Personnel; Deputy Chief of Staff, Plans and Operations; Deputy Chief of Staff, Programs and Requirements; Deputy Chief of Staff, Research and Development; and Deputy Chief of Staff, Systems and Logistics. The Comptroller of the Air Force is also considered a Deputy Chief of Staff.

The Deputies give broad policy guidance in their areas, and make decisions in their area of specialty. Each Deputy Chief of Staff functions more as an individual adviser to the Chief of Staff than as the head of an organization. He exercises personal direction over selected critical matters, but he does not maintain a rigid command relationship of close supervision over his staff, nor does he confine himself solely to the interests within his area of responsibility. Instead, he concerns himself with Air Force–wide systems and resources. A Deputy Chief of Staff can refer a matter to the Chief of Staff or the Secretary for final resolution, or he may seek the review, counsel, and recommendations of the Air Force Council.

An "Assistant For" office is an adjunct to a Deputy Chief of Staff's office. Generally, an "Assistant For" has either a special mission, which needs temporary emphasis, or a unique across-the-board responsibility. At present, they include the following: Assistant For Personnel Systems, DCS Personnel; Assistant For Weather, DCS Programs and Requirements; Assistant For Foreign Development, Assistant For Reconnaissance, and Assistant For Research and Development Programming, all in DCS Research and Development; and Assistant For Logistics Planning, DCS Systems and Logistics.

The backbone of the functional Air Staff is the directorate level. The Chief of Staff assigns basic functions to directorates. Responsibilities of the directorates include the development of policies; review of effectiveness and operational readiness; determination of resource requirements (manpower, financial, and matériel); establishment of priorities; issuance of policy guidance; promulgation of management controls; and the development of current and future plans, programs, and budgets.

In recent years, with the widening scope and growing complexity of Air Force programs and systems, the directorate, which is the "office of primary responsibility," often has team-captained the staff work, worked with other elements and echelons across the Air Staff, kept the Deputy Chief of Staffs informed, and coordinated action with other Deputies as required. Aside from keeping their respective Deputies informed, Directors need refer upward only those matters of the broadest and highest level or those which cannot be resolved at the directorate level.

Division, branch, and section levels are the "working parts" in the directorates. Staff officers assigned at these levels are not barred from working with organizations outside their divisions. On the contrary, the military and civilian staff personnel at these levels are in daily contact with their counterparts throughout all echelons and elements of the Air Staff mission up to the decision-making level of the Directors and Deputies. Staff officers at these levels work as representatives of their Director and his total function, not merely as independent representatives of the particular work assignment of their division, branch, or section.

Under Air Staff doctrine, functional staff officials are responsible for making and defending their own decisions, and for carrying out appropriate actions within their areas of authority. Due to the growth of Air Force resources, the increasing complexity of aerospace systems, and the ever expanding demands made on key USAF officers, it is not always possible for one person to be able to give experienced and due consideration to all of the interrelating facets of a major plan, program, or system. Therefore, advisory bodies are available for the guidance of decision-making Air Staff officials.

These bodies, the Air Force Council and Air Staff Board, help the formal Air Staff organization analyze many questions.

The Air Force Council is the primary advisory body to the Chief of Staff. It is composed of the Vice Chief of Staff (chairman), the five Deputy Chiefs of Staff, the Comptroller of the Air Force, and the Inspector General. The Council may review, evaluate, and make recommendations to the Chief of Staff on all major USAF policies and any fundamental aspect of the USAF mission.

The Air Staff Board is the primary advisory body available to the individual Deputy Chiefs of Staffs and Directors as well as to the Council. It is composed of directorate level members and, for specified purposes only, a representative of the Air Force Systems Command serves as a member. The Board reviews, evaluates, and makes recommendations on such matters as enemy strengths, USAF concepts and objectives, force structure, systems, program documentation, and USAF financial plans and budgets.

The primary purposes of the Air Force Council and the Air Staff Board are (1) to develop conclusions and recommendations for the consideration of the decision-making authorities; (2) to assure that the collective evaluation and experience of senior Air Staff members is brought to bear on important matters; and (3) to expedite coordination when a problem is urgent, major, and complex. Air Staff officials, when they act as members of the Council or Board, are expected to apply a broad Air Force view. The Air Force Council and Air Staff Board do not make decisions, only recommendations. Nor do they operate externally. All their relationships are internal to the Air Staff.

There is a single Secretariat for the Council and the Board. The Board also has several permanent committees and such panels and working groups as are necessary to enable it to fulfill its responsibilities. The Secretariat is an adjunct of the Office of the Vice Chief of Staff.

The operational procedures of the Air Staff are keyed to the basic concept that one element of the staff will always be primarily responsible for each staff transaction, regardless of how many elements are or have been involved in the transaction. The responsible staff element becomes the agent of the Chief of Staff for dealing with the entire Air Staff on the matter. This one staff element is known as the "Office of Primary Responsibility" for the staff action. This is the concept of the "Office of Primary Responsibility–Office of Collateral Responsibility" procedure, and it is the procedural foundation on which all Air Staff actions are based.

The Office of Primary Responsibility (OPR) is any Air Staff component having primary functional interest in, and responsibility for, a specific Air Staff action, project, plan, program, or problem. A staff element automatically becomes the OPR for all transactions which primarily involve its assigned function. An office may also become OPR by being assigned the responsibility for a specific project or action by the Chief of Staff's office.

The Office of Collateral Responsibility (OCR) is any Air Staff component assigned a function as part of a staff transaction that is the primary responsibility of another component. Staff elements assume the role of OCR in contributing to or participating in actions that affect or involve their assigned functions to a secondary degree. When a component becomes an OCR in relation to an individual action, it is then obliged to assist or participate with the office serving as agent of the Chief of Staff, i.e., the OPR.

The major advantages of the OPR/OCR procedural concept are the clearly designated areas of functional responsibility and authority; the organizational concentration of each functional specialty, permitting maximum use of the talent and resources required in that specialty; the flexibility to organize procedurally all interested components around any particular task or program; and the establishment of simple and easily recognizable channels for working level relationships between the Air Staff and any other functionally organized institution.

VI

Organization and Missions of
USAF Major Commands

The United States Air Force provides aircraft and missile forces for the deterrence of war through readiness to respond quickly and effectively to any level of aggression—including general war, limited war, and insurgency activity. It provides the nation's unified and specified commands with their primary forces for aerospace offensive and defensive operations to repel and defeat an aggressor's aerospace forces if deterrence fails. At the same time, it provides the primary capability for air support of ground forces, area air superiority, reconnaissance, strategic airlift for the Armed Services, and research, development, and testing and engineering of certain systems required to support the civilian space agency, the National Aeronautics and Space Administration (NASA).

The major air commands dedicated to these missions are the Strategic Air Command (SAC); Tactical Air Command (TAC); Air Defense Command (ADC); Military Airlift Command (MAC); Alaskan Air Command (AAC); Pacific Air Forces (PACAF); U.S. Air Forces in Europe (USAFE); U.S. Air Forces Southern Command (USAFSO); Air Training Command (ATC); Continental Air Command (CONAC); Air Force Communications Service (AFCS); Air Force Logistics Command (AFLC); Air Force Systems Command (AFSC); Air University; Headquarters Command, USAF; and U.S. Air Force Security Service (USAFSS).

The Strategic Air Command (SAC)

The Strategic Air Command operates the USAF's global strike force—the world's most powerful military force—and the global communications and support systems needed to direct intercontinental weapon systems, including manned bombers and intercontinental ballistic missiles. SAC's primary mission is to deter war by maintaining the ability to deliver conventional or nuclear striking power on demand in such overwhelming power as to discourage aggression and general war. SAC provides a strategic umbrella for the Free World by maintaining a mixed bomber and missile aerospace force of undisputed strength and flexibility. In the event its deterrent mission fails, the SAC force is designed to survive a massive surprise attack and still carry out its wartime mission—the destruction of the enemy's war-making capability.

SAC is a DOD specified command. The chain of command runs from the President to the Secretary of Defense, who acts as the President's agent, through the Joint Chief of Staff to the SAC commander in chief. SAC headquarters, located at Offutt Air Force Base, Nebraska, has four numbered air forces and two divisions.

Bomber and ICBM forces are controlled from the underground command post at SAC headquarters. Here the SAC commander in chief has at his disposal communications equipment that can put him in instant touch with his forces located at seventy bases throughout the world. In addition, alternate command posts are in place at several SAC bases in the United States. They would take over command and control in the event that SAC headquarters were destroyed. If the underground command post and alternate command posts were lost, an airborne command post, complete with communications equipment and manned by an experienced team of controllers, would direct the SAC missile and bomber force and execute the command's emergency war plans under orders of the President. This flying command post has been airborne around the clock since February 3, 1961.

A tested system of codes and communications procedures ensures "positive control" of the SAC retaliatory force. The SAC bomber and tanker force can be launched in minutes by the SAC com-

Chart 4
STRATEGIC AIR COMMAND
Headquarters, Offutt AFB, Neb.

2d Air Force
Hq., Barksdale AFB, La.

4th Strategic Aerospace
Division
19th Air Division
40th Air Division
42d Air Division
825th Strategic Aerospace
Division

8th Air Force
Hq., Westover AFB, Mass.

17th Strategic Aerospace
Division
45th Air Division
57th Air Division
817th Air Division
822d Air Division *
823d Air Division †

15th Air Force
Hq., March AFB, Calif.

12th Strategic Aerospace
Division
14th Strategic Aerospace
Division
18th Strategic Aerospace
Division
47th Air Division
810th Strategic Aerospace
Division
821st Strategic Aerospace
Division

**1st Strategic Aerospace
Division**
Hq., Vandenberg AFB, Calif.

3d Air Division
Hq., Andersen AFB, Guam

*Scheduled to be phased out by July, 1967.
†Scheduled to be phased out by April, 1969.

mander in chief. Getting the force airborne does not send SAC to war, but it does ensure the survival of SAC's ground alert aircraft if the warning were to prove valid. After reaching a certain point on their routes, but still outside enemy territory, SAC bombers automatically return to their bases unless they receive positive coded voice instructions to proceed to their targets.

Day and night, at least 50 per cent of the jet bomber force, which can carry nuclear or conventional bombs, is on ground alert in the United States and overseas, armed and positioned to take off within the warning time of a hostile ICBM attack. Supplementing SAC's manned-bomber force are ICBM's that are constantly on alert. The bomber/tanker force is composed of approximately 600 each of B-52 Stratofortress heavy jet bombers and KC-135 jet Stratotankers, plus 80 B-58 Hustler medium jet bombers having a speed of Mach 2. By mid-1971, the Secretary of Defense has announced, 345 older model B-52's (C through F versions) and the B-58's will be phased out, and 210 FB-111's (bomber version of the new F-111) will enter the inventory.

Twenty-nine B-52 wings are currently equipped with the Hound Dog, a supersonic guided air-to-surface missile with a nuclear warhead and a range of about 500 miles. The Quail is a decoy missile designed for inflight launching to confuse enemy radar by giving a bomber-like electronic pattern, thus improving bomber penetration ability.

The SAC missile forces include three ICBM systems—the Minuteman, the Titan, and the Atlas. The bulk of the forces is made up of hardened and widely dispersed Minuteman missiles. They are solid-fueled, have a 6,300-mile range, and can be launched after a countdown of less than one minute. The Titan II is a liquid fuel missile, loaded at all times. It has an inertial guidance system, a range of over 6,000 miles, and is fired from the bottom of its steel and concrete silo. Atlas "F" missiles are also silo-stored. Older horizontally stored Atlas missiles are being phased out.

The Tactical Air Command (TAC)

TAC is the USAF's long-range, mobile, nuclear or conventional tactical strike force. It is equipped to fight large or small wars using either kind of weapon in tactical fighter, tactical air reconnaissance, Special Air Warfare, and assault airlift operations. Its units operate independently or jointly with other air or surface forces on a world-wide basis.

From its headquarters at Langley Air Force Base, Virginia, TAC directs its three subordinate air forces and three specialized centers.

TAC is both a combat command and a support command. With its array of fighter, reconnaissance, and airlift forces, TAC is the combat-ready strike arm of the United States Strike Command (USSTRICOM), a unified command composed of the ready combat units of the U.S. Continental Army Command and TAC. Responsibility for the tactical air planning functions for the Middle East, Southern Asia, and Africa south of the Sahara have been assigned to TAC.

In its support role, TAC is responsible for the developing and testing of doctrine, tactics, techniques, and procedures for tactical air operations and for performing operational tests on developed equipment. In support of tactical air forces in Europe and the Pacific, TAC provides fighter and assault airlift squadrons on rotation and trained personnel for combat air crews and tactical missile squadrons of U.S. units based overseas.

TAC is the primary USAF agency for developing doctrine, tactics, procedures, and equipment to be used by air forces in counter-insurgency, unconventional warfare, and psychological warfare operations.

Operating at Eglin Air Force Base, Florida, and with detachments in Africa, Southeast Asia, and Latin America, TAC's Special Air Warfare Center (SAWC) has an assigned mission to provide increased counterinsurgency tactical air capability. SAWC consists of the 1st Air Commando Wing, the First Combat Applications Group for development work, and the 4420th Combat Support Group. Combat-ready personnel assist unified commanders in conducting Special Air Warfare operations. Foreign military personnel are also trained in these special operations. The training includes low-level drop techniques, close air support, reconnaissance, and assault airlift transport of ground forces to areas of actual or suspected guerrilla movement, as well as psychological warfare opera-

Chart 5
TACTICAL AIR COMMAND
Headquarters, Langley AFB, Va.

9th Air Force
Hq., Shaw AFB, S.C.

19th Air Force
Hq., Seymour Johnson AFB, N.C.

12th Air Force
Hq., Waco, Tex.

MacDill AFB, Fla.
836th Air Division
15th Tactical Fighter Wing

Shaw AFB, S.C.
363d Tactical Recon Wing
507th Tactical Control Group
USAF Combat Crew Training
School (Tactical Recon)

George AFB, Calif.
831st Air Division
479th Tactical Fighter Wing

Cannon AFB, N.M.
832d Air Division
27th Tactical Fighter Wing

McConnell AFB, Kan.
835th Air Division
23d Tactical Fighter Wing

Forbes AFB, Kan.
838th Air Division
313th Troop Carrier Wing

Pope AFB, N.C.
464th Troop Carrier Wing

Homestead AFB, Fla. (SAC)
31st Tactical Fighter Wing

Dyess AFB, Tex. (SAC)
516th Troop Carrier Wing

Bergstrom AFB, Tex.
75th Tactical Recon Wing
602d Tactical Control Group

Seymour Johnson AFB, N.C.
833d Air Division
4th Tactical Fighter Wing

Lockbourne AFB, Ohio
840th Air Division
317th Troop Carrier Wing

Mountain Home AFB, Idaho
67th Tactical Recon Wing

Nellis AFB, Nev.
USAF Combat Crew Training
School (Tactical Fighter)
4520th Combat Crew Training
Wing

Myrtle Beach AFB, S.C.
354th Tactical Fighter Wing

Orlando AFB, Fla. (MAC)
USAF Tactical Missile School
4504th Missile Training Wing

Davis-Monthan AFB, Ariz. (SAC)
USAF Combat Crew Training
School (Tactical Fighter)
4453d Combat Crew Training
Wing

James Connally AFB, Tex.
4405th Air Base Group

Eglin AFB, Fla. (AFSC)
33d Tactical Fighter Wing

Sewart AFB, Tenn.
839th Air Division
USAF Combat Crew Training
School (Troop Carrier)
4442d Combat Crew Training
Wing

Luke AFB, Ariz.
USAF Combat Crew Training
School (Tactical Fighter)
4510th Combat Crew Training
Wing

Langley AFB, Va.
316th Troop Carrier Wing

4449th Combat Crew Training
Squadron
(Ft. Benning, Ga.)

4441st Combat Crew Training
Squadron
(Williams AFB, Ariz.)

Eglin AFB, Fla. (AFSC)
USAF Tactical Air Warfare
Center

Shaw AFB, S.C.
USAF Tactical Air Recon Center
4411th Combat Crew Training
Group

Hurlburt Field, Fla.
USAF Air-Ground Operations
School
USAF Special Air Warfare
Center

Langley AFB, Va.
4500th Air Base Wing
4444th Recon Tech Group
4440th Aircraft Delivery Group
1st Aerial Port Group
TAC NCO Academy

**4410th Combat Crew
Training Wing**

1st Air Commando Wing
(England AFB, La.)

Pope AFB, N.C.
USAF Tactical Airlift Center

Nellis AFB, Nev.
USAF Tactical Fighter
Weapons Center

tions. Types of aircraft generally used for the special operations include the C-47 Skytrain, C-46 Commando, C-123 Provider, B-26K Counter-Invader, Helio U-10 Courier, T-28 Nomad, and the Douglas A-1E counterinsurgency fighter.

TAC has two general wartime missions: (1) the augmentation of overseas tactical air forces and (2) operations in defense of the Western Hemisphere. Under the first mission, TAC deploys both fighter and assault airlift units to Europe and the Far East to augment peacetime forces in those areas. Under the second mission, TAC augments the Air Defense Command by providing fighter and assault airlift units for the defense of Alaska, Canada, the United States and the Caribbean; provides assessment of bomb damage to the United States, in the event of attack, through reconnaissance operations; and airlifts Army forces to defend critical areas. When required, TAC provides airlift support for SAC and ADC in dispersal operations. TAC's command post contains automated data processing and projection devices to facilitate rapid data assessment and presentation. It maintains constant communications with its airborne command post during tactical operations.

Weapon systems in TAC include the F-84 Thunderstreak, F-100 Supersabre, F-104 Starfighter, F-105 Thunderchief, and F-4C Phantom. The General Dynamics F-111A is expected to be assigned to operational units in 1967 and will materially increase tactical fighter capabilities. Reconnaissance aircraft include the RF-84F Thunderflash, RF-101 Voodoo, RB-66 Destroyer, and the RF-4C Phantom, which entered the inventory in 1965. Assault and cargo transports in service are the C-119 Flying Boxcar, C-123 Provider, C-124 Globemaster, and the new long-range high-speed C-130 Hercules. The backbone of TAC's global and reconnaissance force is the KC-135 Stratotanker. Under the Air Force single-manager concept, SAC furnishes these tankers to TAC for refueling of tactical combat aircraft during exercises and deployments. In the missile field, there are the Mace, Sidewinder, and Bullpup missiles. The first is a surface-to-surface inertial-guidance weapon armed with a nuclear or conventional warhead, deployed with tactical air forces in Europe and the Far East. The Sidewinder is a supersonic air-to-air missile with a passive infrared guidance system. The Bullpup is a tactical air-to-surface missile with a simple command guidance system, a speed of about 1,400 mph, and a high degree of accuracy from a two-mile launching distance. It is in use by tactical air forces in the United States and overseas.

The Air Defense Command (ADC)

The Air Defense Command is the U.S. Air Force component of the United States-Canadian joint service North American Air Defense Command (NORAD). The headquarters of both ADC and NORAD are located at Ent Air Force Base, Colorado Springs, Colorado, and the vital Combat Operation Center of NORAD is now located inside nearby Cheyenne Mountain under tons of nuclear-blast-resistant rock. ADC contributes more than 70 per cent of the manpower and weapons available to the commander in chief, NORAD. The U.S. Army, U.S. Navy, and Royal Canadian Air Force are also part of NORAD. ADC's mission is to organize, administer, train, and equip Air Force aerospace defense forces to a condition of top battle-readiness, responsive to the operational requirements of the commander in chief, NORAD.

ADC has four numbered air forces, the geographical boundaries of which coincide with NORAD's four regions. Its technological back-up includes SAGE (Semi-Automatic Ground Environment) and BUIC (Backup Interceptor Control System). Also, ADC has a weapons center and training range at Tyndall Air Force Base, Florida, and Perrin Air Force Base, Texas. At Ent Air Force Base, Colorado, ADC operates for NORAD a worldwide aerospace surveillance tracking system. This feeds information on man-made objects in space to the NORAD Space Detection and Tracking System.

Recognizing that the natural ocean boundaries of the North American continent were eliminated by the aerospace attack potential of the U.S.S.R., ADC pushed the development of a semi-automatic radar warning and control system to eliminate time lags inherent in manual radar operation. Weapons control was to be hooked into the system to minimize the possibilities of human error and reaction delays. The result of this effort was the SAGE system.

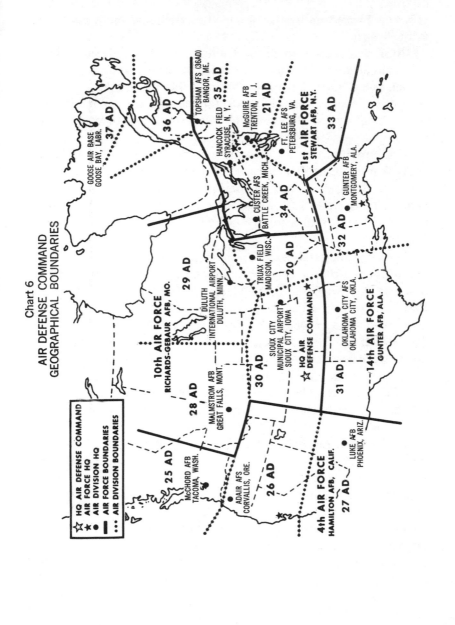

Chart 6
AIR DEFENSE COMMAND
GEOGRAPHICAL BOUNDARIES

It is now backed up by the newer, dispersed, and more automatic, BUIC system.

SAGE was completed in the United States in 1961 and includes a communications network with radar sweeping all avenues of approach to the North American continent. Data is fed through digital computers, which instantly track targets and set up interception courses and control all air defense weapons simultaneously. BUIC was put into service at ADC in early 1966.

ADC provides the facilities for early warning from the Distant Early Warning Line (DEW Line) along the Arctic Circle. To detect hostile ICBM's, ADC has the Ballistic Missile Early Warning System, which operates from ADC sites at Clear, Alaska, and Thule, Greenland, and from a joint RAF-ADC site at Fylingdales Moor, England.

Extending the land-based radar system seaward, ADC employs two wings of airborne early warning and control aircraft with units based at Otis Air Force Base, Massachusetts; McClellan Air Force Base, California; and McCoy Air Force Base, Florida. Altogether, ADC operates approximately 200 radar stations for early warning and detection. They include high-power long-range stations and low-power short-range gap-filler radar to track low-flying aircraft.

In the weapons area, ADC operates six Bomarc B missile sites in the United States. These surface-to-air interceptor missiles have a 400-mile range, a speed exceeding Mach 2, carry a nuclear warhead, and operate under SAGE control.

ADC fighter-interceptor squadrons are all equipped with Century-series aircraft. The F-101B Voodoo, a supersonic long-range fighter armed with Falcon missiles and Genie air-to-air atomic rockets, carries a pilot and a radar observer. The F-102A Delta Dagger, a single-place supersonic fighter, is equipped with Falcon missiles. Nine squadrons of F-101's and seven of F-102's are to be phased out. The F-102's will go to the Air National Guard. The F-104A Starfighter is a high-speed high-performance fighter armed with Sidewinder missiles and Vulcan 20-mm. cannon. The F-106 Delta Dart, a single-place supersonic all-weather interceptor, is equipped with Falcon missiles. It combines a data-link control system with auto-navigation and can be completely controlled by

SAGE to the point of actual missile and rocket firing. ADC hopes it will get operational versions of the advanced all-weather two-place fighter-interceptor aircraft that was first shown to the public on September 30, 1964. This is the YF-12A, which has a sustained speed of Mach 3, can fly higher than 70,000 feet, is equipped with an automatic navigation system and an ASG-18 computer fire-control system, and carries an AIM-47A Falcon air-to-air guided missile. The YF-12A represents a tremendous increase in capability for continental air defense.

The Military Airlift Command (MAC)

The Military Airlift Command is responsible to the Air Force and the Department of Defense for four major types of military missions: global airlift of troops and cargo, including combat air drop of troops and equipment and aeromedical evacuation; air rescue service; air weather service; and documentary photography and aerial photo and electronic mapping of the earth's surface. It is also responsible for the training and inspection of associated units of the Air Force Reserve and National Guard. MAC's headquarters is located at Scott Air Force Base, Illinois.

The global airlift function is performed by two subordinate elements: the 21st Air Force with headquarters at McGuire AFB, New Jersey, which operates from the Mississippi River east to Calcutta, India; and the 22d Air Force at Travis AFB, California, which covers the world westward to Calcutta. Less than half of MAC's airlifts are on a regular schedule, providing transportation of Department of Defense personnel and cargo over 115,000 miles of air routes. The balance of the airlift is available for special purposes: transporting high government officials; humanitarian airlifts; movement of scientific and communications equipment to remote areas; movement of ICBM's; and rapid strategic deployment of U.S. military forces to wherever they are required in the world.

There are two specialized airlift organizations in the Military Airlift Command: the 89th Military Airlift Wing, Special Mission, at Andrews AFB, Maryland, which conducts special air missions to transport the President and other high U.S. and foreign dignitaries on official and state business; and the 443d Military Airlift Wing

Chart 7
MILITARY AIRLIFT COMMAND
Headquarters, Scott AFB, Ill.

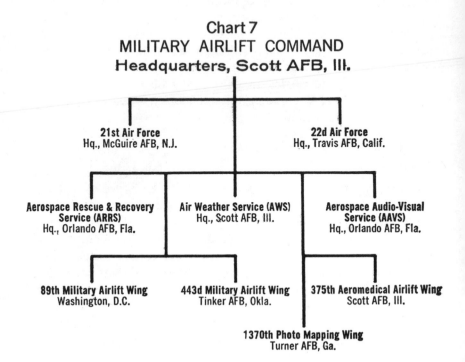

21st Air Force
Hq., McGuire AFB, N.J.

22d Air Force
Hq., Travis AFB, Calif.

**Aerospace Rescue & Recovery
Service (ARRS)**
Hq., Orlando AFB, Fla.

Air Weather Service (AWS)
Hq., Scott AFB, Ill.

**Aerospace Audio-Visual
Service (AAVS)**
Hq., Orlando AFB, Fla.

89th Military Airlift Wing
Washington, D.C.

443d Military Airlift Wing
Tinker AFB, Okla.

375th Aeromedical Airlift Wing
Scott AFB, Ill.

1370th Photo Mapping Wing
Turner AFB, Ga.

at Tinker AFB, Oklahoma, which operates the graduate training school at which air crews and advanced air-transportation personnel are specially trained to operate various MAC aircraft.

The 89th MAW is equipped with about thirty aircraft, including such types as the VC-137C intercontinental long-range jet; VC-137B, a jet similar to the commercial Boeing 707; VC-140 Jetstar, a smaller short-range jet; and a number of conventional propeller-driven aircraft. Aircraft assigned to the airlift forces include the C-135 Stratolifter, C-118 Liftmaster, C-124 Globemaster, C-133 Cargomaster, and the C-130E Hercules. The C-141 Starlifter, a four-fan-jet intercontinental aircraft specifically designed to MAC's needs, was accepted in October, 1964, and joined the operational airlift force in April, 1965; within the next few years, more than 200 of these aircraft will be assigned to the global airlift forces.

The 375th Aeromedical Airlift Wing provides a medical-airlift system of transporting patients from aerial ports of entry and from military installations in the United States to medical treatment centers. It is equipped with C-131's and C-118's designed to meet special requirements for medical airlift.

Three technical air service commands are included in the MAC organization. These commands operate not only for MAC and the USAF but are also available for other military and civilian use: the AWS, ARRS, and AAVS.

The Air Weather Service (AWS), from its headquarters at Scott AFB, Illinois, operates a world-wide weather and environmental network at almost 1,400 locations. It observes, analyzes, and forecasts traditional weather elements and new parameters of aerospace environment, such as solar activity. AWS flies hurricane and typhoon reconnaissance and upper-atmosphere sampling missions. It also supports U.S. missile and space operations by using electronic sensing instruments and computers, jet aircraft, and other modern tools of the aerospace scientist.

Aerospace Rescue and Recovery Service (ARRS), with its headquarters at Orlando AFB, Florida, provides world-wide search and rescue coverage for all Air Force units. It has trained teams, expert in survival, and always ready to fly, hike, swim, jump, or dive to anyone needing assistance. ARRS is responsible for locating and recovering downed airmen the world over, finding and recovering aerospace hardware at sea, locating and assisting astronauts who land outside planned impact zones, and for the direction of the joint military aircraft hurricane evacuation plans. ARRS units are assigned to many Air Force bases to handle search-and-rescue missions of USAF personnel and aircraft.

Aerospace Audio-Visual Service (AAVS), which has its head-quarters at Orlando AFB, Florida, but is scheduled to move to Norton AFB, California, on July 1, 1967, provides the Air Force with photographic services and products. AAVS has the responsibility for Air Force motion picture production, documentary photography, instrumentation photography, commercial motion picture production contracting, management of the Air Force film depository, motion picture distribution, and video tape-recording.

The 1370th Photo-Mapping Wing, based at Turner AFB, Georgia, provides Air Force aerial photography used in making maps, and accomplishes aerial electronic distance measurements, missile site surveys, and stellar-camera satellite measurements.

All the technical air service commands operate specialized aircraft modified for the particular jobs. AWS has about 65 air and weather sampling and support aircraft; ARRS operates about 230 helicopters and four-engine search aircraft; and AAVS employs 30 aircraft for aerial surveying and support.

The Alaskan Air Command (AAC)

The Alaskan Air Command is the air component of the unified Alaskan Command (ALCOM). ALCOM has a tri-service structure, including AAC, with headquarters at Elmendorf AFB near Anchorage; the United States Army, Alaska; and the Alaskan Sea Frontier. The commander in chief, Alaska, is also commander of the Alaska NORAD Region, while the AAC commander is vice commander and operationally in charge, since the Region's headquarters is located together with AAC.

AAC is responsible for early warning of attack on the United States and Canada; air defense of Alaska; support of the Strategic Air Command in Alaska; and support of special projects assigned by ALCOM or the U.S. Air Force.

Chart 8
ALASKAN AIR COMMAND
Headquarters, Elmendorf AFB, Alaska

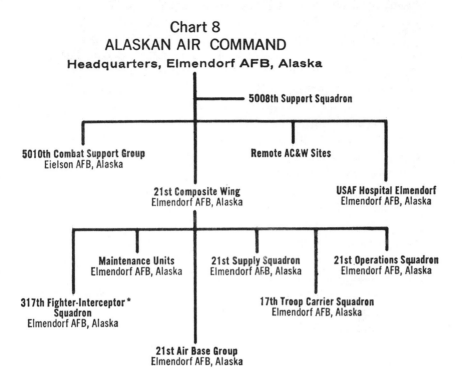

5008th Support Squadron

5010th Combat Support Group
Eielson AFB, Alaska

Remote AC&W Sites

21st Composite Wing
Elmendorf AFB, Alaska

USAF Hospital Elmendorf
Elmendorf AFB, Alaska

Maintenance Units
Elmendorf AFB, Alaska

21st Supply Squadron
Elmendorf AFB, Alaska

21st Operations Squadron
Elmendorf AFB, Alaska

317th Fighter-Interceptor *
Squadron
Elmendorf AFB, Alaska

17th Troop Carrier Squadron
Elmendorf AFB, Alaska

21st Air Base Group
Elmendorf AFB, Alaska

*To be activated July, 1967

Aircraft control and warning tasks are accomplished by two bands of radar sites. The outer band consists of the Alaskan segment of the DEW Line extension along the Arctic Ocean, connecting with early-warning sites ranging the Chukchi and Bering Coasts which, in turn, are linked with the DEW Line extension down the Aleutian Chain. Situated inland, the second band is formed by radars of ground-controlled intercept sites. The data collected from these stations is fed to four master direction centers to be evaluated and forwarded via a Combat Operations Center directly to NORAD.

The aircraft control and warning squadrons and the Aleutian DEW Line stations are manned by AAC. The Alaskan segment of the northern DEW Line is operated by civiliai s ui der contract to the Air Defense Command.

AAC's interception and identification missions are performed by the aircraft control and warning sites and one augmented Delta Dagger squadron having F-102 and F-106 aircraft. The F-102's are to be inactivated by July, ⹁967, to be replaced by rotated units from the United States. Elmendorf is the home base for all-weather interceptors, with elements operating from three forward bases including the Fairbanks-Eielson AFB complex.

Communications in the Arctic and sub-Arctic regions have always been highly unreliable. Adverse atmospheric conditions have an unfavorable effect on ordinary radio communications, and severe weather is a constant hazard to buried cables and landlines. These problems have been overcome by a communications system referred to as "White Alice." It is a radio relay system using over-the-horizon transmission known as "forward propagation tropospheric scatter." Ultra-high-frequency radio beams leap 200 miles in one stride. The system, which serves both military and civilian communications needs, can carry many voice and telegraph messages simultaneously with the audio quality of a local telephone conversation.

AAC has the first military long distance dialing system ever commissioned through the Alaska switching system. It permits site commanders to dial directly to their headquarters, as well as providing immediate communication to the sites from the AAC commander.

Logistical support in Alaska is difficult. Only the main air bases,

Elmendorf and Eielson, have rail service, and only one of the twenty-one radar stations is served by road. Of the remaining twenty sites, two are accessible only by air and the others can be reached by water routes only during the short summer months.

Once a year, after the ice pack recedes from the Arctic Coast, AAC remote stations are served with stockpiles of nonperishable supplies. A massive civilian contract operation called "Mona Lisa" delivers material ranging from bulldozers to razor blades, but it can never meet the full resupply needs of the remote stations. Storage facilities are limited, and there is a continuing requirement for perishables, spare parts, mail, etc. To provide this by airlift, about 250 tons per day, AAC uses C-123 and C-130 cargo aircraft.

C-123 pilots fly to each site about twice a week from their base at Elmendorf. Probably nowhere else in the world is there a continuing aerial resupply faced with such demanding operations. Most of the radar stations are situated in rugged mountainous terrain. Primitive "bush" landing strips have been scraped from the sides of mountains. Often they have only one approach and departure route with no room for a go-around.

AAC provides bases, housekeeping, and air defense for Strategic Air Command aircraft at Elmendorf and Eielson Air Force Bases. SAC bombers and tankers are on rotational alert at these bases around the clock.

AAC also supports annual Arctic maneuvers, rescue operations, weather tests and experimentation, and mapping surveys and geological expeditions to polar regions.

To combat the missile threat, the aerospace defense of Alaska includes a Ballistic Missile Early Warning Station located at Clear, about fifty miles south of Fairbanks. This electronic detection system includes three giant radar screens, each 165 by 400 feet, which continuously monitor space for unidentified objects. Surveillance data from the station flows into a computer at NORAD headquarters.

In the event of an enemy ICBM strike, the retaliatory and defensive agencies and the Joint Chiefs of Staff in the Pentagon would be alerted at the same time. The entire system is designed to give the

North American continent fifteen minutes' warning of a missile attack.

The Pacific Air Forces (PACAF)

Pacific Air Forces is the tactical air arm of the USAF in the Central and Western Pacific, the Far East, and Southeast Asia. It is also the air component of the Department of Defense unified U.S. Pacific Command (PACOM).

The over-all mission of PACAF is to ensure that the United States and its allies maintain control of the air in the Far East. Its major specific peacetime missions include the following: to provide tactical jet strike forces for any contingency; to provide peripheral air defense against enemy attack on the United States from across the Pacific; to maintain an instant alert air defense structure in U.S.–controlled areas; to support the air aspects of the U.S. Military Assistance Program; to maintain close relationships with allied air forces; to perform routine and emergency aerial reconnaissance; to support joint PACOM operations; to provide intratheater airlift support; and to maintain bases and support facilities for augmentation deployments from the United States.

In a general war, PACAF would conduct offensive air operations designed to eliminate or reduce the enemy's ability to attack the PACOM area and the United States and would conduct defensive air operations in protection of the land areas of PACOM and the western approaches to the United States. In addition, PACAF tactical air units would perform a wide variety of theater missions including joint air/ground operations, reconnaissance, and airlift in conjunction with other U.S. forces and with air forces of U.S.–allied countries.

PACAF has about 70,000 personnel and 32 tactical squadrons of strike, support, and air defense aircraft, and operates from some twenty air bases in more than half a dozen countries. In an emergency, PACAF's permanently based air units would be augmented by strike and support units of the Tactical Air Command, and to supplement PACAF's capability, there are more than seventy tactical squadrons, mostly jet equipped, belonging to the free countries of the Far East which might be available.

Chart 9
PACIFIC AIR FORCES
Headquarters, Hickam AFB, Hawaii

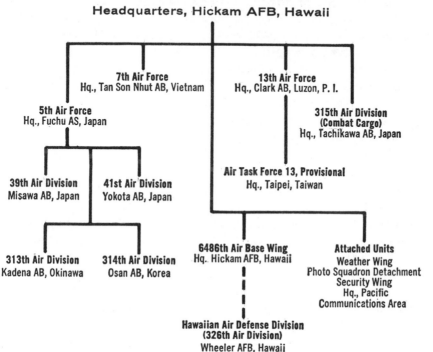

7th Air Force
Hq., Tan Son Nhut AB, Vietnam

13th Air Force
Hq., Clark AB, Luzon, P. I.

5th Air Force
Hq., Fuchu AS, Japan

315th Air Division
(Combat Cargo)
Hq., Tachikawa AB, Japan

39th Air Division
Misawa AB, Japan

41st Air Division
Yokota AB, Japan

Air Task Force 13, Provisional
Hq., Taipei, Taiwan

313th Air Division
Kadena AB, Okinawa

314th Air Division
Osan AB, Korea

6486th Air Base Wing
Hq. Hickam AFB, Hawaii

Attached Units
Weather Wing
Photo Squadron Detachment
Security Wing
Hq., Pacific
Communications Area

Hawaiian Air Defense Division
(326th Air Division)
Wheeler AFB, Hawaii

PACAF's tactical air power includes combat-ready F-100 Super-sabres, F-105 Thunderchiefs, B-57 Canberras, RF-101 Voodoos, F-102 Delta Daggers, and F-4C Phantoms located on bases in the Philippines, Okinawa, Japan, and Korea. Its air power support units are equipped with C-123 and C-130 combat cargo transports, WB-47 Stratojet and WB-50 Superfortress weather reconnaissance planes, KC-135 inflight-refueling tankers, and HC-97, HU-16, and HH-43 rescue helicopters.

As the Air Force component command in the Pacific, PACAF comes under the operational command of the commander in chief, Pacific Command (CINCPAC). From its headquarters at Hickam AFB, Hawaii, PACAF directs its five major subordinate elements. Most of the command's offensive, reconnaissance, and defensive forces come under the 5th Air Force, which turned in a brilliant record in the Pacific in World War II and Korea. Headquarters 5th Air Force is located at Fuchu Air Station, Japan.

The 13th Air Force, which became famous as the jungle air force in World War II, is headquartered at Clark Air Base, Philippines. It maintains forces-in-readiness for tactical air offensive operations and the air defense of the Marianas, the Philippines, Taiwan, and Southeast Asia. The tactical Air Force role in Vietnam is carried out by the 7th Air Force, headquartered in Saigon.

PACAF's intratheater airlift forces are assigned to the 315th Air Division of "Korean Airlift" fame. This airlifting organization, which came into being during the Korean conflict, is headquartered in Japan. Its units provide intratheater airlift and assault capability for all U.S. military forces in PACOM.

In Hawaii, PACAF base command provides logistic and house-keeping support for PACAF bases in the central Pacific and for other commands such as SAC, MAC, and TAC, which use these bases as tenants. Hawaii is also the home of the Hawaiian Air Defense Division (the 326th Air Division) which has operational control over the Hawaii Air National Guard F-102 Delta Daggers. With its headquarters at Wheeler Air Force Base and jet inter-ceptors operating out of Hickam AFB, the Division is responsible for the air defense of Hawaii.

All of PACAF's operational units are on a mobile, combat-ready basis to deal with any contingency in the Pacific. These forces are designed primarily to deter overt aggression but, in case of an attack, can conduct a variety of air operations calculated to terminate hostilities rapidly. PACAF would be augmented by the deployment of U.S.–based Composite Air Strike Forces in the event of a large-scale war.

Not so well-known, but extremely effective, is PACAF's continuous program of cooperative training and operations with the air forces of the United States' Pacific allies. These air forces complement the PACAF offensive and defensive capability. Collectively, the combat air units and equipment of the allies outnumber those of PACAF. The objective of this program is a higher degree of operational standardization and a closer alignment of concepts, doctrines, and procedures. Realistic operational practice in close combined-air-offensive-and-defensive operations has been stepped up in the last six years.

The United States Air Forces in Europe (USAFE)

The mission of the United States Air Forces in Europe is to conduct, control, and coordinate offensive and defensive air operations in accordance with tasks assigned by the commander in chief, United States European Command (USCINCEUR). USAFE is a component unit of the U.S. European Command, along with the U.S. Army and Navy elements in the European area, and comes under the authority of CINCEUR.

USAFE's geographical area of interest sweeps in a giant arc over approximately one-fourth of the globe, from the British Isles and Scandinavia through Western Europe and North Africa to the Middle and Near East as far as Pakistan. It encompasses some of the world's most critically valuable territory, both economically and strategically, along with areas of political instability and unrest. USAFE supports several hundred installations in more than a dozen countries.

USAFE's NATO mission in time of war would be directed by the Supreme Allied Commander Europe from Supreme Headquarters Allied Powers Europe (SHAPE). Tactical units of USAFE's 3d and 17th Air Forces would be assigned to NATO

Chart 10
UNITED STATES AIR FORCES IN EUROPE
Headquarters, Lindsey AS, Wiesbaden, Germany

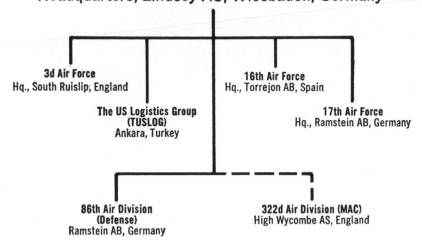

3d Air Force
Hq., South Ruislip, England

**The US Logistics Group
(TUSLOG)**
Ankara, Turkey

16th Air Force
Hq., Torrejon AB, Spain

17th Air Force
Hq., Ramstein AB, Germany

**86th Air Division
(Defense)**
Ramstein AB, Germany

322d Air Division (MAC)
High Wycombe AS, England

duty with the 4th Allied Tactical Air Force (ATAF). The 4th ATAF is commanded by the USAFE commander in chief. USAFE also controls the tactical squadrons rotated from the United States, which would be assigned to the 5th ATAF at Vicenza, Italy, and the 6th ATAF at Izmir, Turkey. One USAFE fighter-interceptor squadron under control of the Royal Netherlands Air Force would be assigned to the 2d ATAF at Moenchen-Gladbach, Germany.

USAFE aircraft designated for NATO use in wartime constitute the largest single contribution of any nation in the Atlantic Alliance, and USAFE is a primary instrument of Western defense. Its principal mission is to train and equip the combat-ready Air Force units that the United States has pledged to NATO. In addition, the command provides tactical air and logistic support for all NATO forces in Europe, assists air forces of other NATO members in developing their combat capabilities, carries out Air Force responsibilities in the Military Assistance Program in Europe, provides command-wide aeromedical service, and operates air search-and-rescue missions from the North Atlantic to the Indian Ocean. USAFE headquarters is located at Lindsey Air Station, Wiesbaden, Germany.

USAFE's principal operational commands are the 3d Air Force, with headquarters at South Ruislip, England, and the 17th Air Force at Ramstein Air Base, Germany. NATO-committed USAF forces under their control include six tactical reconnaissance wings and a tactical missile wing.

The third major USAFE subcommand is the United States Logistics Group (TUSLOG) with headquarters at Ankara, Turkey. It supports U.S. forces, activities, and agencies in Turkey, Greece, and Crete, and in other areas in Africa, the Middle East, and Asia.

USAFE's inventory of weapon systems and support airlift capabilities cover the four classic functions: strike, defense, reconnaissance, and transport.

The greater number of aircraft and missiles support the strike capability. This mixed force of more than 1,000 tactical aircraft maintains an around-the-clock posture. Strike aircraft include the F-100 Supersabre, F-101 Voodoo, and F-105D Thunderchief. The latter is an all-weather fighter-bomber having a Mach 2 speed and capable of delivering heavy bomb loads deep in enemy territory.

All-weather MGM-13A and CGM-13B Mace missiles provide USAFE's tactical missile capability.

For its defense mission, USAFE utilizes the F-102A Delta Dagger, a supersonic all-weather interceptor, armed with air-to-air missiles. The F-102A can fly at Mach 1.2 and is capable of interception at stratospheric altitudes.

The reconnaissance wings operate from bases in England, and Germany, and are equipped with all-weather RB-66 Destroyer and RF-101 Voodoo photo and reconnaissance aircraft.

For airlift, the 322d Air Division (MAC) supports USAFE with C-130 Hercules and C-124 Globemaster transport aircraft. Two TAC rotational squadrons operating C-130's and one MAC rotational squadron with C-124's are on duty with the 322d. These units are used primarily for unscheduled logistic airlift within Europe and aerial delivery of cargo and personnel in conjunction with U.S. Army forces in Europe.

The United States Air Forces Southern Command (USAFSO)

The United States Air Forces Southern Command, with headquarters at Albrook Air Force Base, Canal Zone, is the representative of the USAF for operations throughout Latin America and is the air component of the unified U.S. Southern Command (USSOUTHCOM). It is the oldest major overseas area command in the USAF. Although it did not become a major command until November 20, 1960, when the Panama Canal Department Air Force was established, it had its beginning in 1917 with the arrival of an aerosquadron in the Canal Zone.

The USAFSO area of operations in Latin America is approximately two and one-half times the size of the continental United States and extends from the southern border of Mexico to include all of South America.

The basic mission of USAFSO is the development of Latin American air forces in the interest of internal national security and Western-Hemisphere solidarity, as well as the conducting of various planning and air operations activities in Latin America. The goal in providing assistance to Latin American air forces, is for these forces to achieve that degree of proficiency and self-sufficiency necessary for them to fulfill missions assigned by their national governments to overall Western Hemisphere defense, if required.

As the air component of USSOUTHCOM, the Command's responsibilities include the following specific missions: exercising command of all U.S. military effort in Argentina, Chile, Colombia, Paraguay, Peru, and Uruguay; providing special air operations training for Latin American air forces; conducting contingency planning and operations throughout the area; advising and assisting in the development of the Military Assistance Program in Latin America; providing air defense of the Canal Zone; and conducting and coordinating rescue and recovery operations in the USSOUTHCOM area.

As a major air command, USAFSO conducts the USAF school for Latin America and the USAF Tropic Survival School, both of which are at Albrook AFB. It also develops and exploits sources of air intelligence information, provides logistic and administrative support of the USAF missions, and controls all USAF resources located throughout Latin America.

USAF missions are located in Argentina, Bolivia, Colombia, Chile, Ecuador, El Salvador, Guatemala, Honduras, Nicaragua, Paraguay, Peru, Uruguay, and Venezuela. USAF sections are located in the Dominican Republic and Costa Rica. In Brazil, the USAF is represented by a section of the Joint Brazil–United States Military Commission.

A priority mission of the Command is to provide airlift in support of contingency operations. C-130 Hercules transport aircraft from the Tactical Air Command are maintained at Howard Air Force Base, Canal Zone, on permanent rotation for this purpose. C-118 Liftmaster aircraft assigned to USAFSO for logistic support operations also would be committed in the same role as required. These aircraft fly the logistics pipeline "Andes Run," one of the most hazardous in the world. The Command supports a logistics pipeline throughout the entire area. The round-trip distance on a pipeline flight to Rio de Janeiro, Brazil, from Panama approximates that of a direct flight from Albrook to Peking, China—more than 9,000 miles.

One of the Command's most important functions is the special air-operations training for Latin American air forces. The training is tailored to specific country requirements and encompasses the full spectrum of special tactics, ranging from counterguerrilla air operations to civic actions. Thus far, fourteen Latin American countries have received this training, part of which is conducted jointly with Canal Zone–based U.S. Army 8th Special Action Forces.

USAF standards of technical competence are introduced to Latin American air forces through the USAF School for Latin America at Albrook AFB. In Spanish, bilingual USAF instructors at the school teach approximately thirty different subjects, including aircraft maintenance, electronics, supply, and personnel administration to about 500 students—officers and men—a year. Since it was opened in 1943, more than 6,400 students from Latin American countries have been graduated from the school, and many USAFSO personnel have taken its Spanish-language courses.

The school also conducts a preventive-medicine training program. This USAFSO program is designed to train five-man teams in basic preventive medicine, including pest control, sanitation, and immunization. The teams are composed of two preventive-medicine veterinarian technicians, two medical-services technicians, and one medical-laboratory technician. Upon completion of training, teams are provided medical equipment and supplies and returned to their home countries. Countries participating in the program are furnished aircraft for the transportation of mobile air-medical teams.

Tropic survival training is conducted at the USAF Tropic Survival School at Albrook AFB. In addition to training all USAFSO flying personnel, the school trains pilots of the Army, Navy, Marine Corps, Latin American air forces, and other federal agencies. The unique value of the training has been recognized by NASA. Mercury and Gemini astronauts were required to undergo the week-long course.

USAFSO is also responsible for providing search-and-rescue services through its Rescue Coordination Center at Albrook AFB. Air and surface craft assigned to all USSOUTHCOM components are employed in these operations. More than 100 missions are conducted yearly in Panama, mostly on a humanitarian basis to assist sick and injured Panamanians.

The Air Training Command (ATC)

The Army Air Force Training Command was organized in 1943, and redesignated the Air Training Command in 1947. Its headquarters is located at Randolph AFB, Texas. It is one of the largest single commands in the Air Force, having an assigned strength of about 133,000. As one of the largest educational organizations in the Free World, ATC operates 18 training detachments in the United States and 200 field and mobile training detachments at bases around the world.

Its mission is to recruit and provide military, technical, and flying training of personnel for the U.S. Air Force.

The USAF Recruiting Service operates 7 groups, 54 detachments, and 753 recruiting offices throughout the United States. Recruiters, generally technical sergeants of ten years' service, annually interview 1,000,000 persons, from which about 100,000 are enlisted. Generally, recruits must be high school graduates, and all new officers must have a bachelor's degree.

Basic military training is conducted at ATC's Lackland Military Training Center, San Antonio, Texas. New airmen attend a six-week basic training course, which teaches military skills, identifies aptitudes and knowledge of each recruit, and assigns and trains them according to the needs of the Air Force.

Officer Training School (OTS), also at Lackland, provides a three-month training program for college graduates who have skills needed by the Air Force. OTS is also attended by airmen who obtain a college degree through the Airman Education and Commissioning Program. The OTS course emphasizes military knowledge and abilities required of all commissioned officers. Accredited law school graduates also attend OTS. Ministers, priests, and rabbis are trained to become Air Force chaplains at the Chaplains' School at Lackland.

Processing and basic military and medical service orientation are performed under the supervision of ATC at the USAF Medical Service School at Gunter AFB, Alabama, where thirty-nine specialized medical courses are given for officers and airmen.

Technical training in nonrated USAF specialties is provided

Chart 11
AIR TRAINING COMMAND
Headquarters, Randolph AFB, Tex.

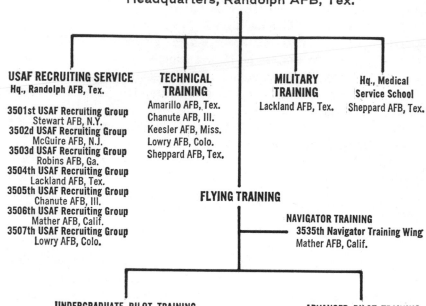

USAF RECRUITING SERVICE
Hq., Randolph AFB, Tex.

3501st USAF Recruiting Group
Stewart AFB, N.Y.
3502d USAF Recruiting Group
McGuire AFB, N.J.
3503d USAF Recruiting Group
Robins AFB, Ga.
3504th USAF Recruiting Group
Lackland AFB, Tex.
3505th USAF Recruiting Group
Chanute AFB, Ill.
3506th USAF Recruiting Group
Mather AFB, Calif.
3507th USAF Recruiting Group
Lowry AFB, Colo.

TECHNICAL TRAINING
Amarillo AFB, Tex.
Chanute AFB, Ill.
Keesler AFB, Miss.
Lowry AFB, Colo.
Sheppard AFB, Tex.

MILITARY TRAINING
Lackland AFB, Tex.

Hq., Medical
Service School
Sheppard AFB, Tex.

FLYING TRAINING

NAVIGATOR TRAINING
3535th Navigator Training Wing
Mather AFB, Calif.

UNDERGRADUATE PILOT TRAINING

3500th Pilot Training Wing
Reese AFB, Tex.

3550th Pilot Training Wing
Moody AFB, Ga.

3575th Pilot Training Wing
Vance AFB, Okla.

3640th Pilot Training Wing
Laredo AFB, Tex.

3525th Pilot Training Wing
Williams AFB, Ariz.

3560th Pilot Training Wing
Webb AFB, Tex.

3615th Pilot Training Wing
Craig AFB, Ala.

3646th Pilot Training Wing
Laughlin AFB, Tex.

ADVANCED PILOT TRAINING

3510th Flying Training Wing
Randolph AFB, Tex.

3630th Flying Training Wing
Sheppard AFB, Tex.

3636th Combat Crew Training
Group (Survival)
Fairchild AFB, Wash.

officers and airmen at five bases, where more than 700 courses are given. These bases graduate in excess of 100,000 USAF personnel each year. In addition, some 300,000 specialists complete the technical training conducted by ATC mobile and field training detachments each year.

Technical training bases and some of their courses are:

Keesler AFB, Mississippi (electronics, air traffic control, radio and radar, missile guidance systems, and communications);

Sheppard AFB, Texas (helicopter and conventional aircraft mechanics, data processing, transportation, Atlas and Titan missiles, and the Titan III space booster);

Chanute AFB, Illinois (advanced aircraft mechanic specialists, Minutemen, Bomarc and Hound Dog missiles, motorized equipment, firefighting, and weather observation);

Lowry AFB, Colorado (armament, intelligence, photography, special weapons maintenance, Mace and air-to-air weapons); and

Amarillo AFB, Texas (jet mechanics, airframe repair, guided missile systems, metal-working, utilities, personnel administration, and supply).

Flying training is given at twelve ATC bases. Eight of these conduct undergraduate pilot training (UPT), and four conduct aircrew training programs. The aircraft used in these programs are the T-37, a primary jet trainer, which cruises in excess of 400 miles per hour at 35,000 feet; the T-38, a supersonic trainer with a speed exceeding 800 mph at 50,000 feet; the T-29 "Flying Classroom," with room for fourteen student navigators and two instructors; and the T-39, with a cruising speed of 500 mph and a ceiling above 40,000 feet. Student pilot training includes preflight instruction, 120 hours of primary training, and 120 hours in the T-38. The new single-engine propeller-driven T-41A entered the ATC inventory in 1965, and primary training includes 30 hours in the T-41A and 90 hours in the T-37.

Helicopter pilots, all of whom are pilot training graduates, are trained in a 102-training-day basic helicopter course. Training is given in the H-19, CH-21, HH-43B, and CH-3C helicopters.

Students at the undergraduate navigator school at James Connally AFB, Texas, receive 177 hours of airborne instruction. Advanced courses for navigator-bombardiers and electronic warfare officers are conducted at Mather AFB, California, where approximately 800 students are trained annually.

Headquarters ATC has a staff agency, Training Development, which investigates and evaluates new training methods, technologies, and devices. Programmed instruction tests conducted by ATC indicate that electronic teaching methods can provide faster and more efficient training for ATC students in the courses used in test programs.

Concurrency-training began in 1963 in such new weapon systems as the Titan III, F-111A, and F-4C. Under this concept, personnel training begins at the industrial plants before the new systems become operational. Thus, trained crews and instructors are on hand when the new systems reach operational status.

The Continental Air Command (CONAC)

The over-all mission of the Continental Air Command is to furnish logistical, budgetary, administrative, and personnel support for all Air Force Reserve units and for assigned and attached individual members of the Air Force Reserve designated in USAF orders. It also provides training and inspection support for Air Force Reserve units to be assigned to CONAC in an emergency and for assigned and attached individual Air Force reservists as directed by Headquarters U.S. Air Force. In addition, CONAC orders to extended active duty in the event of war or national emergency those Air Force Reserve units to be gained by CONAC, and those individual Air Force reservists as specified by Headquarters U.S. Air Force.

CONAC also performs certain special functions. These include:

(1) Supervision of and liaison with the Civil Air Patrol in the continental United States, Alaska, Hawaii, and Puerto Rico (the Civil Air Patrol, a national organization and an auxiliary of the USAF, flies extensive inland search missions in the United States, maintains a communications network of 14,500 radio stations, and conducts a comprehensive aerospace education and youth training program);

(2) Liaison with the Selective Service System;

Chart 12
CONTINENTAL AIR COMMAND
Headquarters, Robins AFB, Ga.

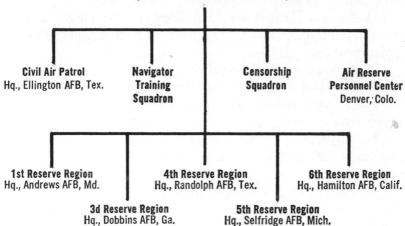

Civil Air Patrol
Hq., Ellington AFB, Tex.

Navigator
Training
Squadron

Censorship
Squadron

Air Reserve
Personnel Center
Denver, Colo.

1st Reserve Region
Hq., Andrews AFB, Md.

4th Reserve Region
Hq., Randolph AFB, Tex.

6th Reserve Region
Hq., Hamilton AFB, Calif.

3d Reserve Region
Hq., Dobbins AFB, Ga.

5th Reserve Region
Hq., Selfridge AFB, Mich.

TYPICAL REGION

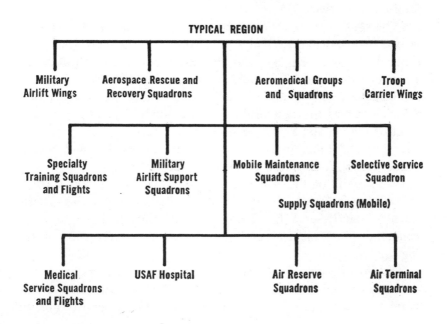

Military
Airlift Wings

Aerospace Rescue and
Recovery Squadrons

Aeromedical Groups
and Squadrons

Troop
Carrier Wings

Specialty
Training Squadrons
and Flights

Military
Airlift Support
Squadrons

Mobile Maintenance
Squadrons

Selective Service
Squadron

Supply Squadrons (Mobile)

Medical
Service Squadrons
and Flights

USAF Hospital

Air Reserve
Squadrons

Air Terminal
Squadrons

(3) Formulation of USAF civil defense plans and coordination of such plans with those of the Army;

(4) Representation of the Air Force on Regional Civil Defense Coordinating Boards;

(5) Provision of necessary assistance to other major air commands in recruiting reserve personnel to meet augmentation requirements;

(6) Action as a single Air Force contact in cooperating with Army and Naval districts in the United States in carrying out the Air Force responsibilities prescribed in the Basic Plan for Defense (other than air defense) of the United States;

(7) Provision of representatives in conjunction with the Army and Navy for the State Reserve Facilities Board in the United States;

(8) Supervision of Air Force cooperation with the Air Explorer Program in the United States—including Alaska—and in Puerto Rico; and

(9) Supervision of the CONAC portion of the Military Affiliated Radio System (MARS).

CONAC is organized into eight subordinate commands: Air Reserve Personnel Center, Civil Air Patrol–USAF, and six Air Force Reserve Regions. Regions are the focal points for all Reserve activities within their geographical boundaries. Below the Regions are Reserve Flying Units and sixteen Air Force Reserve Sectors. Reserve Sectors are responsible for all nonflying units. Management of Region and Sector headquarters is accomplished partly by reservists. All other units subordinate to the Region and Sector headquarters are managed entirely by reservists.

Flying units of the Air Force Reserve include Troop Carrier Wings, Troop Carrier Groups, and Air Rescue Squadrons. Additionally, the Reserve has many support units including mobile communications, medical service, air terminal, and navigation training squadrons.

The Air Reserve Personnel Center, Denver, Colorado, is the "manpower bank of the Air Force." The Center maintains current, correct, and complete records of all Air Force reservists not on extended active duty—approximately 370,000—to assure rapid and economical mobilization in the event of a national emergency.

The Air Force Communications Service (AFCS)

The Air Force Communications Service was established on July 1, 1961. From its headquarters at Scott AFB, Illinois, it operates and maintains on-base and global communications, air traffic control services, and air navigational aids for the Air Force and other governmental and civilian agencies. It provides major support to the Defense Communications Agency.

AFCS stands seventh among the sixteen major Air Force commands in terms of military population. It has nearly 50,000 individuals, military and civilian, at more than 500 locations around the world. Sixty per cent of AFCS personnel are stationed overseas. AFCS units, being tenants on bases under the jurisdiction and control of other commands, are dependent on such bases for support and housekeeping services.

AFCS provides five principal services: on-base communications, long-line continental and intercontinental communications as components of the Defense Communications System, navigational aids, air traffic control, and emergency mission support.

On-base communications support includes communications services on air bases such as telephone, teletype, intercom, fire and crash alarm, air-police and security alerting systems, and on-base closed-circuit television.

AFCS operates long-line communications including global radio and teletype and telephone networks, which link Air Force activities world-wide. Special networks provide communications for aircraft and missile early-warning systems. As part of the Defense Communications System, AFCS operates within the Air Force the Automatic Digital Network and the Automatic Voice Network. These high-speed data, teletype, and voice communications systems tie together hundreds of bases, supply depots, major command headquarters, and other members of the defense team.

Air navigational aids include radio ranges, direction finders, homing beacons, radar beacons, marker beacons, instrument landing systems, and tactical navigational aids. Using T-33 and C-140A

Chart 13
AIR FORCE COMMUNICATIONS SERVICE
Headquarters, Scott AFB, Ill.

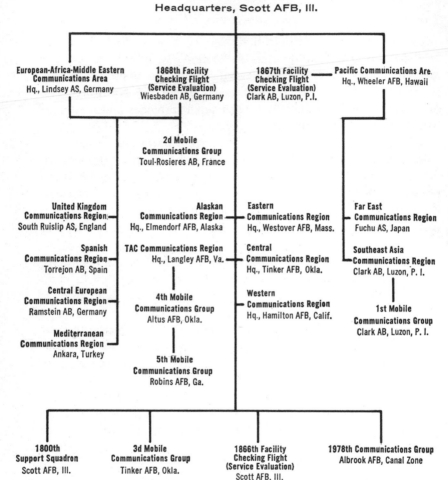

European-Africa-Middle Eastern
Communications Area
Hq., Lindsey AS, Germany

1868th Facility
Checking Flight
(Service Evaluation)
Wiesbaden AB, Germany

1867th Facility
Checking Flight
(Service Evaluation)
Clark AB, Luzon, P.I.

Pacific Communications Are.
Hq., Wheeler AFB, Hawaii

2d Mobile
Communications Group
Toul-Rosieres AB, France

United Kingdom
Communications Region
South Ruislip AS, England

Alaskan
Communications Region
Hq., Elmendorf AFB, Alaska

Eastern
Communications Region
Hq., Westover AFB, Mass.

Far East
Communications Region
Fuchu AS, Japan

Spanish
Communications Region
Torrejon AB, Spain

TAC Communications Region
Hq., Langley AFB, Va.

Central
Communications Region
Hq., Tinker AFB, Okla.

Southeast Asia
Communications Region
Clark AB, Luzon, P. I.

Central European
Communications Region
Ramstein AB, Germany

4th Mobile
Communications Group
Altus AFB, Okla.

Western
Communications Region
Hq., Hamilton AFB, Calif.

1st Mobile
Communications Group
Clark AB, Luzon, P. I.

Mediterranean
Communications Region
Ankara, Turkey

5th Mobile
Communications Group
Robins AFB, Ga.

1800th
Support Squadron
Scott AFB, Ill.

3d Mobile
Communications Group
Tinker AFB, Okla.

1866th Facility
Checking Flight
(Service Evaluation)
Scott AFB, Ill.

1978th Communications Group
Albrook AFB, Canal Zone

jet aircraft, dual-rated AFCS pilot-controllers evaluate all air traffic controllers manning the system. AFCS also performs service evaluation to ensure the safe and effective operation of these navigational systems.

AFCS air traffic controllers operate and maintain point-to-point and ground-to-air radio stations, airdrome control towers, and precision radar-control approach services to permit aircraft landings under all weather conditions.

Emergency mission support provides mobile communications that can be transported quickly to any place in the world. AFCS has five mobile communications units strategically located around the world. Elements with necessary equipment can be transported by the Military Airlift Command to establish voice and teletype communications to support any U.S. contingency operation. These highly mobile units ensure reliable and secure communications for field commanders.

AFCS is divided into geographic areas comparable to numbered Air Forces and independent regions similar to air divisions. The command is responsible for training more than 6,000 Air Reserve forces personnel assigned to Air National Guard and Air Force Reserve communications units. On mobilization, these units would augment active-duty communications units.

The Air Force Logistics Command (AFLC)

The mission of the Air Force Logistics Command is to keep the Air Force's aerospace weapon systems at "go." This mission, which is constantly growing in size and complexity, must be performed at the lowest possible cost. Its vital task is to ensure that the combat commands have the logistics management needed to keep their aircraft, missiles, and electronic devices constantly at top efficiency.

AFLC headquarters is at Wright-Patterson AFB, Ohio. The large units that carry out most of the Command's operational functions are known as Air Matériel Areas (AMA). In 1966, there were nine AMA's in the United States. The largest two employ up to 20,000 people each. Over-all, AFLC employs about 141,000 people, of whom nine out of ten are civilians. The number of

Chart 14
AIR FORCE LOGISTICS COMMAND
Headquarters, Wright-Patterson AFB, Ohio

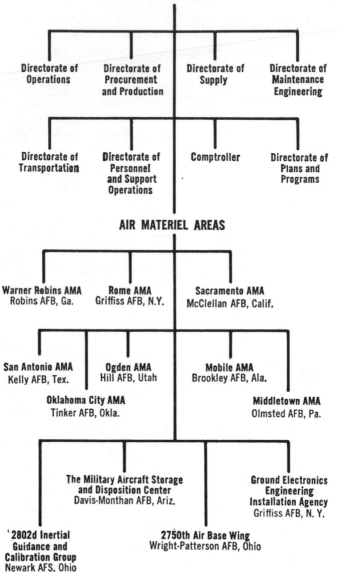

Directorate of Operations

Directorate of Procurement and Production

Directorate of Supply

Directorate of Maintenance Engineering

Directorate of Transportation

Directorate of Personnel and Support Operations

Comptroller

Directorate of Plans and Programs

AIR MATERIEL AREAS

Warner Robins AMA
Robins AFB, Ga.

Rome AMA
Griffiss AFB, N.Y.

Sacramento AMA
McClellan AFB, Calif.

San Antonio AMA
Kelly AFB, Tex.

Ogden AMA
Hill AFB, Utah

Mobile AMA
Brookley AFB, Ala.

Oklahoma City AMA
Tinker AFB, Okla.

Middletown AMA
Olmsted AFB, Pa.

The Military Aircraft Storage and Disposition Center
Davis-Monthan AFB, Ariz.

Ground Electronics Engineering Installation Agency
Griffiss AFB, N. Y.

2802d Inertial Guidance and Calibration Group
Newark AFS, Ohio

2750th Air Base Wing
Wright-Patterson AFB, Ohio

AMA's and their primary responsibilities are changing as the Air Force closes various installations in compliance with Department of Defense directives.

The AMA's divide the country into geographical areas. All are system-support managers providing world-wide logistics management of specific weapon systems, such as the B-52 and Minuteman ICBM, and for specific classes of commodities, such as jet or missile engines. Each AMA furnishes logistic and administrative support, including technical advice and assistance, to the Air Force and certain Department of Defense activities within its area. The AMA's also provide support and technical assistance outside the United States as required.

AFLC has revolutionized its logistics operations within the last decade. With the advent of missiles, the USAF today is geared for instant retaliation, prepared to strike with whatever is on hand when hostilities begin. In the face of this military reality, the day of costly stockpiling in overseas warehouses, along with slow supply lines, is obsolete. Direct support is needed. Direct support means the high-speed movement from the United States of priority and high-value materials. It calls for rapid communications and electronic data processing. Today, an Air Force activity requisitions and receives directly from AMA's whatever it needs, regardless of the unit's location in the world.

In addition to providing more effective and flexible support, the direct-support approach in logistics management has contributed to the closing of more than forty installations since 1950, and a reduction in manpower from 224,000 to 141,000. Requirements for spare parts have been reduced by billions of dollars during this same period.

The main activities of AFLC are procurement, supply, depot maintenance, and transportation.

(1) Procurement, amounting to approximately $3 billion a year, is for modification, replenishment spares, initial spares for aircraft and missiles, propellants, munitions, electronics and communications, contract maintenance, motor vehicles, ground-support equipment, and local purchases. By establishing policies and procedures

and directing them through staff visits, AFLC also has surveillance over $1.2 billion in local transactions by Air Force bases.

(2) Supply activities are concerned with the more than a million items used by the Air Force. All of these items are catalogued and most of them are stocked at the AMA depots. Supply also computes requirements of spare parts for future Air Force needs.

(3) Depot maintenance accounts for the work of 100,000 persons, about half of whom are off-base contract personnel, and sees to it that all matériel is capable of performing its intended function. Data is constantly collected to improve performance and reduce costs. The AMA's modify and overhaul matériel that using organizations cannot maintain. Technical publications are provided for the operation and maintenance of all Air Force matériel, prescribing maintenance systems, methods, and procedures to be used. The basic philosophy is to minimize the need for maintenance through improved reliability and to provide top performance at the smallest cost.

(4) Transportation manages LOGAIR, an around-the-clock airlift whose fleet of 82 cargo aircraft, making 156 departures daily, supplies 82 domestic air bases and ties in the Military Airlift Command's five aerial ports for overseas airlift. AFLC also develops systems and procedures for the world-wide movement of Air Force matériel and passengers; sets transportation policies in support of missiles, space, and satellite systems; and gives technical direction to all Air Force packaging and materials-handling activities.

AFLC's Ground Electronics Engineering Installation Agency has its headquarters at Griffiss AFB, New York. It provides single-point management for the engineering, installation, and maintenance of all Air Force ground communications-electronics equipment including radar, microwave, and early warning systems. About 8,000 people, mostly military, make up fourteen squadrons operating in five regions located throughout the world.

The 2802d Inertial Guidance and Calibration Group, located at Newark AF Station, Heath, Ohio, is under the direct jurisdiction of Headquarters AFLC. As the single point within the Air Force for the test and repair of inertial guidance systems, Newark provides direct support to the Minuteman, Titan, and Atlas missile systems, and to the navigational system of the F-4C Phantom II interceptor. Other advanced systems, such as the F-111 aircraft now in development, will be added to the workload as they reach operational status.

AFLC's Military Aircraft Storage and Disposition Center, located at Davis-Monthan AFB, Arizona, stores aircraft not currently in use by the operating Air Force commands so that they remain available when needed by other Department of Defense services or by Military Assistance Program countries. Residual aircraft are disposed of by reclamation, demilitarization, or sold as surplus property.

AFLC also operates the Air Force Museum at Wright-Patterson AFB and manages the Air Force matériel portion of the Military Assistance Program, including both the grant aid portion and the Military Assistance Sale. The grant aid portion involves about $400 million annually. These programs are managed for the benefit of more than fifty nations in the Free World.

The Air Force Systems Command (AFSC)

The Air Force Systems Command, established in April, 1961, as successor to the Air Research and Development Command, is responsible for the advancement of military aerospace technology and the development of operational aerospace systems. It is designed to provide the most up-to-date and effective management of Air Force scientific and technical resources.

AFSC meets major space responsibilities of the Department of Defense by providing research, development, testing, and engineering of satellites, boosters, space probes and associated systems to be used by DOD. AFSC also supports National Aeronautics and Space Administration projects.

From its headquarters at Andrews AFB, Maryland, AFSC directs the operations of eight divisions, five development and test centers, two test ranges, and three contract management regions. The strength of the command is approximately 29,000 officers and airmen and 37,000 civilian employees.

In coordinating the military and civilian scientific and industrial development effort of aerospace weapon systems, AFSC directs the expenditure of about 32 per cent of the Air Force budget, or about

Chart 15
AIR FORCE SYSTEMS COMMAND
Headquarters, Andrews AFB, Md.

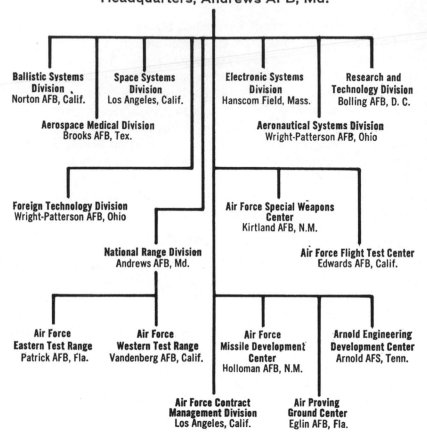

Ballistic Systems Division
Norton AFB, Calif.

Space Systems Division
Los Angeles, Calif.

Electronic Systems Division
Hanscom Field, Mass.

Research and Technology Division
Bolling AFB, D. C.

Aerospace Medical Division
Brooks AFB, Tex.

Aeronautical Systems Division
Wright-Patterson AFB, Ohio

Foreign Technology Division
Wright-Patterson AFB, Ohio

Air Force Special Weapons Center
Kirtland AFB, N.M.

National Range Division
Andrews AFB, Md.

Air Force Flight Test Center
Edwards AFB, Calif.

Air Force Eastern Test Range
Patrick AFB, Fla.

Air Force Western Test Range
Vandenberg AFB, Calif.

Air Force Missile Development Center
Holloman AFB, N.M.

Arnold Engineering Development Center
Arnold AFS, Tenn.

Air Force Contract Management Division
Los Angeles, Calif.

Air Proving Ground Center
Eglin AFB, Fla.

7 cents of each federal tax dollar. It also administers more than 15,000 contracts having a total obligation of around $45 billion.

AFSC manages and controls some 300 installations or separate activities in the United States and overseas, including England, South Africa, Greenland, Alaska, Hawaii, Eniwetok, and Singapore. It also manages sixty-nine systems programs in varying stages of development acquisition.

Briefly stated, the functions and responsibilities of AFSC's subordinate divisions are:

(1) The Ballistic Systems Division plans, programs, and manages the acquisition of ballistic missiles and related equipment. It provides for activation of selected missile sites for the Atlas, Titan, and Minuteman programs. This effort has been the largest construction program in the history of this country.

(2) The National Range Division plans, develops, operates, maintains, and controls assigned Department of Defense range facilities in support of national ICBM and space programs. Its Eastern and Western Test Ranges maintain, operate, and modify the Atlantic and Pacific Missile Ranges in support of the U.S. missile and space programs.

(3) The Space Systems Division plans, programs, and manages military space systems and related equipment, including responsibility for research, development, engineering, testing, in-orbit tracking, telemetry control, recovery, evaluation, procurement, production, quality assurance, installation, and checkout. It also manages the acquisition of related items such as space boosters and aerospace ground equipment necessary to provide launching, control, and recovery of space equipment, and to support space programs.

(4) The Aeronautical Systems Division manages the development and acquisition of aeronautical systems and related equipment. It also manages AFSC's priority programs to strengthen Air Force capabilities in limited war, Special Air Warfare, and counterinsurgency operations. The division program includes managing aircraft and nonballistic missile systems supporting all Air Force operational requirements.

(5) The Electronic Systems Division plans and manages information and communications programs and projects to develop com-

mand, control, warning, and surveillance and support (weather and intelligence) functions. Responsibilities include electronic systems acquisition, test, and support for the Air Force and other U.S. Government agencies.

(6) The Aerospace Medical Division manages bio-astronautics research and development programs in support of Air Force systems development, assigned research programs supporting the Air Force personnel system, and clinical-medicine and aerospace-medicine requirements. It also supervises specialized aerospace-medical educational programs.

(7) The Foreign Technology Division acquires, evaluates, analyzes, and disseminates foreign aerospace technology in concert with other AFSC divisions and centers. Information collected is screened, processed, and analyzed to provide reports, studies, technical findings and assessments of potential hostile technology or operational environments with which the Air Force weapon systems must cope. The division provides foreign-technology support for USAF research and development activities.

(8) The Research and Technology Division (RTD), at its laboratories, plans and manages AFSC's exploratory and advanced development programs aimed at creating a broad base of research and technology for timely application in the development of superior advanced aerospace-weapon-and-support systems and equipment.

The laboratories under RTD supervision and their functional areas are the AF Weapons Laboratory, which performs research in nuclear weapon applications, effects, ballistics, safety, etc.; the AF Rocket Propulsion Laboratory, which studies rocket propulsion components, propellants, and associated ground equipment; the Rome Air Development Center, which does research in electromagnetic energy conversion, signal detection and processing, computation and display, command and control, and test and evaluation; and the AF Armaments Laboratory, which works on munitions.

Four laboratories at Wright-Patterson AFB are under program direction of RTD. These are the AF Aero-Propulsion Laboratory, studying air-breathing, electric and advanced propulsion, fuels, lubricants, and flight vehicle power; the AF Materials Laboratory, which does research in material sciences, metals, ceramics, non-metallic materials, manufacturing technology, and materials application; the AF Flight Dynamics Laboratory, which studies flight vehicle dynamics, performance, control, launching, structures, crew station, environmental control and escape, and aerodynamic decelerators; and the AF Avionics Laboratory, which performs research on electronic components, optics and photo materials, navigation and guidance, vehicle defense, electronic warfare, communications, and reconnaissance.

In addition, five AFSC Centers are maintained under RTD. They are:

(a) the AF Flight Test Center which conducts aircraft testing and provides facilities for contractor tests and a final functional test to determine the capability and suitability of a complete system in meeting USAF requirements and design objectives;

(b) the AF Special Weapons Center which provides engineering support and testing of nuclear weapons, their components, associated equipment, and related phenomena and environment;

(c) the Air Proving Ground Center which develops, operates, and maintains the Gulf Test Range for aircraft and missile systems' tests and an electromagnetic test environment for electronic countermeasure tests, conducts development engineering tests of missile and aircraft systems, subsystems, and equipment, carries out combat effectiveness tests, and operates the USAF Climatic Laboratory;

(d) the AF Missile Development Center which conducts research and development testing of air-to-air missiles and drones, maintains and operates an inertial guidance test facility, performs rocket firings, and conducts research and development in human factors relating to biodynamics and space biology; and

(e) the Arnold Engineering Development Center which provides test support in the fields of gas dynamics and propulsion to government agencies and contractors and educational and research institutions in the largest wind tunnel center in the Free World. (This center's mission is to plan, construct, and operate a series of wind tunnels, high-altitude test cells, and aerospace simulation chambers for the development, testing, and evaluation of aircraft, guided missiles, aerospace systems, and rockets and air-breathing propulsion systems. It includes four major laboratories.)

(9) The Contract Management Division is responsible for Department of Defense contract management activities in those plants assigned to the Air Force under the DOD National Plant Cognizance Program. Three regional offices manage the administration of contracts executed by AFSC organizations, AF Logistics Command procurement activities, major air commands, Defense Supply Agency, NASA, and other U.S. Government purchasing agencies when required.

The Air University

The Air University is the educational center of the U.S. Air Force and conducts the professional education program to provide selected Air Force officers with the knowledge and abilities essential for increasingly responsible command and staff positions. To fulfill its mission, the Air University operates colleges, schools, institutes, and supporting agencies from its headquarters at Maxwell AFB, Alabama. The core of the Air University system is its three professional military schools:

(1) The Squadron Officer School prepares junior officers for command and staff duties at lower organizational levels. Students are lieutenants and captains with three to seven years' commissioned service. Selected officers from the air forces of other Free World nations are also admitted. Lectures, seminars, and individual leadership exercises combine with independent research and practice in communicative skills to form a well-rounded educational program. The quota for each of the three classes given annually, which run for fourteen weeks, is about 850.

(2) The Air Command and Staff College, the intermediate level of education, aims at increasing the professional qualifications of selected USAF captains and majors. The school directs its effort toward expanding the scope and depth of the students' staff and command abilities and toward contributing to the development of doctrine, strategy, and tactics. The nine-month course includes military management, bases of international conflict, integration of

Chart 16
AIR UNIVERSITY
Headquarters, Maxwell AFB, Ala.

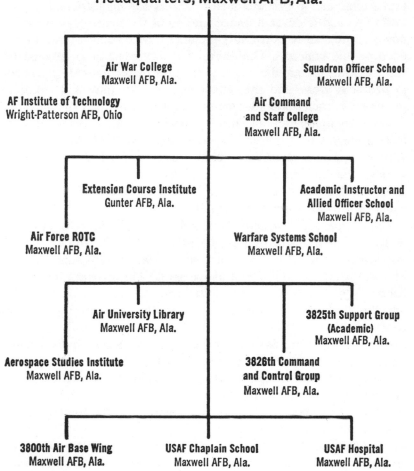

Air War College
Maxwell AFB, Ala.

Squadron Officer School
Maxwell AFB, Ala.

AF Institute of Technology
Wright-Patterson AFB, Ohio

**Air Command
and Staff College**
Maxwell AFB, Ala.

Extension Course Institute
Gunter AFB, Ala.

**Academic Instructor and
Allied Officer School**
Maxwell AFB, Ala.

Air Force ROTC
Maxwell AFB, Ala.

Warfare Systems School
Maxwell AFB, Ala.

Air University Library
Maxwell AFB, Ala.

**3825th Support Group
(Academic)**
Maxwell AFB, Ala.

Aerospace Studies Institute
Maxwell AFB, Ala.

**3826th Command
and Control Group**
Maxwell AFB, Ala.

3800th Air Base Wing
Maxwell AFB, Ala.

USAF Chaplain School
Maxwell AFB, Ala.

USAF Hospital
Maxwell AFB, Ala.

command and staff efforts, and present and future aerospace power employment doctrine. Each class has about 600 students.

(3) The Air War College is the senior Air Force school. Its prime aims are to prepare senior officers for high command and staff duty, and to develop understanding of the elements of national power. A related responsibility includes development of Air Force doctrine and concepts. One-third of the curriculum is devoted to student seminars, another third to lectures by recognized specialists in pertinent areas, and the remaining third to study and research on the thesis each student writes on a subject of military significance.

By participating in an off-duty program, Air Command and Staff College and Air War College students and selected Air University faculty members may earn master's or bachelor's degrees through the Air University–George Washington University Center.

In addition to its major professional schools, the Air University conducts various specialized activities:

(1) Academic Instructor and Allied Officer Schools have as their mission to increase the effectiveness of selected Air Force instructors, to raise the level of communicative skills, and to prepare Allied officers for school assignments. The six-week instructor course is given six times annually, and the class quota is 170. Allied officers receive a special orientation before enrolling in other courses.

(2) The Warfare Systems School aims to orient, indoctrinate, and instruct key officers and civilians in the effective utilization of aerospace power. Through its own courses and by instruction given in other Air University schools, the Warfare Systems School promotes a better understanding of the capabilities and limitations of modern aerospace weapon systems.

(3) The Air Force Institute of Technology operates two programs to provide sufficient technically and scientifically educated Air Force officers. The Institute's Civilian Institutions Program enrolls promising Air Force officers in civilian colleges, universities, and technical institutes throughout the country. This program has graduated more than 20,000 students since 1946 in fields including medical, advanced management, training with industry, and special short courses. The Institute operates an accredited resident engi-

neering program through which officers may receive bachelor's and master's degrees in such fields as astronautics, air weapons, electrical, nuclear, and aeronautical engineering. The Institute also operates the School of Systems and Logistics, Civil Engineering Center, and the Airman Education and Commissioning Program.

(4) The Air Force Reserve Officers Training Corps program, administered by the Air University, gives students a streamlined course of Air Force instruction while they are enrolled as undergraduates at civilian universities and colleges that maintain a cadet program. Upon satisfactory completion of Air Force instruction and graduation from college, Air Force ROTC cadets receive commissions in the Air Force Reserve and begin active duty.

(5) The Air University's Extension Course Institute offers more than 100 correspondence courses using principally the study materials of certain resident courses conducted by the Air University and the Air Training Command. Members of the Regular Air Force, Air Force Reserve, Air National Guard, Civil Air Patrol, members of other services, and civilians employed by the Armed Services make up the student body of about 350,000. The Institute has awarded more than one million diplomas.

(6) The Aerospace Studies Institute supports the Air University's other educational programs and conducts specialized research. Staff members prepare special studies in political, social, economic, military, and geographic fields and assist in formulating current aerospace doctrine. The divisions of the Institute are (a) Arctic, Desert, Tropic Information Centers; (b) Communications-Electronics Doctrinal Project Office; (c) Concepts Division; (d) Documentary Research Division; (e) Air Force Historical Division; and (f) *Air University Review,* the USAF professional journal of the aerospace age. The Institute also operates the USAF historical program.

(7) The Air University Library provides complete bibliographic and reference service for students, faculty, and staff personnel who seek to expand their knowledge about aerospace power. The library's books and bound journals exceed 200,000, and its military documents collection contains more than 500,000 items. The Authority Section maintains complete files of regulations, manuals,

and directives from Headquarters USAF, numbered air forces, and major air commands. The Cartographic Branch provides a vast collection of maps and charts essential for instruction in Air University schools.

Headquarters Command, USAF

The primary mission of the Headquarters Command is to support and service Headquarters USAF and other Air Force units in the Washington, D.C., area. It is directly involved with the nation's capital, the President, national and international dignitaries, and various ceremonials. In addition, it supports administratively some 12,000 Air Force personnel in more than 600 world-wide operating locations. These include personnel in the Federal Aviation Agency, National Aeronautics and Space Administration, Defense Intelligence Agency, Air Attaché offices, the North Atlantic Treaty Organization, and unified commands and other organizations.

From its headquarters at Bolling AFB, Washington, the Command is responsible for the supervision of Bolling AFB, nearby Andrews AFB, the USAF Band, the 1100th Support Group, and the Malcolm Grow USAF Clinical Center.

The 1100th Air Base Wing operates Bolling AFB, which has tenant units of the Strategic Air Command, Office of Aerospace Research, Air Force Systems Command, and Air Force Communication Service as well as the command headquarters of the Headquarters Command. The USAF Band and the USAF Ceremonial Unit are also based at Bolling.

The command missions performed at Bolling include providing administrative and logistical support to USAF Headquarters and other USAF organizations in the Washington area; providing administrative support to many worldwide Air Force activities; furnishing, through the 1100th Support Group, accounting and finance support to USAF Headquarters and all other USAF units in the Washington area; and providing housing and dining facilities for Air Force enlisted personnel on duty in the Washington area.

The 1001st Air Base Wing operates Andrews AFB, which is the home base for Presidential aircraft and the aerial port of arrival and departure for distinguished official visitors to Washington.

Command missions performed at Andrews include providing aircraft for and supervising administrative and proficiency flying of all Air Force personnel assigned to the Washington area; and supervising the Malcolm Grow USAF Clinical Center, one of the major military medical installations in the nation, which serves about 100,000 military personnel and their dependents. The Headquarters of the Air Force Systems Command is a tenant on Andrews AFB.

The United States Air Force Security Service (USAFSS)

The USAF Security Service was organized and designated a major command in October, 1948. Its mission is to monitor all USAF communications to ensure compliance with established communications security practices and procedures. USAFSS units occasionally conduct research in communications phenomena in support of various elements of the U.S. Government.

From its headquarters at Kelly AFB, Texas, the USAF Security Service directs five major subordinate units: (1) the Air Force Special Communications Center, at Kelly AFB, Texas, which provides technical assistance to all operating elements of USAFSS; (2) the 6940th Security Wing at Goodfellow AFB, Texas, which trains officers and airmen in the many skills and techniques used solely by USAFSS; (3) the European Security Region at Frankfurt, Germany, which exercises command and administrative control over USAFSS units deployed in the European theater; (4) the Pacific Security Region at Wheeler AFB, Hawaii, which exercises command and administrative control over USAFSS units deployed in support of the Pacific Air Command; and (5) the 6981st Radio Group Mobile, located at Elmendorf AFB, Alaska, which exercises command and administrative control over USAFSS units deployed in support of the Alaskan Air Command.

VII

USAF Separate Operating Agencies

In addition to the major air commands described in the preceding chapter, the Air Force includes four separate operating agencies. As distinguished from a major air command, a separate operating agency is a subdivision of the Air Force directly subordinate to Headquarters USAF and is assigned a specialized mission that is restricted in scope when compared to the mission of a major air command. It does, however, have the procedural responsibilities of a major air command. The four separate operating agencies of the USAF are described in this chapter.

Aeronautical Chart and Information Center (ACIC)

The mission of the Aeronautical Chart and Information Center is to provide the Air Force with aeronautical charts, graphic air target materials, geodetic data, astronautical and geophysical charts, flight information publications and documents, terrain models, maps, evaluated intelligence on air facilities, and related carto-graphic services.

All ACIC publications are developed concurrently with weapon or support systems. Concurrently, ACIC maintains close liaison with operational commands to assure that the ACIC support item is available when a system becomes operational in the field.

Most of the major sciences and approximately sixty-five special skills are involved in the ACIC cartographic process—from simple arithmetic to complicated mathematics, from fundamental camera procedures to sophisticated photographic techniques, and from sciences required for charting the earth to sciences required for the development of space reference systems.

There are four major programs of production and related services within the ACIC mission:

(1) Air Target Materials include 1:200,000 and 1:50,000 scale air target charts, mosaics, and missile-target data sheets that position potential military objectives for air or missile attack through graphics and text. With the advent of long-range missiles, Target Materials production of data for determining launch-site target-position relationships has greatly expanded.

(2) Air Navigation and Planning Charts are primarily for manned-aircraft preflight planning and inflight operations throughout the world. They are also extensively used by air operations and planning staffs, air control centers, command posts, etc. They include the 1:250,000 scale aeronautical and the 1:500,000 pilotage charts used primarily for close-air support and tactical air operations, the 1:1,000,000 operational navigation charts, the 1:2,000,000 jet navigation charts, which mainly support high-speed and strategic air operations, the 1:5,000,000 global navigation charts for very long-range operations or planning, and many other charts to fulfill the requirements of advanced weapon and guidance systems.

(3) Flight Information Publications are used for planning departure, en route, and terminal phases of flight. They provide complete up-to-date air traffic control and air navigation data for all-weather operations by manned aircraft of U.S. military air forces. The publications cover the entire Free World.

(4) ACIC services include a photographic laboratory in Washington, D.C., the maintenance of libraries, and the production of special cartographic products and projects such as the tactical situation displays, which are miniaturized cartographic items in the form of 35mm film strips and electronic data—computer tapes produced to support the F-106. Aeronautical video mapping plates for ground control of flights are among the many miniaturized items produced for new weapon systems.

ACIC supported NASA's Project Mercury with test charts, training charts, orbit charts, and recovery charts and designed a series of charts to support NASA's Project Gemini.

A lunar atlas and two lunar reference mosaics have been published at scales of 1:5,000,000 and 1:10,000,000, and a portion of the 144 lunar aeronautical charts required to cover the moon have been published at the 1:1,000,000 scale.

About 100,000,000 copies of the 38,000 separate items ACIC publishes are distributed annually to users all over the world.

To carry out its responsibilities, ACIC is organized with a headquarters, production and distribution plant, field organization, and four overseas units. The headquarters and plant are located in St. Louis, Missouri. A detachment of the field organization is located in Washington, D.C., and performs liaison with the mapping, charting, and geodetic agencies located there. It also maintains the USAF Historical, Pictorial, and Documentary Library for the Air Staff and provides photographic services for the Department of Defense.

The four overseas units support requirements of Air Force commands within their areas of responsibility. The four units are located at Albrook AFB, Canal Zone; Elmendorf AFB, Alaska; Wiesbaden, Germany; and Hickam AFB, Hawaii. Subdetachments of these units are located elsewhere in Europe and in the Philippine Islands, Okinawa, and Japan.

The Air Force Accounting and Finance Center (AFAFC)

The Air Force Accounting and Finance Center, located at Denver, Colorado, is responsible for providing technical supervision and advice and guidance to Air Force accounting and finance field activities, as well as centralized Air Force accounting and finance operations. AFAFC is directed and supervised by the Comptroller of the Air Force through the Director of Accounting and Finance, Headquarters USAF.

AFAFC is the link between 399 accounting and finance field offices throughout the world and the Directorate of Accounting and Finance. Field accounting and finance offices report through their major air commanders to the Center where 2,800 reports a month are audited, balanced, summarized, and analyzed. From this data, about 200 reports each month are prepared for such offices as the Air Staff, Secretary of Defense, Bureau of the Budget, and Department of the Treasury.

The Center also performs a number of centralized operations for the Air Force. It maintains more than 1,600,000 allotment accounts for some 800,000 military personnel. Nearly 140,000 changes to these accounts, such as authorizations, discontinuances, and changes in amounts and addresses, are processed each month. More than 330,000 checks are written monthly in payment of these accounts. The number of checks issued does not equal the number of accounts because several allotments going to the same address are covered by one check, plus a listing of accounts to be credited.

Retired Air Force personnel are also paid by AFAFC. The Center writes more than 100,000 checks a month to retired members, and the figure is increasing at the rate of 2,000 a month. These checks amount to $96.6 million a month. The checks are written and mailed to arrive on time—a service important to the morale of Air Force dependents and retirees.

AFAFC issues U.S. savings bonds Air Force–wide—more than 134,000 bonds a month and an additional 219,000 quarterly.

The electronic data-processing system currently in use is capable of handling alpha-numeric data with magnetic tape, punched paper tape, punched card input and output, and printed output. With magnetic tape, the computer can read and write 33,333 alphabetic letters or numerals per second. Printed reports, vouchers, and listings are prepared at the rate of 1,500 lines a minute. Checks are turned out at the rate of 18,000 per hour.

The main categories of operations performed by the computer system are:

(1) Merged Accountability and Fund Reporting, a system providing disbursement accounting information and reports for the management of Air Force funds;

(2) Military Pay Allotments File Maintenance, a file of more than a million pay allotment accounts including Air Force members' pay allotments to dependents, payment of insurance premiums, deposits to credit unions, and purchase of U.S. savings bonds through payroll deductions;

(3) Military Pay Data Reporting, a computer system that verifies debit and credit entries from each record and extracts pay accounting information, social security information, and allotment deduction data;

(4) Civilian Payroll, a master file of payroll accounts for about 4,800 AFAFC, tenant agency, and Lowry AFB civilian employees, computing gross and net pay and leave balances and issuing checks automatically;

(5) Air Force Retired Pay, a system that produces data for checkwriting, voucher listings, and accumulative pay information, computes withholding taxes, and prepares annual dependency verification cards; and

(6) Magnetic Tape to Treasury, an operation that produces magnetic tapes designed to meet Treasury requirements to record some 450,000 checks issued monthly by AFAFC.

The Office of Aerospace Research (OAR)

The Office of Aerospace Research is the prime agency of Air Force exploratory research. It is responsible for conducting research within its own laboratories, and for sponsoring some exploratory efforts by universities and other outside institutions through its grants and contracts program. OAR operates laboratories and field sites under the direction of Air Force scientists who are engaged in those areas of research most likely to contribute to the continued technological growth of the Air Force. OAR also draws upon the scientific talent of the Free World through its sponsorship of grants and contracts in areas of Air Force interest to leading scientists in colleges, universities, nonprofit, and industrial organizations.

By stimulating work with top scientists, OAR gains an insight into the general increase in the body of scientific knowledge. This provides the means for identifying concepts that will enable the USAF and its contractors to design superior weapon systems. OAR pursues its activities for the Air Force in such fundamental scientific disciplines as physics, mathematics, chemistry, psychology, biology, astronomy, and meteorology. These disciplines are organized within four general areas of research: life sciences, environmental sciences, engineering sciences, and physical sciences. Categories that relate to OAR's exploratory development interests are environment and aerospace environment.

Although OAR is concerned primarily with research in the general areas listed above, studies are not limited to systems development, nor even to specific problems. Similarly, exploratory development performed or financially supported is normally of broad applicability rather than system-oriented. Headquartered in Washington, D.C., OAR has eleven subordinate units, four of which are major research organizations, four research-supporting units, and three field liaison offices.

The Air Force Cambridge Research Laboratories (AFCRL) at L. G. Hanscom Field, Massachusetts, is the focal point for research in environmental, physical, and engineering sciences. The nine laboratories conduct a large and varied research program in radio physics, gaseous and plasma physics, solid-state electronics, electronics, mathematics, and energy conversion. They also do exploratory development in the environment and aerospace environment.

The Air Force Office of Scientific Research (AFOSR), located in Washington, supports extramural research in those sciences that offer the greatest potential for improving the USAF's operational capability. AFOSR carries out its research program through more than 1,200 grants and contracts with about 200 colleges, universities, and research organizations in the United States and abroad. Research is supported in nuclear and general physics, chemistry, mathematics, electronics, mechanics, energy conversion, astronomy and astrophysics, and the behavioral, biological, and information sciences.

AFOSR programs may be regarded as supporting research in areas of recognized Air Force problems, such as pioneering research leading to new technologies or concepts to meet unforeseen Air Force requirements, and maintaining contact with world-wide scientific developments for possible future application.

The Aerospace Research Laboratories (ARL) at Wright-Patterson AFB, Ohio, are a major Air Force in-house research facility in physical and engineering sciences including general physics, solid-state physics, general and physical chemistry, fluid dynamics, flight mechanics, mechanics of solids and energetics, and theoretical and applied mathematics. Along with AFOSR and AFCRL, ARL also supports contractual research.

The Frank J. Seiler Research Laboratory at the U.S. Air Force Academy, Colorado, is an in-house facility in an academic setting engaged in research in the physical and engineering sciences, primarily general chemistry, physical chemistry, mathematics, fluid dynamics, and flight mechanics.

The Office of Research Analyses (ORA) at Holloman AFB, New Mexico, performs analysis and evaluation of future Air Force systems. These technically complex and independent studies are made for any Air Force activity. Through this study activity, ORA is provided with critical technology for incorporation into the research program.

The European Office of Aerospace Research (EOAR) in Brussels, Belgium, is responsible for the administration of contracts and grants in Europe, the Near East, and Africa. The office is a point of contact for European research scientists and helps to identify unique research abilities abroad. All funds for the support of foreign research and development come from laboratories in the United States as part of their total program.

The Latin American Office of Aerospace Research is located in Rio de Janeiro. It extends Air Force grant and contract support of unique research capability to Central and South American countries.

The Churchill Research Range, Fort Churchill, Canada, is located in the Arctic on Hudson Bay, near the earth's magnetic pole and zone of maximum auroral activity. This is an OAR-managed rocket-and-balloon launch, tracking, and telemetry-recording complex. Operated for the Department of Defense, NASA, and the Canadian research agencies, its primary purpose is to launch high-altitude research rockets and balloons for collecting data on the aerospace environment at high altitudes. A year-round capability has been developed that holds rockets in firing positions under the most adverse climatic conditions, in order to take advantage of geophysical events of scientific interest.

Other supporting aerospace research organizations are the field offices located at Patrick AFB, Florida, Vandenberg AFB, California, and in Los Angeles. These field offices maintain liaison among the scientists, the launch team, and the contractors. Small scientific experiments are installed on rockets fired for other purposes, thus ensuring that the Air Force receives maximum payload utilization.

Several elements of the Air Force Systems Command conduct and monitor a portion of OAR's research program. The studies of these AFSC organizations are in fields related to their primary exploratory-development mission. Laboratories involved include the following: Arnold Engineering Development Center, Tullahoma, Tennessee; Detachment 4, Research and Technology Division, Eglin AFB, Florida; Air Force Avionics Laboratory and Air Force Materials Laboratory, both at Wright-Patterson AFB, Ohio; Air Force Weapons Laboratory, Kirtland AFB, New Mexico; and Rome Air Development Center, Griffiss AFB, New York. Also participating are the Aerospace Medical Research Laboratory at Wright-Patterson AFB and the Aeromedical Research Laboratory at Holloman AFB, New Mexico, both of the Aerospace Medical Division.

The United States Air Force Academy (USAFA)

The concept of an Air Force academy evolved during World War I, when the employment of American military aviation indicated the growing importance of air power to national defense. During World War II, the decisiveness of aerial warfare clearly demonstrated the future dominant role of air power in the defense of the Free World and the need for officers trained specifically in the use of that power.

When the Air Force became a separate service of the Department of Defense, proposals were made to establish an air academy similar to the Military and Naval academies. With air and space technology in full development, an institution dedicated to preparing a nucleus of career officers skilled in leadership, imbued with desirable traits of character, and oriented in the techniques of the aerospace age seemed increasingly important. The Korean conflict interrupted the proposals for an air academy but, at the close of that war, Congress authorized establishment of the Air Force Academy and President Eisenhower signed the legislation on April 1, 1954.

The Air Force Academy began operations at Lowry AFB, Colorado, on July 11, 1955, when the first class of 306 cadets was sworn in. The Academy opened at its permanent location, a 17,900-acre site at the foot of the Rampart Range of the Rocky Mountains, eight miles north of Colorado Springs, in 1958. In keeping with its spirit of modernity, all buildings are constructed in contemporary style of glass, steel, and aluminum. The cadet wing reached its authorized strength of 2,512 in 1962, and, in 1964, Congress increased the authorized strength to 4,417 cadets. At about the same time, the authorization that had allowed graduates of the service academies to transfer to other services was ended.

The mission of the Air Force Academy is to provide instruction, experience, and motivation to each cadet so that he will graduate with the knowledge, character, and qualities of leadership essential to his progressive development as a career officer in the United States Air Force.

The Academy accomplishes its mission through a four-year curriculum composed of academic courses, leadership and military training, physical education and athletics. Completion of the curriculum entitles the cadet to graduate with a Bachelor of Science degree in a major study of his choice, and a regular commission as a second lieutenant in the Air Force.

The North Central Association of Colleges and Secondary Schools recognized the Air Force Academy as an accredited institution of higher learning in 1959. In 1962, the Engineers' Council for Professional Development granted accreditation to the Major in Engineering Sciences.

Since the Academy has the same general educational objectives for all students, the framework of the curriculum is based on standardized or prescribed courses. A total of 145 semester hours is included in the four-year prescribed curriculum. In addition to the prescribed courses, each cadet must complete a minimum of 43 semester hours to earn an academic major, bringing the total curriculum requirement to 188 semester hours.

To allow for the wide variances in individual student abilities, preparation, and achievements, the Academy has developed a program of elective courses and major subjects beyond the prescribed curriculum known as the "enrichment program." The basic objective of the program is to challenge a cadet to advance academically as far and as fast as his abilities permit.

The enrichment program also includes graduate-level courses, which may be applied toward a Master's degree. Under cooperative arrangements between the Academy and certain civilian universities, selected cadets may earn Master's degrees from these universities within seven months after their graduation from the Academy. Master's degree programs are presently available in Astronautics and International Affairs.

The leadership and military training program prepares and motivates the cadet for a career of leadership as an officer in the USAF. Training in this program provides experience in leadership, promotes professional attitudes, and provides the basic military knowledge required of an Air Force officer. Specialized courses of instruction are given in military training throughout the cadet's four years at the Academy. The instruction is both academic and practical. Each cadet visits military installations in the United States and overseas to view the Armed Forces in operation.

The Air Force Cadet Wing provides an opportunity for personal development of leadership competence. The Wing consists of a headquarters with a cadet commander and staff and subordinate units of groups, squadrons, flights, and elements. The squadrons and groups are supervised by USAF officers. Upperclass cadets are appointed to positions of responsibility within the cadet wing to perform command and staff functions and to assist in the military training of the fourth (freshman) class. Cadet officers are selected from the first class and senior noncommissioned cadet officers from the second class. Training in command and staff functions within the wing allows cadets to practice leadership techniques and provides situations for the development of character and discipline.

The Air Force Academy is responsible for supporting the Frank J. Seiler Laboratory (described earlier in this chapter), which is under the command jurisdiction of the Office of Aerospace Research. It also operates the USAF Academy Preparatory School, whose purpose is to provide intensive instruction to assist active-duty servicemen in preparing for the Academy entrance examinations on an equal basis with civilian candidates who are still in high school or have recently graduated. The school is located on the Academy site and is open to selected members of the Regular and Reserve components of the armed forces.

VIII

The Role of Women in the USAF

During World War II, woman military volunteers held down a wide variety of jobs in all the services, freeing men for other duties. Since the war, women have played an important role in helping to maintain American air power. Currently, there are three distinctly separate organizations in the United States Air Force in which women perform significant functions: Women in the Air Force (WAF), the Air Force Nurse Corps, and the Air Force Medical Specialists. The WAF has both officers and enlisted women. The Nurse Corps and the Medical Specialists have officers only. Personnel of the three organizations come under the same rules and regulations for promotion, education, leave, medical and dental care, pay and allowances, and retirement as the male members of the Air Force.

Women in the Air Force (WAF)

Long before Pearl Harbor, military planners foresaw the potential of a women's corps in the military service. As far back as 1936, American observers in Spain had noted the important role played during the Spanish Civil War by nonmilitary women employees in key administrative and communications posts.

Shortly after the United States entered World War II, the Women's Army Corps was created, and its members became known as WAC's. General H. H. Arnold, commanding general of the Army Air Forces, impressed upon his staff officers and field commanders that Air Force efficiency required the widest possible employment of qualified women to compensate for manpower shortages. Of the 100,000 WAC's who composed the peak strength of the Corps, more than 40,000 served in the Army Air Forces and were called Air-WAC's.

On June 12, 1948, the Women's Armed Service Integration Act gave permanent status to Women in the Air Force. By mid-October, the first women recruited directly into the USAF reported to Lackland Air Force Base, Texas, for basic training. The following January, WAF's were first admitted on a coeducational basis to the Air Force Officer Candidate School. The wartime policy of integration had proved so successful that WAF was not organized into a separate corps; instead, the Office of the Director of the WAF was established as a directorate in the Office of the Deputy Chief of Staff for Personnel, Headquarters USAF. The Director is a full colonel whose specific responsibility is to advise the Chief of Staff, USAF, and the Air Staff on all matters pertaining to WAF, as well as to coordinate and formulate plans and policies for the organization.

WAF airmen serve within the continental United States and in selected overseas areas in a variety of career fields. These are administration, medical, dental, communications, personnel, air traffic control, transportation, supply, accounting and finance, statistical analysis, data systems, photomapping, procurement, education and training, special services, and food services. The assignment of WAF's is generally made in terms of their Air Force skill and capability without reference to sex.

All WAF airmen receive six weeks of basic military training. After completion of the training, approximately 55 per cent attend technical training courses of from four to twenty weeks' duration along with male airmen. The other 45 per cent are sent to their duty assignments and receive on-the-job training. There are approximately 5,000 enlisted women serving in the U.S. Air Force.

Thirty per cent of the WAF airmen are considered in career status. While the retention rate is improving, the loss of young women before completion of their first enlistment continues to be a problem. The primary reason for leaving is marriage. Studies on women in the civilian labor force support the concept that the interval between school and marriage is about two years and that

50 per cent of all women marry before they reach 21 years of age. This statistic also applies to the Air Force, which loses a number of WAF airmen just as they become valuable to the work force. The Air Force makes every effort to keep married military couples together, thereby encouraging married women to remain in the service.

WAF officers are employed in all officer jobs except those requiring aeronautical ratings or combat duties. While the majority are assigned in administration, personnel, supply, intelligence, information, accounting and finance, education and training, and procurement, some WAF officers are also assigned in weather and research and development activities.

Each year, approximately 125 young women are commissioned as second lieutenants in the Air Force. They, like their male counterparts, must be college graduates to qualify for a commission. In addition, they must be above average academically and pass stringent mental and physical examinations. Selected applicants attend the Officers Training School (OTS) at Lackland AFB. After successfully completing the three-month course of instruction and orientation, graduates are commissioned as second lieutenants in the Air Force Reserve and begin an obligatory four-year tour of duty.

Insofar as possible, the more than 700 WAF officers are assigned duties closely related to their civilian education, training, and experience. However, in many instances, newly commissioned WAF officers go directly from OTS to a technical school for more specialized training in such areas as communications, accounting and finance, meteorology, intelligence, and data systems.

WAF officers receive further professional schooling in the Squadron Officer School and the Air Command and Staff College. Additional education and training are available through subsidized Air Force programs at selected colleges and universities.

Air Force Nurse Corps

The Air Force Nurse Corps was established as an integral part of the Air Force Medical Service in July, 1949. At that time, 1,199 nurses were permitted to transfer from the Army to the Air

Force. Of these, 307 nurses were members of the Regular Army Nurse Corps and the remainder were members of the Reserve component of the Army Nurse Corps.

Although the Air Force Medical Service was established as a separate service from the Army in 1949, its history dates back to 1907, when the Aeronautical Division of the Army was created. During World War I, the Aviation Medicine Division of the Surgeon General's Office expanded rapidly as the Air Corps realized the importance of the physical evaluation of flying personnel and the need for research in the field of aviation medicine. These requirements were greatly accentuated after the entry of the United States in World War II.

The urgent need for nurses to care for the sick and wounded being transported by aircraft during World War II marked the beginning of a new chapter in the history of nursing. Even at that early date, the prospective flight nurse had to meet rigid requirements which, to a great extent, limited the applicants to the young and physically fit who were eager to fly and practice their profession close to the combat area.

The first class of nurses was graduated from the Army Air Forces School of Air Evacuation at Bowman Field, Kentucky, in February, 1943. The school conducted a four-week course of instruction and training in the professional, technical, tactical, and administrative procedures involved in the air evacuation of the sick and wounded. Graduates were designated as "Flight Nurses" and were authorized an identifying insignia. Personnel trained for air evacuation duties at Bowman Field included 109 medical officers, 1,097 nurses, and 558 medical technicians.

In October, 1944, the school was incorporated into the School of Aviation Medicine and transferred to Randolph AFB, Texas. Between November, 1944, and October, 1950, 1,421 flight nurses were trained. The Flight Nurse Course was moved to Gunter AFB, Alabama, at the outbreak of the Korean conflict. It is presently a part of the School of Aerospace Medicine at Brooks AFB, Texas.

Male nurses have been appointed in the Nurse Corps as Reserve officers to meet the needs of the service since October, 1955. In 1963, male nurses were integrated into the Regular Air Force Nurse

Corps. The strength of the Nurse Corps is now around 3,400 officers, of whom about 150 are male.

Nurses completing the Flight Nurse Course return to hospital duty until a vacancy occurs in one of the aeromedical evacuation squadrons. Following two years of "air-evac" duty, nurses are again assigned to hospitals. In this way, a ready pool of experienced flight nurses is available in the event of a national emergency. A large number of Air Force nurses are assigned to Air Force hospitals and dispensaries. Others are assigned to staff positions in Headquarters USAF and, in other major commands, as instructors in various Air Force teaching facilities.

Specialties in a nursing career are Administrative Nurse, Psychiatric Nurse, Operating Room Nurse, Nurse Anesthetist, and General Duty Nurse.

The educational level of the Air Force Nurse Corps is keeping abreast of the total nursing profession. Every year a designated number of career nurses are enrolled as full-time students under the Air Force's education program to obtain their baccalaureate or master's degree in the various fields of nursing. An eighteen-month course in anesthesia is conducted annually for students who have an interest and qualification for training in this specialty. Nurses may also apply to attend short courses, workshops, or institutes in the various specialties conducted by either military or civilian institutions. In addition, many nurses study part time at local colleges or universities during their off-duty hours.

In July, 1965, the first students were enrolled in the Aerospace Nursing Course at Cape Kennedy, Florida. This year-long course, given annually, provides the Air Force with nurses possessing the additional knowledge, skills, and understanding necessary to meet the diverse requirements for performance on the aerospace medical team. The Aerospace Nursing Course is the first and only course of its kind in existence today.

Air Force Medical Specialists

Like the other components in the Air Force Medical Service, the establishment of the Medical Specialist Corps dates back to July 1, 1949. At that time, eighty officers transferred from the Army Medical Service to the Air Force Medical Specialist Corps. On March 15, 1965, the Medical Specialist Corps was abolished and made part of a new scientific group called the Biomedical Sciences Corps. Medical specialists continue to retain their identity within the framework of the new Corps and are headed in the Surgeon General's Office by a senior officer designated as Chief, Air Force Medical Specialists. There are approximately 250 such officers on active duty, most of whom are female.

The Air Force Medical Specialists is composed of officers who are qualified in one of three professional groups: occupational therapy, physical therapy, and dietetics.

Occupational therapy is a medically prescribed activity carried out by the patient under the supervision of a trained therapist. Fourteen Air Force hospitals are now using occupational therapy in the rehabilitation of patients. Patients receiving occupational therapy fall into three general categories: physical disabilities, of which orthopedic, neurosurgical and neurological cases are in the majority; special adjustment, with tuberculosis patients being the largest group; and neuropsychiatric patients. Approximately thirty occupational therapy officers are on active duty.

There are forty-eight physical therapy clinics in the Air Force operating under the supervision of physical therapists. Subprofessional personnel in the physical-medicine career field are qualified and authorized to administer certain treatments. Air Force policy in regard to the utilization of physical therapy equipment conforms with the standards established by the American Congress of Physical Medicine and Rehabilitation and the American Physical Therapy Association.

Officers selected for appointment are graduates of physical therapy schools approved by the Council on Medical Education and Hospitals in collaboration with the American Physical Therapy Association.

Dictitians are assigned to fifty-four Air Force hospitals. The dietitian serves as an adviser to the surgeon at command or subcommand level on dietetics and hospital food service, directs the planning of regular and therapeutic diets, and manages hospital food service activities to stay within the monetary allowances established by the Bureau of the Budget. Her duty assignment is normally at a large Air Force hospital.

The medical food service consultant program has achieved excellent results. Under it, certain dietitians also serve as consultants to small hospitals operating without the full-time services of a dietitian to enable these institutions to meet the professional standards required by the Joint Commission on Accreditation of Hospitals.

The dietetic intern program is the main source of Air Force dietitians. It is an eighteen-month training program; the first twelve months are spent completing an internship in a civilian hospital, and the dietitians then take part in a residency program in an Air Force teaching hospital for at least six months. Residency training provided by USAF hospitals has improved work performance, retention, and career progression of dietitians in the Air Force.

IX

Manpower Requirements

One of the most acute problems in the United States today is the effect of rapid technological advance on the national labor force. Highly mechanized and increasingly automated industry does not demand the untrained labor readily available but the scarcer scientists, engineers, and technicians.

In a country of large organizations, the U.S. Air Force is one of the largest, employing more than one and one-half million people. Of these, nearly 850,000 are officers and airmen on active duty, 300,000 are civilian employees, and 375,000 are members of the Air Force Reserve and Air National Guard.

Within the Air Force's operational aerospace medium, there has been a technological revolution equaled in magnitude only in a small segment of private enterprise. With rare exceptions, the many dramatic breakthroughs in science and technology of recent years have had a direct application to the research, development, operation, and support of aerospace systems. The success of the Air Force mission increasingly depends upon knowledgeable and skillful people able to operate in a highly technological environment.

Today, machines sell food, soft drinks, and cigarettes, wash clothes, and calculate income taxes. But machines alone cannot defend a nation. Man remains the essential element in the military equation. It is men who fight and men who make the peace. Electronic circuits do not have courage. Dedication cannot be built into a black box.

The Air Force–industry team is working on the machinery of aerospace national security: advanced aerospace craft, space ex-

162

ploration systems, space boosters, missiles, electronic command, control and warning systems, rapid-response aerospace defenses, multiple-purpose support systems, and many others. But, in many cases, the highly trained airmen and officers needed to run this vast array of gadgetry are hard to retain in the Air Force.

It takes three years to train an Air Force electronics specialist at a cost of many thousands of dollars. Since he enlists for four years, the Air Force gets about one year of useful skilled service from him for its investment. The Air Force spends hundreds of millions a year training such skilled technical specialists, less than one-third of whom make the Air Force a career. Many of them have scarcely been trained to the technical proficiencies required to operate new and complex weapons when they leave the military for more lucrative jobs in industry. This annual loss is estimated at more than half a billion dollars. In 1960, the Air Force required and trained 13,000 highly skilled technical specialists. Only 70 per cent re-enlisted. In 1961, 17,000 skilled specialists were required and trained, and only 60 per cent re-enlisted. The situation is not improving.

If the Air Force is unable to recruit and retain support and operating people for the systems being developed, a very real threat to national security develops. All aerospace systems can be visualized as pyramids. At the top is the end product, the system or vehicle minutely small in comparison to the great bulk of the supporting structure. In the pyramid are thousands of trained workers; aircraft and missile-launch crews; maintenance, communications, radar and electronics technicians; supply, transportation and administrative personnel; and research, development, procurement, intelligence, medical, and management specialists.

Manning such a pyramid is a herculean task that increases in proportion to the complexity of the vehicle at the top. The job is not made easier by the theory of "noncomparability," the long-accepted doctrine that the Government cannot afford to match industry's pay rates, that part of the military man's reward must lie in the satisfaction of service to country, plus some tangible fringe benefits.

Recent pay increases do not provide comparability with industry, but they have helped to remind the military man that he is not completely forgotten and that his service to his country is recognized. Still, many people in the Air Force today work more than seventy hours a week, live in substandard housing, and pay excessive rent. There is constant separation of families. There are hardship tours at isolated radar sites in the extreme North and on remote islands in the Pacific. There are missile-launch and support crews on underground duty and aircraft ground crews on week-long alerts. And there is fighting in distant lands. These hardships are the realities and necessities of modern-day national security. Early warning of attack is possible only if airmen on the fringes of the Free World scan radar scopes twenty-four hours a day. Nor can there be a credible deterrent in the missile-nuclear age unless airmen are constantly poised beside strike aircraft and missiles. National security also demands that armed-forces personnel be subject to military law. There can be no collective voice on working conditions, no unions, no brotherhoods, no sit-downs, slow-downs or picket lines to attract public support.

For all of these reasons, the Secretary of the Air Force and the Chief of Staff frequently stress the importance of the individual Air Force man and the need to improve his working conditions and the standard of living of his family. Recognition and response is necessary to prevent erosion of a dedicated professional force.

Beyond Pay

Air Force management is concerned with several factors other than pay that affect the retention of personnel:

(1) Housing. Inadequate or high-cost housing is one of the most undesirable features of an Air Force career. An urgent need exists for more and better housing, bachelor officers' quarters, etc., on base or Government-leased housing near Air Force installations.

(2) Family separation. Airmen and officers consistently report separation from family and too frequent changes of station as an undesirable career feature. When not dictated by military necessity, this problem can be alleviated by better internal Air Force management.

(3) Medical care. Although generally excellent, current medical care does not provide some benefits, such as dependents' dental

care. Medical care for retired military personnel and their dependents is sometimes not immediately available due to lack of facilities.

(4) Officer promotion. Field grade officer authorizations in the Air Force are not equal to those of the other services. Improvement in promotion opportunities has been reported as one of the most urgently needed retention incentives.

(5) Junior officers. Since these young officers will determine to a great extent the scope and capability of tomorrow's aerospace force, Air Force commanders are making a strong effort to encourage these future officers to recognize the challenges and opportunities awaiting them. Air Force ROTC is the major source of new officers. The Air Force Academy alone cannot produce enough career officers to meet service requirements.

(6) Educational opportunities. A broad program of educational opportunities, competitive with industry, to meet Air Force educational requirements and to serve as an effective career incentive should be maintained.

(7) Fringe benefits. One of the most frequently mentioned irritants among Air Force career personnel is the steady erosion of the so-called military fringe benefits, available at commissaries and base exchanges, as well as other similar privileges.

(8) Military retirement. Although traditionally and overwhelmingly reported by officers and airmen as the most important reason for staying in the Air Force, current policies are considered by many to contain a number of inequalities.

The Qualities Sought

The day has passed when any officer was considered automatically qualified for any job in his grade. The military establishment has become too large, too technical, too complex for complete interchangeability of personnel. The range of skills required in the military service covers most of the fields of specialized civilian competence—engineering, accounting, law, management, medicine, teaching, public relations, etc.—and, especially, the ability to supervise, to inspire and direct people, to lead.

Personal qualifications among individuals vary considerably. Some men are combat leaders. Some have a natural talent for operational planning. Others have the unique analytical qualifications and the military-political insights required for the development of strategy. There are also those who are expert in and naturally adapted to the business side of the military—the management of resources. For each general area, distinct expertise is required.

The application of talents is not confined solely to one specialty, however. Each specialty demands to varying degrees other talents, too. And for key command and staff assignments, the Air Force draws its top-level generalists from among officers who have a wide range of talents and who have acquired a broad, across-the-board understanding of the Air Force and its missions.

Today's Air Force officers and airmen are a new breed. In 1957, only 64 per cent of all first-term airmen were high school graduates. Today, more than 96 per cent of all airmen in the lower four grades have earned high school diplomas. One out of every seven airmen has completed at least two years of college. Among officers, 65.7 per cent have at least one college degree, and one out of every ten holds an advanced degree. Before a new officer can qualify for an active-duty commission in today's Air Force, he must possess a college degree.

Complicated weapon systems are demanding and receiving more and more from Air Force people. They are not only mastering the new systems but learning to do so in shorter periods of time. Highly qualified personnel are one reason; their effective management is another. Science and technology have provided valuable assistance in this area, as in the effective employment of weapons and equipment. For example, automation enables personnel officers to devote more time to the individual. Using the "inquiry technique," a computer can identify all people qualified for a specific manning requirement, thereby allowing personnel managers to arrive at a decision with all the facts at hand to choose the best qualified individuals for specific Air Force duties. Automation was successfully introduced for officer personnel management in 1964. In 1966, a completely automated personnel data system streamlined administration and assignment procedures for all airmen.

Many attributes are required of the new breed of Air Force personnel. The first is possession of knowledge. Although a good education has always been important, today it is essential. In the research, development, procurement, and production of new systems, its value is obvious. In an increasing number of other military tasks, even undergraduate education is not enough. There is an ever-growing need for men with advanced degrees in a wide variety of subjects. In addition to the scientific and technical knowledge required, the military man must also have some understanding of the complex political, diplomatic, and economic factors that affect military decisions. He should be able to express himself clearly and concretely and know how to manage men.

Today's military man must have imagination. No one has yet designed a computer with true creative ability. Only men can produce radically new concepts and recognize their value. This quality is particularly important today because of the accelerated pace of scientific advancement, and the importance of not overestimating what can be achieved in a short time or underestimating what can be accomplished in a longer period of time. More than ever, the military man must be able to look ahead with imagination.

Another essential quality is courage—the courage found in the laboratory, the test facility, the staff office, and around the conference table, as well as in combat. It is the daring to accept new ideas, the determination to fight for one's convictions, and the persistence to stick with difficult, tiresome, time-consuming work. Only through the courageous persistence and dedication—and patriotism that puts national security ahead of personal security—of pilots, astronauts, managers, scientists, and researchers has the United States been able to build its military air strength.

Educational Opportunities

To help meet manpower requirements, the Air Force offers many training and educational opportunities for both on-duty military and off-duty nonmilitary education.

The major objective of on-duty military education is to improve the efficiency of the individual in his professional duties. This training is conducted by the Air Training Command, the Air University, and Air Force Service schools.

The off-duty nonmilitary academic instruction is provided by the

Air Force Education Services Program. Its objective is to raise the general educational level of Air Force members. Nonmilitary education consists of general academic work on the elementary, high school, college, university, and postgraduate levels. Vocational training is also available. Practically all Air Force Service schools include some academic instruction as part of their on-duty programs, but the greater portion is offered in voluntary off-duty study programs.

Nearly 250,000 Air Force members have earned college credits while in the Service, most of them taking their schooling during off-duty hours. The "Bootstrap" program, for example, through tuition assistance and permissive temporary duty, allows some 800 officers and 300 airmen to earn degrees each year.

Since a higher proportion of Air Force officers now hold undergraduate degrees, increased attention is being given to graduate-degree programs. A program leading to an M.S. in Aerospace Management has been established in Europe with the cooperation of the University of California. In addition, large numbers of officers have completed advanced degrees through the George Washington University–Air University Cooperative Program. Graduate programs are also available at several Air Force bases in the United States.

The educational opportunities provided by the Education Services Program are not confined to the United States. Officers and airmen selected for overseas assignment may continue their education in college and university programs available at or near most Air Force installations around the globe.

The Air Force today has a vital manpower requirement for well-educated and highly trained men and women to accomplish its diverse missions; and, as technological developments continue, its requirement for intellectual excellence will increase. The thousands of industrious, talented, and ambitious men and women who continue their education and training in the Air Force will help meet the challenge of the aerospace age and contribute to the security of the United States.

X

Problems and Prospects

The complex force requirements and high costs involved in maintaining superior military strength pose many difficult problems for Air Force planners. This chapter traces some of them.

The Advanced Manned Strategic Aircraft (AMSA)

Although Air Force leaders recognize the tremendous importance of ballistic missiles and have created the most powerful ICBM force in the world today, they believe that missiles must continue to play a partnership role in a balanced mixed force of unmanned weapons and advanced manned aircraft. Missiles have great advantages in terms of speed to target, facility of penetration, and accommodation to dispersal and hardening of their sites.

There are, however, important limitations. A missile cannot report the results of its mission. It cannot find targets that have not been located previously. It cannot be used efficiently against portable or mobile targets. It cannot seek out and destroy imprecisely located targets nor discriminate in destroying pinpoint targets. It cannot provide a national command center with wartime assessments of target damage. In sum, it lacks the flexibility demanded by the variety of tasks that aerospace forces must perform.

In those areas in which the missile is lacking, manned-weapon systems offer many strengths. The Air Force believes that a mixed force containing both missiles and aircraft continues to be required to meet the need for a strategy of controlled response, so that enemy aggression may be met at any level. Such a strategy requires

169

a capability to bring about military decisions compatible with a variety of political situations. Therefore, to support a strategy of controlled response, aerospace forces must be flexible enough to be used in a number of ways.

At the higher intensities of conflict, where inflicting a high order of damage on enemy territory is compatible with U.S. policy, the ICBM plays an important role. But manned systems are needed for the many other kinds of wars this country may have to fight. ICBM's are economically feasible and operationally effective only for the delivery of nuclear weapons, while manned vehicles can deliver either nuclear or conventional weapons. Whereas the missile is used once, the manned vehicle may be used many times. Also—and vitally important in a world where error could set off accidental war—the launching of an ICBM is irrevocable, but an aircraft is subject to recall and retargeting.

Whereas a missile can go astray in flight and cause highly provocative, unintended destruction, the men who fly aircraft can exercise judgment, correct malfunctions, and hold weapons rather than loose them on unintended targets. Further, although missile accuracies will improve, new devices will continue to give weapons employed by manned systems increased precision and discrimination capacities. For such reasons, Air Force planners believe manned-weapon systems are a vital part of the mixed aerospace force demanded by our controlled-response strategy.

Currently, our strategic retaliatory force is composed of such a mixed array of missiles and manned bombers. The missile force is growing as additional Minuteman squadrons are activated and become operational. Its effectiveness is improving as the Minuteman I missile is replaced by the Minuteman II, which is more accurate, has a greater range, and carries a greater payload. But the current mainstays of the manned-bomber force—the B-52's and B-58's—are aging. And the Air Force is hopeful that an advanced strategic bomber for the 1970's will be authorized. To date, the closest thing to such an aircraft is a bomber version of the F-111 scheduled for SAC use but considered by many inadequate to the task.

During Air Force budget hearings, the House Armed Forces

Appropriations Committee has shared the Air Force concern for an Advanced Manned Strategic Aircraft research and development program. In 1965, both the House and the Senate approved a $52 million appropriation for the AMSA. Subsequent to the budget hearings, the Air Force, with contractor support, conducted additional studies on operational concept and submitted a Program Change Proposal (PCP) to utilize the funds for project definition and advanced development work on avionics and propulsion. The PCP, approved by the Joint Chiefs of Staff, including the Chairman, was forwarded to the Secretary of Defense for review and approval. However, approval for the $52 million expenditure by the House and Senate Armed Forces Appropriations Committees and the Joint Chiefs of Staff did not mean that the Defense Department automatically proceeded with the AMSA effort. In such matters, final determination rests with the Secretary of Defense, and in every instance since his arrival in the Pentagon, Secretary of Defense McNamara has declined to use funds he has not himself specifically requested.

Thus, for example, when Congress directed the Secretary of the Air Force to spend the money to proceed with production and long lead-time procurement of the proposed B-70 bomber, the Secretary of Defense decided not to spend the additional funds and was supported in his decision by the President. The reluctance of several administrations to approve a major program for the B-70 has reduced the program to an aircraft prototype program designed to study supersonic flight problems. Meanwhile, surface-to-air defense missile performance has improved to such an extent that survivability of high-flying bombers even at Mach 2 has become questionable to many experts. After the U-2 and Cuban incidents, it was apparent that a low-altitude penetration capability was necessary, and existing USAF bombers were modified to withstand the stresses imposed by this change in operational concept. These developments convinced the Department of Defense that the high-speed high-altitude B-70 approach no longer made sense, and this experience with the B-70 concept may have caused the Secretary to be even more critical of AMSA.

The views of Secretary of the Air Force Harold Brown are also significant in this connection. In 1964, when he was Director of Defense Research and Engineering, he said:

> . . . in recent years considerable effort has been devoted to upgrading the capabilities of the B-52's and B-58's of our strategic bomber force. Sizable modification programs have been funded to tailor the B-52 airframe and systems for low-level penetration under enemy defenses. . . . Bombers . . . should and will remain in the strategic inventory in the foreseeable future. But this need not be a convincing argument for a new, large, specially designed bomber whose development and deployment cost would approach $10 billion. There are several alternate approaches to provide us with a mixed bomber and missile force even through the 1970's, including retention of existing aircraft, adaptation of new ones, and development of entirely new systems.

There are also international political considerations regarding AMSA. The President has proposed freezing the production of strategic nuclear delivery vehicles for international arms-control purposes, provided others do the same. But there were provisions for continued research and development of such systems contained in the fine print of the proposal.

The fiscal year 1966 appropriations bill contained $22 million in New Obligational Authority for AMSA, which, together with funds made available from earlier programs, provided $46 million for the development of AMSA components. To produce AMSA in significant operational numbers might take nine to ten years. In the face of developments in Southeast Asia, the possibility that the NATO alliance may be materially modified in 1969 when the treaty comes up for renewal, and the other worldwide commitments of the United States, most Air Force leaders believe that a bomber mission will still exist in the 1970's.

The Aerospace R&D Community

Many Air Force leaders are worried about what may be a current loss of momentum in science and technology. This concern dates back to 1961 when the Defense Department adopted what many consider an overly cautious approach to research, development, and procurement of new weapon systems. Also, direct investments in research, development, test, and evaluation (RDT&E) have declined since 1961. The net effect has been to reduce the pressures and monies for aerospace research and development considerably below the levels maintained during the 1950's.

The USAF by no means advocates a return to the high-risk, high-cost, often wasteful methods of the 1950's nor to a massive increase in direct investments in RDT&E. It does, however, recommend that certain classified projects should be funded, that the processing time and procedures associated with the advocacy and acceptance of new systems or technology developments should be reduced, and that, where necessary, the development of high-cost prototypes should be authorized without having to define a specific priority mission or going through currently required stringent justification procedures. Finally, USAF believes that the current low-risk approach to systems development ought to be somewhat compensated for by greater efforts and greater expenditures in the RDT&E area.

A second concern is the growing tendency within the Defense Department to await the appearance of an identifiable threat before initiating any R&D effort in response. Air Force leaders point out that there is often a wide gap between what is known about basic Soviet research, as published in Russian scientific journals, and the appearance and identification of specific new military threats that stem from such research.

It is believed that the United States' greatly improved space and intelligence systems' ability to identify new Soviet military hardware should not be the sole determinant of the scope and nature of U.S. efforts in basic, exploratory, and advanced defense research. Modern advanced weapon systems have a long lead-time measured in years. For this reason, if the United States waits to react to new threats until they appear as hardware under test—or even later—it can find itself unable to match or respond rapidly to a new Soviet capability.

What seems desirable is that national policy "user" requirements, arms-control considerations, etc., should influence only the decision to procure weapon systems for inventory, not the R&D funds or efforts to·put science and technology to work in all sectors of military interest so that a response may be made quickly when a new threat is identified.

A third area of concern in the Air Force is the current Department of Defense organization for R&D. This concern stems from what many consider the lack of effective and expeditious means of processing new projects and a resulting tendency to involve developmental efforts and programs in red tape. One problem, in the view of many Air Force observers, is the increasing separation of authority and responsibility in the RDT&E chain of command, and a consequent overcentralization of detailed decision-making. Organizational changes, they say, should be made to reduce the number of layers in the RDT&E chain of command and improve the long-range process within the Air Force itself.

A fourth area of concern is that of the technological threat *per se.* Soviet efforts to increase scientific and technological capabilities, as evidenced by the manpower channeled into higher education in the sciences, the number of scientific institutes being created, the amount of effort devoted to science and technology in general in the U.S.S.R.—all these are day-to-day worries of Air Force planners.

Today's technological threat is not one associated solely with the identification of new Soviet military hardware. It stems more from an analysis of what the U.S.S.R. could produce in the way of surprise in this area if the Russians managed to range far ahead of the United States in all fields of basic exploratory research. For instance, Soviet efforts in the field of cybernetics cannot now be directly related to a potential military threat or even to a U.S. military requirement. Yet imagination suggests that such progress could have military importance.

Another major worry of Air Force leaders is the tendency in the Defense Department to make budget and manpower cuts at the expense of future capabilities. It is difficult to plan an equitable share of available defense funds for R&D in an era of declining defense spending on the strategic-weapon side and increased spending for conventional weapons and ground forces.

This problem has been aggravated sharply by the pressures of the Vietnamese War.

Times and Choices

Since World War II, evolutionary developments have divorced a large portion of R&D activities from the direct concern of the combat commands, historically the sole users of military R&D. Since combat commands limit their requirements to the visibility of the threats facing them, their real military hardware threats can hardly be forecast more than three to five years ahead. With ten-year lead-times to consider, the R&D community can no longer await the appearance of a military threat before starting its technological response. Longer lead-times, therefore, argue for R&D efforts somewhat more independent of combat command requirements as well as of identifiable military threats. The high cost of new weapon-system developments, together with the many alternatives to choose from, force planners to be selective early in the game. If the R&D community is to be selective long before the combat commands can identify their interests, threats, or requirements, it will have to make weapon-system-for-force-structure decisions that will have a major impact on the future aerospace force.

By the time operating commands identify the military threats they face and establish requirements for new weapon systems to cope with them, most of the associated basic and exploratory research should have already been completed. Therefore, the ability of the R&D community to respond to future military dangers will be largely dependent upon the extent to which it may have maintained an adequate research effort on its own initiative and without benefit of the user's requirements. This effort has to match potential Soviet technological and scientific threats, not be concerned merely with foreseeable military applications.

As long as R&D is considered a support activity, its research programs will be restricted in scope, nature, and funding to efforts that are primarily of interest to hot- and cold-war user commands. Subordinated in a support role to combat command requirements, the R&D community cannot hope to compete on an equal footing for an equitable share of available defense funds. Hot- and cold-war requirement plans will dictate the distribution of available funds, and such plans do not give adequate recognition of an independent technological threat and the associated need for an independent technological response to such a threat.

Generally, future proposals for new weapon systems are considered only if they fit within the generally accepted, present national policy goals. Although national policy constraints are clearly pertinent to decisions to acquire new weapon systems, these considerations should not necessarily affect decisions on whether or not to pursue basic and exploratory research and development in a given area, many R&D people believe.

There is a tendency to apply policy restrictions to both basic R&D and acquisition decisions alike. Arguments are heard against funding basic and exploratory research in space-based nuclear weapons because current policies preclude their deployment. Yet many critics claim that such restrictions could result in inability to catch up in time with enemies who might be proceeding with similar systems.

In recent years, aerospace R&D has taken on an increasing number of operating functions. These operational activities have been primarily in the area of missile and space-range management, space activities and, in some limited instances, intelligence and communication activities. In the Air Force of the 1940's and early 1950's, operating activities were assigned to the major combat commands and the role of R&D was limited to the development and procurement of equipment for these commands. As such, R&D reacted to the operating command requirements and seldom found itself in sustained operations paralleling or competing with combat commands.

For national policy reasons, with the advent of the space age and the associated efforts to identify space with peaceful purposes, space operations within the Department of Defense were not assigned to the combat commands, except for space surveillance, which, as described in an earlier chapter, is a responsibility of the Air Defense Command. The net effect of this policy is that the operation of both manned and unmanned space systems, as well as their development and procurement, is the business of the R&D community.

The coming into being of long-range missiles and space systems created the need for test ranges of such scope and size as to create both research and development and operating problems in themselves. To consolidate these national test-range resources, the Defense Department created the National Range Division (NRD) within the Air Force Systems Command to operate the ranges in support of both test and operational launches for missiles and spacecraft. Although research and development is associated with range development, NRD is essentially an operational activity. As such, with NRD the R&D community finds itself in the business of operating a major activity.

It has other operating responsibilities in addition to space systems and ranges. Normally, completed new aircraft and missile systems are turned over to the combat commands for operation. This is not true, however, of all the intelligence, warning, and electronic systems built by the Air Force to support defense activities. Because of their special nature, complexity, or one-time missions, some of these facilities have remained under the operational cognizance of the Air Force Systems Command.

The above trends and developments, it is argued, present a case for recognition of the new operating responsibilities of the R&D community, particularly in the space system and missile range areas, and for organizational, procedural, and policy adjustments to accommodate these activities within the framework of the over-all defense structure on equal terms with the operating responsibilities of competing unified, specified, or service commands.

The long lead-time in advanced weapon-system development and the resulting need to commit the United States to new weapon systems, frequently before the military threats they are to deal with can be clearly foreseen, have increased the R&D role in shaping future aerospace forces. In the past, combat command and Joint Chiefs of Staff plans established the requirements for forces quite independently of technology and then gave R&D the job of equipping these forces with the latest weapons. In the future, the equipment preselected by R&D policy decisions will increasingly determine the level and nature of the forces themslves. This trend emphasizes the importance of a stronger link between the R&D community and the Joint Chiefs of Staff strategic planning.

Part of the problem of establishing a sound future aerospace force, which takes into account technological, political, and economic realities, operating command aspirations, and threat forecasts, lies in the predominantly short-term orientation of Service

Chiefs and Joint Chiefs of Staff planning. The business of running today's aerospace forces and reacting to short-term policies and considerations tends to restrict long-term planning unduly because leaders have to spend so much time on the "here and now." Thus, long-term planning often degenerates into programmed "projectism" and frequently winds up with unrealistic, unachievable goals.

Long-range planning has usually suffered from inadequate personnel and effort, ivory-tower environments, inadequate consideration of nonmilitary factors, inherent resistance to change, and committee or "consensus" review and approval procedures.

Most attempts to improve long-range planning for aerospace forces have resulted in the establishment of leadership or study groups subject to day-to-day Air Force direction. Since long-range planning requires change in force structure, concepts, doctrines, tactics and weapon systems, and since change often is opposed by those responsible for the current Air Force posture and policies, many experts believe that planning for future aerospace forces must be separated from planning and operating today's aerospace forces and should be linked with efforts to maintain the technological base and wage the technological war. It is true that the most successful efforts in the past were accomplished by *ad hoc* groups, heavily influenced by technology and responsible directly, if not solely, to senior commanders or to the Chief of Staff personally. The "Teapot Committee" of the early 1950's, which helped convince the Air Force of a "crash requirement" for ICBM developments, is an example.

R&D was once solely a support activity of the commands, but today it not only supports those commands but also is waging an independent technological war and conducting separate operations equivalent to and as important as those of the combat commands.

As long as the R&D effort is regarded as a support activity, its priority on funding will be subordinate to the combat commands. To ensure that an equitable percentage of defense funding is devoted to the technological effort and to space, range, and other R&D operations, recognition of the independent nature of the R&D community's role in those areas is essential. This recognition should be reflected by equal consideration in Joint Chiefs of Staff strategic and operations plans and Department of Defense and Service programs. Such action would ensure adequate momentum in U.S. science and technology quite independently of military requirements and applications.

Finally, the long lead-times required to develop future weapon systems, and the frequent need for decisions that ultimately affect both weapons and force structures long before the military threat becomes clear, imply that science, technology, and planning for the 1975–80 aerospace force weapons and structure are inextricably interrelated. This effort should therefore be centralized under the R&D community and given coequal stature with that now devoted to planning and operating the current Air Force.

Such are the arguments of the R&D planners—and they are persuasive.

Management in the Pentagon

Since 1961, the capabilities of the U.S. armed forces have tremendously expanded. Navy strength has grown, and Army combat-ready divisions have increased significantly. New high-performance sophisticated interceptor, fighter, fighter-bomber, and reconnaissance aircraft are assigned to operational squadrons in significant numbers, and the replacement of older combat aircraft is proceeding rapidly. In the strategic-alert area, the number of nuclear-warhead missiles has tripled. There are approximately ten times as many counterinsurgency forces now as in 1961. Further, airlift capability has more than doubled since that date and is still rising sharply.

Much of the credit for successful management of this phenomenal build-up of military strength goes to Robert S. McNamara, who became Secretary of Defense in 1961. Most observers credit Mr. McNamara with being the first Defense Secretary actually able to employ and enforce the authority conferred on that office by Congress.

Although his accomplishment of rapid military build-up has been widely acknowledged, the Secretary's management program has been controversial, especially among military leaders, with criticism directed chiefly against what is considered overcontrol and overmanagement and "computerization" of decision-making at the highest levels of Pentagon command.

Management control has been more and more centralized in the Office of the Secretary of Defense, although, as critics point out, many of the highest achievements of the military in the past have been traceable to the fact that military commanders have exercised command freely within a general-mission framework.

The Defense Department has grown into the world's largest corporate organization and, as a consequence, has a management problem of the greatest magnitude. Its difficulties are not created solely by its size and complexity. The Department of Defense exists to provide the United States with armed forces to deter war and win wars if deterrence fails. This responsibility requires an efficient team of fighting forces and supporting forces, both composed of highly professional, dedicated, and skilled men.

The concern is that overmanagement and overcontrol may be carried to extremes. Many military men voice a wariness over the tendency in government quarters to equate Defense Department management with that of large corporations—despite obvious differences. There is a fundamental dissimilarity between managers and commanders. The manager is responsible for providing the commander with the maximum efficient support—quality equipment and personnel delivered on time at the proper place; the commander is responsible for the success or failure of his military actions and should not—critics say—be under the control of a "business manager." In the attainment of U.S. objectives dependent on full coordination between management and operational planning, over-control and overmanagement are pitfalls to be avoided.

Most controversial, in the press and among many officers, is the increasingly important role being played in the Pentagon by systems analysts, many of whom have had little or no experience with actual military operations.

Systems analysis—or operations analysis, as it was called in earlier days—is the technique of relating, at the national policy level, production schedules, inventory levels, and distribution costs of new weapon systems as a series of variables. Systems analysts acknowledge that their methods are more successful when applied to technical questions rather than to involved policy decisions. Critics maintain that the judgments of experienced individuals must continue to play an equal role with systems analysis in decision-making. Systems analysis has provoked considerable irritation not only among military personnel but within Congress.

Cost-effectiveness studies, which are a prime feature of systems analysis, are also viewed with misgiving by many. Such studies are frequently regarded as refined explanations for not procuring items needed by the armed forces or for procuring inadequate or second-rate equipment to save money. Cost-effectiveness is not a new concept. Businessmen have been using the process for decades. But where businessmen measure "effectiveness" by the return on their capital investments, the DOD analyst endeavors to show what x dollars will buy in terms of military capabilities. Critics say that preoccupation with cost-effectiveness arguments on defense matters can sometimes lead to major planning errors.

All of these considerations deeply concern the long-range planners of U.S. aerospace forces. Defense is a complex and dynamic enterprise—as the heated current debates over national security policy underscore.

XI

USAF Aerospace Power Today

Peace continues to depend on military strength. Yet, the destructive power of today's most advanced weapons, which can be delivered anywhere on the globe in minutes, makes armed conflict a matter of the gravest concern to all countries. This fact poses a dilemma. Nations need military might, but they recognize that the uncontrolled use of military power can defeat its purpose.

The realities of a divided world have made it necessary for the United States to stand as a strong, ready, and vigilant nation, prepared and determined to defend its freedom and the freedom of others. At the same time, the U.S.S.R. maintains its military forces in a high state of readiness and training and is improving and developing its own military capabilities. Communist China has also demonstrated its military-technological progress by detonating its first nuclear devices. Chinese Communists and their puppets have demonstrated by their actions their intention to dominate Southeast Asia. In response, the build-up and operations of the U.S. armed forces have assumed substantial proportions in Southeast Asia.

As long as world domination remains a basic Communist goal, conflict in many spheres may be expected. There is no longer a clear distinction between peace and war in the pre–World War II meaning. This is an era of "twilight wars," of guerrilla aggression combined with what has come to be known as limited conventional warfare. Today, the United States must be able to deal effectively with a wide range of military threats and attacks. Further, it must face, in each such conflict, the question of whether it is a shooting war or a power play (such as the Cuban crisis in 1962), with the possible danger of escalation to general war. Thus, the United States must somehow maintain the ability to fight low-level conflicts while at the same time holding decisive nuclear superiority. This combination is vital if it is to deter general war by convincing enemies that they risk their very survival by threatening the vital interests of the United States.

The many forms of aggression that the Communists have at their disposal and the unpredictable crises resulting from political upheavals around the world require the U.S. Air Force to maintain a force posture adequate to cope with a broad range of tasks. The tools for these tasks are:

(1) Strategic aerospace systems, aircraft and missiles, both capable of carrying nuclear destruction to an enemy's homeland in hours and minutes;

(2) Flexible, "damaging-limiting" defensive weapon systems, capable of dealing with space-age threats posed by both manned and unmanned enemy weapon systems;

(3) All-weather and night-capable reconnaissance vehicles that can collect accurate and comprehensive intelligence;

(4) Tactical aircraft and missiles, equipped with conventional or nuclear weapons, that can perform discriminating and selective military tasks;

(5) Airlift to respond rapidly to emergencies world-wide; and

(6) Command and control networks that will provide flexible, rugged, and mobile communications that can operate in any environment.

The cost and complexity of air-power weapons have increased so much in recent years that no military service can have every feasible weapon and support system proposed by planners. Nevertheless, the Air Force is attempting to meet its broad range of assignments through the careful expenditure of its resources and use of its people. Today's Air Force posture is designed to meet the complex military challenge it faces.

The Manned Bomber Force

The Strategic Retaliatory Forces presently include some 600 B-52 bombers, well dispersed, half of them on fifteen-minute alert and backed up by an improved warning system. Three hundred and forty-five older-model (C through F) B-52's are to be phased out by 1971. The 80 supersonic B-58's are also to be phased out by then, and 210 bomber versions of the F-111, the FB-111, are expected to join SAC's inventory. Thus, by 1971, the Defense Department plan is for a force of 465 manned bombers: 210 FB-111A's and 255 B-52G's and H's.

The Strategic Air Command's reconnaissance capability will be greatly improved by the addition of the SR-71. This aircraft flies above 80,000 feet at a speed over Mach 3, carries a two-man crew, and is equipped with improved reconnaissance sensors. The first SR-71's were delivered to operational units in 1965.

The Ballistic Missile Force

The USAF's ballistic missile force has progressed to the point where first-generation missiles have been retired. All Atlas and Titan I cryogenic missiles were phased out of the operational inventory by July, 1965. Their places have been taken by the less expensive, faster-reaction solid-fueled Minuteman and the Titan II, which is powered by easier-to-handle storable liquid propellants.

The Minuteman is the mainstay of the more than 850 land-based ICBM force. It is a three-stage, solid-propellant missile. The Minuteman I force reached its peak in July, 1965, and the greatly improved Minuteman II entered the inventory during fiscal year 1966. As a result of a modernization program, the USAF plans to obtain maximum capability from the Minuteman force by replacing the older missiles with Minuteman II's, which have greater range, accuracy, and destructive power. Launchers and launch control facilities will be modified accordingly to provide the full Minuteman II capability. A further improved Minuteman model—Minuteman III —is being developed and will be added to the inventory. A force of 1,000 Minuteman ICBM's and 54 Titan II's is the current plan.

The two forces described above represent a striking power that requires swift and reliable command and control. During 1964, substantial improvements were achieved in the command and control capability of the Strategic Air Command when a major portion of the new system reached its initial operational capability.

SAGE and BUIC—Air Defense Elements

One of the most vital elements of the aerospace defense system is the electronic command and control system referred to as SAGE (Semi-Automatic Ground Environment). Refinements have been incorporated into the SAGE Air Defense Command and Control System and the new version of the BUIC (Back-Up Interceptor Control System) is being installed. The more modern BUIC III hardware, tied in with networks of radars, can handle the air-defense-command-and-control problems of a single air-defense sector and feed data into the NORAD Combat Operations Center now relocated underground deep in the Cheyenne Mountain cave near Ent Air Force Base, Colorado.

Manned Interceptor Force

The present manned interceptor force was designed to counter the long-range bomber threat of the late 1950's, when Soviet long-range bombers carrying nuclear weapons were considered to be the primary threat. ICBM's were only beginning to be important then. Since 1959, the interceptor force in the United States has been reduced in both numbers of squadrons and manned aircraft. As a result, the USAF relies heavily on the Air National Guard interceptor units. A significant portion of the active duty force is on fifteen-minute-or-less alert.

To increase the capability of the interceptor force, a construction program of dispersal bases in the United States was begun. Currently, it provides an interim capability that permits temporary interceptor dispersal, similar to the action taken during the Cuban crisis.

Air Defense Command has hoped for addition of the new YF-12A into its fighter-interceptor force for defense against manned bombers. Its high cruise rate and extended radius of action would permit interception of bombers far beyond U.S. borders and provide a more effective defense, but to date no such decision has been made by the Defense Department.

In 1964, the Air Force withdrew all of its all-weather air defense interceptor forces from Spain and some from Japan, and the following year withdrew additional interceptor squadrons from Japan, Okinawa, and Clark Air Base, Philippine Islands. To offset the loss in capability of the squadrons at Okinawa and Clark, the USAF has programmed deployment of tactical rotational F-4C squadrons in their place. It is hoped that local foreign air forces, which have been trained to USAF standards with USAF equipment, will provide air defense coverage of facilities in Japan, Spain, and Korea.

Ballistic Missile Defense Systems

One of the most critical problems confronting the USAF is active defense against missile attacks from land, sea, and space. The Ballistic Missile Early Warning System (BMEWS) with sites at Clear, Alaska; Thule, Greenland; and Fylingdales Moor, England, provides an effective warning system of a surprise ICBM attack. To increase the warning time, the USAF has installed a complex of new over-the-horizon radars, which give almost instantaneous reports of ballistic missiles launched for attack. Authority has also been received for radar modification of certain Air Defense Command SAGE radars to provide warning of a submarine-launched ballistic missile (SLBM) attack.

For defense against possible actions by enemy satellites orbiting in space, the Air Force has improved its space tracking and neutralization capabilities. New sensors have been developed for the Air Force Spacetrack System, a system which is responsible for cataloguing all man-made satellites and component parts orbiting the earth. Because of the potential threat from space and the necessity to counter a psychological threat from space, two weapon systems capable of intercepting and destroying hostile orbiting space satellites were developed. These are based on the Air Force *Thor* space booster and the Army's Nike-Zeus antimissile system.

Close Air Support of the Army

The primary tactical missions of the USAF are to gain and maintain air superiority in the combat area and to provide further support to the Army through interdiction, close air support, and reconnaissance. The Air Force ability to perform these missions has steadily improved over the years.

In addition to maintaining a general war posture by means of a nuclear and conventional alert overseas, portions of the USAF tactical forces are organized into Composite Air Strike Forces. These forces, which consist of fighter, reconnaissance, airlift, and tanker elements, can be rapidly deployed to any area of the world and can conduct sustained operations from bases having only an airstrip and a place to park aircraft.

The operational readiness of these forces, and of the Army units working with them, is frequently tested through joint exercises conducted under the unified control of the U.S. Strike Command. Two recent exercises, "Desert Strike" and "Gold Fire I," significantly improved Air Force operational techniques. An actual emergency situation best illustrates the value of such exercises. In August, 1964, in response to the Tonkin Gulf incident in Vietnam, a force consisting of tactical fighters, tactical reconnaissance aircraft, and assault transport aircraft completed rapid deployment to bases in the Pacific. Because of the availability of prepositioned munitions and support, they were prepared upon arrival to go promptly on alert.

To provide a focal point for its continuing effort to improve tactical air support capabilities, the USAF has established a Tactical Air Warfare Center at Eglin Air Force Base, Florida. During the fall of 1964, the center conducted "Exercise Indian River," the purpose of which was to test and evaluate USAF tactical air support concepts under field conditions. The Army provided brigade-size forces to participate in this operation.

Tactical Fighters

In addition to improvements in concepts and techniques, the capabilities of the equipment have been increased. The F-4C tactical fighter is in the operational inventory of many USAF units. It is a two-man, twin-jet, all-weather weapon system having a speed of Mach 2 plus, a ceiling of about 60,000 feet, and it is armed with missiles, 20-mm. cannon and other weapons, both nuclear and non-nuclear.

The latest development in tactical aircraft is the F-111, designed for Air Force and Navy use. It is a short take-off and landing, variable-geometry aircraft with the wing folding back along the fuselage for high-speed flight. It is designed to take off within 3,000 feet, go supersonic on the deck, and in excess of Mach 2 at altitude, and will have an intercontinental ferry range with refueling. It was successfully test flown in December, 1964, and is expected to eventually replace F-100's and F-105's. Its ability to perform varied tactical air missions, including reconnaissance and air defense, and to operate from relatively crude bases will provide greater flexibility and better security from enemy attack and will add tremendously to the USAF's tactical air capabilities. The bomber version, the FB-111, has been announced for the Strategic Air Command.

Aircraft Developments

Joint tactical exercises with the Army have emphasized the importance of timely and accurate intelligence to support military operations. Currently, the RB-66 and RF-101 aircraft are providing this capability. The RB-66's are being replaced and the RF-101's are being modernized. The first RF-4C's, the reconnaissance version of the tactical F-4C, which will replace the RB-66, were delivered to the Air Force in September, 1964. Eventually, the RF-4C will comprise the bulk of the USAF reconnaissance force.

The USAF has also developed a preliminary operational concept for the first generation V/STOL (Vertical/Short Takeoff and Landing) aircraft. The concept envisages the V/STOL as a predominantly offensive weapon system capable of operating under centralized control from dispersed or main operating bases. The aircraft has the potential of performing all tactical fighter and tactical reconnaissance missions in both nuclear and non-nuclear war. Continued research experimentation and refinement of operational doctrine and procedures are necessary in this area; however, the V/STOL shows promise of significant improvement in combat capability in tactical operations.

Special Air Warfare Activity

The Air Force has placed increased emphasis on the planning for operations at any level of conflict and with many force options.

Of particular concern are the need to reduce collateral damage to a minimum, the necessity for discriminating and selective use of weapons, and the ability to control the intensity of response to aggression. Of growing importance, also, is the requirement to improve Air Force skills in counterinsurgency (COIN) and unconventional and psychological warfare operations.

The U.S. military forces have long been aware of the insurgency threat in Latin America and the need to help improve the technical skills of our military counterparts in that area. The USAF Special Air Warfare forces have increased their activity there as well as in Southeast Asia. The Air Force has a group of specialists working on improvements in all types of conventional ordnance, tactics, and techniques. Special provisions have been made to permit accelerated procurement and testing of equipment which may have Special Air Warfare applications.

Vulnerability of Overseas Aircraft

In recognition of the problem of vulnerability of theater tactical aircraft, there are several corrective actions under way. One of the approved programs entails shelters to protect aircraft and key facilities from non-nuclear weapons. This program also provides for a rapid runway repair capability to ensure that tactical aircraft will be able to launch and retaliate before re-attack. In addition, the Air Force is developing and operationally testing other active and passive defense measures to provide a balanced long-term program for overseas tactical force survivability.

The Airlift Force

For many years the airlift force consisted primarily of piston-engine aircraft. The need to respond immediately to requirements has made the creation of a modern, flexible, fast-reaction, jet-powered airlift force a matter of urgency. Modernization of the current airlift force is proceeding as programmed. The advanced turboprop C-130E is continuing to enter both the strategic and tactical airlift inventories. The first operational C-141 aircraft have been phased into the operational squadrons, and more than 200

C-141's are programmed to be operating in 1968. This total will provide a 70 per cent increase in airlift capability over 1965 levels. The giant C-5A, now entering development, will enormously enhance USAF airlift power.

The Indian River/Gold Fire exercises demonstrated the Air Force ability to support ground forces in a combat environment. New delivery techniques and refinement of joint coordination and control procedures have given new dimensions to USAF assault and intratheater airlift effectiveness. The Air Force objective is to enhance effectiveness by providing fast-reaction logistical support and mobility to Army units located in the most forward part of the combat zone.

The C-5A

During 1964 and 1965, the Air Force reviewed its airlift requirements with a view toward improving its outsize capability. A number of comprehensive studies using airlift in support of contingency operations have been completed. All concluded that there was a requirement for a large, efficient outsize cargo aircraft to add a higher degree of credibility to the United States contingency posture.

Air Force analyses of studies conducted by industry showed the development of such an aircraft, the C-5A, to be technically feasible and indicated that a highly economical and effective airlift system would be achieved with it. This jet transport program was approved by the Secretary of Defense in December, 1964, and a $2 billion contract to develop and produce fifty-eight C-5A's was awarded to Lockheed in September, 1965. The C-5A is slated to be in operation in 1969. It will carry all the combat and support equipment normally assigned to Army forces and can be configured to accommodate from 500 to 700 troops. Using the Berlin airlift for comparative purposes, on a daily tonnage basis, only five C-5A's would have been needed to do the job performed by 142 C-54's.

The ability of the U.S. Armed Forces to respond to aggression in a timely and appropriate manner requires the utmost in airlift flexibility and capability. The Air Force envisions a mixed airlift force consisting of the C-5A, the C-141, and a V/STOL transport, supported by a Reserve force equipped with the C-130. The Air

Force believes that such a force will create new vistas in military management and economy, leading to revolutionary logistical concepts that will significantly increase the combat effectiveness of U.S. military forces.

Air Reserve Forces

Under the current concept of utilization, the Air Reserve forces are an integral part of the USAF's deterrent strength. The Air Force reviews their roles and missions annually in conjunction with the active force and assigns them appropriate missions in general war and contingency plans. The USAF goal for the Reserve forces is a "ready now" element, fully capable of carrying out a wartime operational mission. To attain this goal, the Air Force has assigned peacetime operational tasks to its Reserve units as opposed to having them perform training exercises merely for the sake of proficiency. Transport units, for example, airlift MAC cargo. During 1964, they airlifted nearly 25 million pounds overseas. During the Tonkin Gulf incident, Air Reserve forces' C-124's flew 1,350 hours airlifting MAC cargo to the Far East, while C-97's and C-121's augmented MAC efforts on the East Coast and transported 250 tons of cargo to Europe.

The Air National Guard attained its current "ready now" status as the result of steady progress since the end of the Korean conflict. For example, 215 aircraft of eleven ANG squadrons were sent to Europe in 1961 during the Berlin crisis. They crossed the Atlantic in an island-hopping operation, landing several times to refuel. Total deployment time was five days. In August, 1964, the 113th TAC Fighter Wing made the same deployment in nine hours and fifteen minutes. The difference was airborne refueling by Air National Guard tankers—a technique the Air National Guard has mastered since the Berlin crisis. Air National Guard units are also strengthening U.S. air defenses and taking a heavy load off Regular fighter-interceptor squadrons by taking over runway alert functions under Air Defense Command control.

Although Air Reserve forces have materially increased their capability during the past years and have made significant contributions to the over-all defense effort, their contribution in the immediate future will be even more important. Some Reserve air rescue units are getting long-range HC-97's, which will enable them to operate more effectively over much wider areas. All Air National Guard KC-97 tankers have been modified by the addition of two jet engines. This gives the ANG units a self-contained capability for greater global deployment. The Air Force considers that the augmentation of its Regular forces by Reserve units is essential in this period of frequent and unpredictable crises.

Research and Development

In the area of research and development, the Air Force is primarily concerned with ensuring that the best technology is available to provide superior weapon systems and a flexible response strategy.

Major new developments in weapon systems include SRAM (Short-Range Attack Missile) to be deployed operationally with the on-coming FB-111 to permit the bomber to attack a larger number of targets, and to do so from beyond the range of local defenses. Also under consideration is a series of new payloads for strategic missiles. These include penetration aids, to assure that the missile reaches its target through any defense; guidance and re-entry vehicle designs, to increase manyfold the effectiveness of USAF missiles against various kinds of targets; and methods of reporting the arrival of missiles on target, up to and even including the time of explosion. A third R&D program proposed for implementation during 1966 was in the area of propulsion, to enable industry to move some of their best engine ideas from experimental status into development.

Space Programs

Air Force space programs are focused on the defense aspects of space. The objective is to make sure that no nation secures a position in space that could threaten the security of the United States. The Air Force realizes the dangers to national security that could arise from unchecked military exploitation of space by a hostile power. The military value of space systems has been established in several distinct areas, but USAF knowledge of space has not progressed to the point where all possible military uses can be identified.

The Air Force is seeking to identify those areas in which man can contribute to military space capabilities through an orderly progression of controlled experiments. These will be performed aboard the Manned Orbiting Laboratory (MOL), which will carry military crews in space in the late 1960's, using a Gemini spacecraft, a Titan IIIC booster, and a canister-shaped laboratory vehicle. The MOL will enable the USAF to assess man's ability in performing spaceborne military functions. The Secretary of Defense recommended funds in the fiscal year 1966 proposal for design studies to assist in obtaining the cost and technical information required to proceed with full-scale development of the MOL. On August 25, 1965, President Johnson announced final approval for the project, expected to cost some $1.5 billion.

The Air Force is also working on the new Advanced Re-Entry and Precision Recovery Program, which will permit further study and test of maneuvering re-entry and data retrieval.

The X-15, a manned rocket airplane, has flown more than 4,000 miles per hour at altitudes exceeding sixty miles. A plane of this type may be the forerunner to manned spaceflight from earth to space and back to earth. The X-15 has been used in a program designed to provide navigational reference points for astronauts in the future Apollo mission.

One of the most significant milestones in the Air Force's Titan III Standard Space Launch Vehicle program occurred on June 18, 1965, when the first Titan IIIC was launched. With a lift-off thrust of over 2 million pounds, it became the most powerful rocket launched in the Free World. Twelve minutes after lift-off, the Titan IIIC put a 21,000-pound payload into orbit 115 miles above the earth. Russia, however, still remains ahead of the United States in payload weight orbited with a record 26,880-pound satellite hurled aloft on July 16, 1965.

Civilian Support

The Air Force Association is an independent, national, nonprofit air-power organization, incorporated February 4, 1946. Since its establishment, the AFA has served the United States and the cause of peace through its primary objective "to assist in obtaining and maintaining adequate aerospace power for national security and world peace."

AFA is organized into twelve regions, each composed of three or more states and divided into state organizations and chapters. Each region, state, and chapter is administered by a group of elected officials, all dedicated to AFA's goals. Its world-wide membership is approximately 82,000, of whom about 35,000 are USAF officers and airmen on active duty.

In addition to its continuing campaign for adequate U.S. air power, the AFA over the years has supported many military personnel programs of the Air Force, including additional slots for officer promotion, additional on-base housing, the continuation of commissary stores and exchanges, and moving allowances for civilian employees dislocated by base closings. AFA has pushed hard to streamline job placement of military retirees and took the initiative in securing coordination and action on the problem with the Department of Defense, Department of Labor, the Small Business Administration, and other agencies. For many years, it has spoken out strongly in support of fair and adequate pay and deserves a large measure of credit for the military pay-raise bills passed by Congress.

AFA publishes the authoritative magazine *Air Force/Space Digest,* written and edited by professionals and covering the whole spectrum of aerospace power and the military, scientific, political, and economic factors that influence it. Its average monthly circulation is around 98,000. In January, 1965, AFA introduced a new magazine, *Air Force/Space Digest International,* with the object of extending to readers abroad a useful monthly review of U.S. aerospace developments, both military and commercial.

In the field of aerospace education, through its affiliate, the Aerospace Education Foundation, AFA sponsors educational seminars around the nation to provide current information on U.S. aerospace efforts to educators at state, county, and city levels, national and local educational associations, parent-teacher associations, and school boards.

More than 250 corporations and companies interested in aerospace power are affiliated with the AFA through its Industrial Associate Program. This program disseminates information about USAF missions and requirements to Industrial Associate members by means of briefings and published materials.

XII

The Aerospace Outlook for Tomorrow

Any study of the U.S. aerospace posture in the decade ahead must take into consideration both future threats and technological developments. These elements will undoubtedly lead to the establishment of new military requirements not only for the United States Air Force but for the entire armed forces establishment.

The Future Threat

Since the end of World War II, power in the world has been polarized in two great blocs, the North Atlantic Treaty Organization, led by the United States; and the Communist countries, led by the Soviet Union. The United States has been the leading member of the Atlantic Alliance because of its great economic and military strength. Russia has been the leading power in the Communist camp, not only because of its economic and military strength, but also because it has dominated the international Communist apparatus.

These conditions have begun to change. Western European nations and Japan in the Far East are prospering economically. The United States is no longer the only important economic and political power in the Free World. Nor is NATO as unified as it was a few years ago. Not only France's dissatisfaction but also such quarrels between NATO members as that of Greece and Turkey over Cyprus threaten the Alliance. And the pressures for a greater share in nuclear planning by NATO allies create strains.

On the Communist side, the once unquestioned domination by the

196

Soviet Union of the Communist bloc has been successfully challenged. Yugoslavia, Rumania, Poland, and, to a lesser degree, other Communist regimes in Eastern Europe are following policies geared to their own national interests. Red China demands recognition as the new leader of the Communist world. In moving away from their former dependence on the Soviet Union, the Chinese Communists continue to rely for military strength upon large ground forces armed with conventional weapons, but, at the same time, are working slowly toward strategic nuclear capabilities. The withdrawal of Russian technicians and specialists in the nuclear fields, and the ideological differences in the Russian and Chinese approach to world Communism will certainly delay, but are not likely to prevent the equipping of the Chinese Communist armed forces with modern weapon systems.

Meanwhile, the U.S.S.R.'s Warsaw Pact partners in Europe continue to be a threat to NATO forces and U.S. overseas bases. The arms and equipment of the satellite countries are being steadily improved, although some reports indicate that the reliability of the troops is open to question. Nevertheless, as satellite air force units improve in quality, Russian units are released and become available for other assignments. Thus, the value of the military forces of the satellite countries must be considered in any examination of the future threat to the Atlantic Alliance partners.

Current strategic studies and past history suggest that the Russians will continue to expand their military capabilities through advanced weapons programs. It has been reported that the Russians are working hard on advanced aerodynamic systems, nuclear weapons, space systems, advanced ballistic missiles, and missile-defense systems. A supersonic transport with a speed of Mach 3 is also reported to be included in their R&D effort. Their pre-nuclear-test-ban detonation of a 57-megaton thermonuclear device was widely reported.

Russia has four types of operational bombers—to which the USAF has assigned the code names of Badger, Bear, Blinder, and Bison. These have been operational for a number of years. Despite their age, their effectiveness has been updated by the incorporation of air-to-air refueling capabilities and stand-off weapon systems in addition to their normal bomb loads. Follow-on bombers may appear in Soviet operational units by the mid-1970's.

In the air-to-surface missile area, four types of missiles have been identified and are operational: the Kangaroo, carried by the Bear; the Kipper, carried by the Badger; the Kitchen, which may be launched from the Blinder, Badger, and Bison; and the Kennel, a turbojet-powered missile carried by the Badger. Improved air-to-surface missiles are most likely being developed.

The Russians have not neglected the offensive capabilities of their naval forces. Soviet submarines have been and are continuing to be equipped with intermediate-range ballistic missiles. Their early ranges were reported to be between 300 and 400 nautical miles. Informed military sources believe that subsequent improvements in the weapon have increased the operational range approximately twofold.

It has been established that land-based operational medium- and intermediate-range ballistic missiles are located at sites within the U.S.S.R. and many of its satellites. Intercontinental ballistic-missile sites, however, are located only within the U.S.S.R. To be effective, Soviet ICBM's need an operational range of about 6,000 nautical miles and must carry warheads having nuclear yields of from one to fifteen megatons, perhaps even greater, depending upon the target. Soviet ICBM's are emplaced on both soft and hard sites, the latter capable of withstanding substantial pressure.

At the May Day parade in Moscow in 1965, a three-stage solid-fuel missile, described as intercontinental in range, was displayed. Since Russia already has some 270 liquid-fuel ICBM's that are capable of reaching the North American continent, the display of one solid-fuel rocket in a parade was not considered startling. But it could indicate Soviet efforts to shift to solid-fueled "instant" ICBM's similar to the United States' Minuteman and submarine-carried Polaris. And it should be noted that chemical or bacteriological agents may be used as well as nuclear warheads as the payloads of missiles.

The Russians are reported to be developing supersonic long-range interceptors carrying long-range missiles and utilizing long-range air-intercept radar. These aircraft are designed for a speed of about

Mach 2.5 at 70,000 feet altitude. They could appear in the Soviet inventory in the early 1970's.

During World War II, the Russians relied largely on U.S. designs and Lend-Lease aircraft to meet their transport requirements. After World War II, when they decided not to produce heavy bombers in quantity and had an adequate inventory of "Badger" bombers, they turned their design and production facilities to the development and manufacture of long-range transports. As a result, their civil and military air fleet includes many turboprop and jet long-range transports (AN-10, IL-18, TU-104, and TU-114). It is possible that the Russians will develop, in the late 1960's, a supersonic transport that will have such offensive-combat applications as troop transport, missile launching, and reconnaissance.

At the International Air Show in Paris in June, 1965, the Russians unveiled the world's largest airplane. According to its designer, Oleg Antonov, the AN-22 can carry 720 passengers or 80 tons of cargo. It is 187 feet long, has a wing span of 211 feet and, with its maximum load, weighs 250 tons. It is powered by four 1,500-horsepower turboprop engines, each engine having twin propellers rotating in opposite directions. Its maximum speed is 460 miles per hour, altitude 36,000 feet, and range 3,100 miles with maximum load.

The Soviets also displayed a model of a proposed supersonic passenger plane, the delta-wing TU-144, to be designed, they said, by Andrei N. Tupolev. It would carry 121 passengers, cruise at 1,550 miles per hour, and have a range of 4,000 miles.

Soviet Space Aims

Ever since the Russians launched their first Sputnik in 1957, it has been their aim to exploit their space achievements to the maximum by using political and psychological warfare programs to impress the world with Soviet technical and military prowess. These programs will likely be continued into the future. For several years, they have developed and perfected massive boosters capable of placing sizable payloads in orbit. They have consistently stressed manned space systems and rendezvous in space. Their policy statements often refer to the military potential of space.

If they were able to achieve a technological breakthrough such as an effective spaceborne antimissile system, they might be in a position to seriously damage U.S. strategic retaliatory forces as well as interfere with the U.S. space program. Such a breakthrough is not considered easy by most experts, but, at the same time, most experts see the significance of such potential feats.

U.S. policy is to use space for peaceful purposes. In announcing the Air Force Manned Orbiting Laboratory program, President Johnson stressed that the United States would orbit no weapons, that MOL's aim is only to get a crew into orbit to see what military jobs can be done effectively in space. The United States has already developed unmanned space systems for strategic reconnaissance, navigation, meteorology, and communication. The Russians are aware of the relation of these systems to U.S. strategic and tactical capabilities and, except for occasional propaganda purposes, have not protested strongly.

However, as these U.S. systems grow in importance, the Russians could conceivably find provocation to attack them first politically and then militarily. The United States would be equally determined to protect them, and the relation between space activity and overall strategic balance could become extremely critical. The United States might adopt passive defense measures, or initiate reprisals against Soviet space systems, or attempt active space-to-space defense. The latter, however, requires a technical capability equivalent to what would be needed for the spaceborne antimissile defense. Such systems require complex sensing devices, extensive maneuverability, and complicated command and control operations.

Reprisals against Soviet space systems could result in limited space war, while reprisals against Soviet land-based forces could expand into a general war. If neither side considered the elimination of its satellite capability a major strategic setback, the danger of the war's escalation would be reduced. Just as the Strategic Air Command is a deterrent force, so a proven U.S. capability to effect an antisatellite reprisal could serve to deter Soviet attack on U.S. space systems. Thus, a prime reason for having a U.S. military space capability is that it could actually add to international stability. If, however, the Russians were to successfully challenge the United States in space militarily, the United States might be forced to change the location of the conflict from space to earth. Under present national policy, the initiation of antisatellite attacks by the United States would require considerable certainty that the satellites were menacing. The United States would have to have an inspection-and-capture capability to make certain of the danger of a Soviet space threat.

Technological Developments

In the past quarter-century, basic and applied research have introduced a greater change in military science and technology than took place in all the years before 1940. Research and development are the keys to the future USAF posture. The scientific and technological changes that have drastically influenced the nature of weapons and warfare show no signs of abating. The Air Force must anticipate changes and direct some aspects of scientific exploration and investigation along lines that will enable it to build soundly for the future.

The Air Force is not only actively engaged in basic and applied research through its own laboratories. It also sponsors basic research at universities and other civilian agencies. Generally, the research conducted in its own laboratories or sponsored in outside agencies is in areas unique to the Air Force or in areas of Air Force interest not adequately covered by other participants in the national research program.

The Air Force's in-house and sponsored basic research have contributed to the development of many new systems and techniques. Its current studies also show that new developments in metallurgy, airframe design, propulsion, and avionics can be combined to produce manned aircraft with performance characteristics not heretofore attainable. This improved performance will give manned aircraft a better ability to survive enemy attack, to penetrate enemy defenses, and to strike enemy targets with precision. It is interesting to consider certain possible technological developments within the next decade and speculate on their application to new military capabilities:

(1) Metallurgy. Solutions to the difficult problem of developing lightweight materials that can withstand high temperatures gener-

ated by the great speed of missiles and advanced aircraft may be expected. High-strength titanium and steel alloys will be able to withstand the aerodynamic heating in aircraft structures up to Mach 4 speeds. Nickel-base super alloys will be used in turbines having temperatures up to 1,800 degrees Fahrenheit. Plastics will be vastly improved. Advances will be made by combining the ideal properties of several materials into a single composite material. These high-strength, high-temperature materials will be used in the construction of re-entry vehicles as heat shields and in tubing for nuclear reactors. Some future vehicles will require the use of fiber materials but, at the moment, the fiber technology is not in hand—although boron fiber composites, for one, hold great promise for the future.

(2) Airframe structures. The advance in metallurgy technology will enable the Air Force to build stronger and lighter structures for its aircraft, missiles, and space vehicles. Space applications will place special emphasis on collapsed structures that can be packed in a small space and then be unfolded or inflated to their normal functional shape after a moon landing or after injection into orbit.

(3) Propulsion. Improvements in existing turbofan engine technology should lead to lower fuel consumption and the development of significantly more thrust for little increase in weight. Beryllium may be used in V/STOL aircraft to improve the thrust-to-weight ratio. Storage batteries and fuel cells will be improved or replaced by more efficient and reliable systems.

(4) Avionics. The F-111 with its variable sweep-wing geometry is the most advanced air-weapon system approved for production. Further developments in the variable geometry principle and improvements in boundary layer control could very well result in substantially higher aircraft performance. V/STOL aircraft should be practicable within a few years. Prototypes of V/STOL combat aircraft are being flown in Europe, and, in August, 1965, the USAF accepted delivery of the second XC-142A all-service V/STOL for operational suitability tests to continue through 1966. V/STOL technology in the decade ahead should develop to satisfy a requirement for a combat and transport V/STOL aircraft. The NASA lunar program is advancing the technology of manned spaceflight.

•

Development of this technology should provide a capability for maneuvering in space, rendezvous with spacecraft, and selecting the point of return to earth. The USAF's Manned Orbiting Laboratory and other orbital exploration projects will provide a wealth of knowledge about the space environment.

In addition to the above, technological developments will probably result in improved performance in command and control, guidance and communication through improved sensors, computers and data-processing equipment, and communications satellites in synchronous orbit.

In almost every area of aerospace technology, future developments seem so limitless that by 1976 the problem may well be to determine *which* high-priority projects to undertake, not *how*.

Current USAF development programs of major consequence include the SR-71 Mach 3 strategic reconnaissance aircraft, the F-111 Mach 2 plus tactical fighter, the C-5A 500- to 700-passenger transport, and the Manned Orbiting Laboratory. The SR-71 breaks new ground in engine technology, materials, structures, and reconnaissance systems. The F-111 will introduce the first operational use of the variable-sweep wing. But in all other important areas, these four development programs are presently feasible and do not push technology. The lead-time from initial planning to full operational readiness of any major system is approximately ten years. Thus, despite the great future possibilities, and unless circumstances force the United States into crash programs, the USAF technological efforts in the next decade will be spent on systems that are essentially possible now.

Advanced Aircraft

The USAF has carefully studied numerous proposed versions for a follow-on bomber for SAC. Technology offers some very promising options, and these have been subjected to detailed cost-effectiveness analysis. Former Air Force Chief of Staff General Curtis E. LeMay, a combat veteran who gained his experience during peace and in war, is firmly convinced that an advanced manned strategic aircraft (AMSA) is needed as part of the force structure for the

1970's. The technology is available, the development risks acceptable. He and many others believe that the United States should not have to rely on updated B-52's or on modifying the F-111 or SR-71 for a retaliatory posture. The Air Force envisions the AMSA as having intercontinental range without refueling, able to penetrate enemy territory with refueling, able to operate at tree-top level as well as at high altitude, and armed with an assortment of weapon systems.

In the improved manned interceptor field, no decision on the production of the YF-12A for the Air Defense Command has been made. If a decision were made to go ahead with operation deployment of a YF-12A-type aircraft, the Department of Defense might well authorize an interceptor version of the larger SR-71 aircraft, which has a considerably greater range, since both the YF-12A and SR-71 come from the same family tree. The Defense Secretary's statements suggest that ADC's prospects for having YF-12A's in the inventory of operational squadrons by the mid-1970's are not bright.

The General Purpose Forces include most of the Army's combat and combat support units, virtually all Navy units, all Marine Corps units, and the tactical units of the Air Force. These are the forces upon which the United States relies for all military actions short of nuclear war, i.e., limited war and counterinsurgency operations. The greatest developments in the USAF will likely occur in this area. The variable sweep-wing F-111 will tremendously increase the Air Force's supersonic fighter-bomber capabilities. Originally referred to as the TFX, the F-111, on August 23, 1965, flew 1,520 miles an hour at 40,000 feet. It is doubtful, however, whether this high-cost, high-performance aircraft will be employed in counterinsurgency operations in which it might be extremely vulnerable to anti-aircraft fire and missiles.

By 1976, V/STOL aircraft developments should provide the USAF with greatly increased capabilities, particularly in troop airlift and close battlefield missions. The XC-42A is a four-engine tiltwing assault transport capable of taking off vertically like a helicopter and flying in a conventional manner at speeds as high as 430 miles per hour.

The outlook in the airlift field for 1976 is bright. C-141's have been assigned to squadrons of the Military Airlift Command and have already demonstrated their superiority over the present fleet of transport aircraft for airlift and supply of U.S. armed forces on a global basis. Great logistic savings may be expected when MAC is operating on an all-jet basis. The new transport in the 725,000-pound class, the C-5A, with four newly developed engines, will be in operational units within the coming decade. This aircraft will deliver cargo 40 per cent more cheaply per ton delivered than the C-141 and about 70 per cent more cheaply than the C-130. It will have rapid loading and unloading capacity and be able to operate from short runways and airfields. Including development and procurement, the C-5A program will cost about $2.2 billion but, since one C-5A should be able to do the work of three to five C-141's in deploying typical Army units, it is considered a better buy than additional C-141's. A force of C-5A's would go far toward solving the problem of deploying large Army forces from the continental United States in the first thirty days of a limited war.

An examination of the Defense Secretary's recent statements gives the impression that since both the United States and Russia have ICBM's armed with nuclear warheads, the two nations are at a relative technological stand-off, which may continue for the next five or ten years. The development of a superior weapon system to replace the ICBM or the development of an effective defensive weapon system are not considered likely within the next decade.

If this interpretation is correct, the Air Force can only hope for an improved manned interceptor, such as described above, to bolster its defensive forces by 1976. Conceivably, the USAF might develop improved Airborne Early Warning and Command and Control systems. Currently, all man-made objects in orbit around the earth are detected, identified, tracked, and catalogued by the USAF Spacetrack System, operated by the Air Defense Command's 9th Aerospace Defense Division as part of the multiservice NORAD Space Detection and Tracking System. This system will be improved and expanded by 1976.

The USAF's Manned Orbiting Laboratory should be in orbit within the next decade and should make valuable contributions to the military aerospace defense program through a variety of missions described earlier.

Present U.S. military policy is to refrain from any truly advanced technological developments for the next five years. What about other countries?

The development of weapon systems of significant military impact requires great resources in manpower, money, and facilities. England is eliminated because it cannot afford such a program. France will need years to attain its nuclear-force goals, which are modest by comparison with those of the United States and the Soviet Union. Russia is the only other nation that can afford the resources to develop truly advanced weapon systems. And Russia and the United States are at a relative stand-off in missiles.

Barring any break of the ICBM impasse by the Russians, which would result in a crash program of some sort on the part of the United States, USAF forces in 1976 will probably consist essentially of aircraft, missiles, weapon systems, and equipment designed and developed from technology some of which dates as far back as the early 1950's.

XIII

Aerospace Doctrine in Modern Conflict

BY

LIEUTENANT COLONEL WALTER S. VANCLEAVE, USAF

NOTE: *The following chapter, written especially for this book, is designed to acquaint the reader with current Air Force doctrinal thinking on the roles and capabilities of air power in the nuclear-space age. While it is not an official document, Lieutenant Colonel Vancleave's contribution is representative of present Air Force philosophy. The author is a staff officer in the Aerospace Doctrine Division of the Air Force Directorate of Plans at Headquarters, United States Air Force in Washington.*

Technological developments during the twentieth century have made a dramatic impact on concepts of warfare. Perhaps the most significant result of technology was the expansion of the existing conflict arena by exploiting the potential of aerospace as a military medium. The evolution of the airplane—and later the ballistic missile—compressed the dimensions of time and space so that a nation's degree of immunity from attack was no longer necessarily a factor of geographic location. The introduction of weapons of mass destruction during the latter part of World War II, and their later refinement, further increased the complications and magnified the dangers of modern warfare.

These technological developments were also influencing factors in the evolution of the United States from an isolationist state to a nation with world-wide commitments. The major problem confronting the United States in its Free World leadership role has been the increasing power of the Communist bloc in pursuit of its objective of world domination. To date, the Communists have chosen to avoid high-intensity warfare as a means of achieving this goal. (The reason most commonly attributed has been the obvious capability of the United States to prevail in a nuclear exchange.) Instead, the Communist nations have chosen measures less likely to jeopardize their existence as viable societies. These measures have included psychological pressures, subversion, and limited military aggression.

The world today is dominated by the interaction of the forces of freedom and Communism in seeking divergent objectives. Courses of action available to these opposing factions embrace a vast spectrum of international conflict ranging from political, economic, social, educational, and technological competition at one extreme to unrestrained nuclear warfare at the other.

The most common method of categorizing modern conflict is to divide it under the several headings of cold, limited, and general war. The *Dictionary of Military Terms for Joint Usage* provides the following explanation of these terms:

> (1) *Cold War.* A state of international tension, wherein political, economic, technological, sociological, psychological, paramilitary, and military measures short of overt armed conflict involving regular military forces are employed to achieve national objectives.
>
> (2) *Limited War.* Armed conflict short of general war, exclusive of incidents, involving the overt engagement of the military forces of two or more nations.
>
> (3) *General War.* Armed conflict between the major powers of the communist and free worlds in which the total resources of the belligerents are employed, and the national survival of a belligerent is in jeopardy.*

We should recognize, however, that within each of these broad categories exists a wide variety of conflict possibilities. Furthermore, modern conflict is fluid and can fluctuate rapidly from one level to another. Therefore, it may be difficult, in some instances, to de-

---

* Technically this definition does not specifically require the employment of nuclear weapons on an intercontinental basis. However, in considering a general war in which the United States would be involved, we commonly interpret it to require the employment of nuclear weapons by both sides, since only a major nuclear power can inflict unacceptable levels of destruction on our nation.

fine a specific conflict as a "pure" example of one of the above forms of warfare. For example, the initial conflict in South Vietnam could be classified as a cold-war engagement. The U.S. involvement initially was limited to military assistance and nation-building activities designed to restore stability to that nation. Later, this involvement was expanded to active and large-scale military effort, with the intensity increasing to a limited-war level; however, the United States continued to support, and, in fact, expand the nation-building cold-war activities in South Vietnam.

All wars may be limited to a degree. Some restraint will usually be exercised on the number or type of targets, kinds of weapons, size of forces, zone of combat, or nature of objectives.

Escalation

It is possible for conflict to expand rapidly to a higher intensity if the national interests of the major world powers are involved. For example, the 1962 U.S.–U.S.S.R. confrontation in Cuba was a very tense cold-war situation, which had the potential of spontaneously escalating to a general-war nuclear exchange. Conflict escalation may also occur slowly and in measurable steps.

It is essential that we recognize these complexities of modern conflict and the multitude of operating conditions they suggest. With this in mind, one can achieve a better understanding of the wide range of situations with which military forces may have to contend, along with some of the basic factors that influence modern conflict.

The development of significant nuclear-delivery capabilities by the opposing major world powers has had a profound effect on military doctrine. Unrestrained nuclear conflict could be disastrous, for it could create damage levels to one or more of the major combatants incompatible with continued national existence. In this circumstance, even the "victor" could suffer a level of destruction unacceptable in terms of the specific issues at stake. For this reason, opposing nations may not seek "total defeat" in the initial stages of conflict. Instead, limited objectives that will produce favorable terms may be pursued by the side holding the advantage, in order to avoid placing the adversary in an untenable position. Therefore, the traditional meaning of the terms "win" and "defeat" must be re-evaluated in the light of the current environment and defined within the limitations of a stated objective.

The 1962 Cuban crisis provides an illustration of this rationale. The U.S. objective was limited to securing the withdrawal of Russian intermediate-range ballistic missiles—not the total defeat of Communism in Cuba. The limits of this objective may be argued, pro and con, many times; however, the necessity of action to avoid a nuclear conflict was recognized by the leadership of both the United States and Russia. The trend toward limitation of conflict can be further illustrated by evaluating the United Nations' limited objectives in Korea—to re-establish the 38th parallel as the geographic dividing line between the North and South; and in Vietnam, where the repeatedly declared U.S. objective has been limited to halting aggression in the South—not the unconditional surrender of the North Vietnamese.

Strategic Superiority

Although "total victory" may not be sought in the initial stages of conflict, the possibility of unrestrained warfare always exists, requiring U.S. strategic superiority over all potential enemies. For this reason, priority must be given to maintaining survivable offensive and defensive general-war forces, which can assure destruction of an enemy society as a viable entity while effectively limiting damage to one's own and allied homelands. The ability to convince an aggressor that an all-out attack will not attain his objectives reduces the effect of blackmail threats and thus influences the deterrence of aggression at lower levels of intensity.

It is a paramount objective of the United States to deter provocation or attack by convincing a potential aggressor that he will risk more than he can hope to gain. If it is clear that the United States has both the resolve and the range of capabilities to defeat aggression, then deterrence will probably result. To ensure retention of a credible deterrent posture, the United States must maintain strategic superiority at the upper levels of conflict, while at the same time maintaining the ability to provide a flexible and selective response to enemy aggression at all levels of intensity.

To effectively deter enemy aggression, the forces must be credible for the crisis at hand. Since our objective is to achieve a favorable termination of the conflict at the lowest possible intensity, it is essential that we provide the enemy a clear indication of our intentions. This can be accomplished by communicating with him and, also, by the manner in which we apply force. Prompt reaction to an aggressive act provides a convincing signal that aggression will be opposed. Force must be applied with selectivity through precise attacks on military forces and systems, by avoiding collateral damage, and by limiting force to that required to resolve the specific issues at stake.

The Doctrine in Vietnam

U.S. air attacks on North Vietnam during 1965 provide a perfect example. While there could be no doubt of U.S. capability to devastate North Vietnam, we chose to strike carefully selected targets in an attempt to persuade that nation to end its aggression in the south. The degree of ultimate success achieved in such actions may be attributed in part to the limitations observed and the perseverance in application.

Proper management of each crisis, then, is dependent upon selecting an appropriate option to accomplish a limited objective, while avoiding the risks of unnecessary escalation.

The aggressor must also be convinced that we will oppose him in a manner advantageous to us, even if it means increasing the scope or the intensity of the conflict. This is especially applicable to the lower levels of conflict, since an aggressor will seek conditions favorable to him. This may have influenced our increasing the intensity of the conflict in South Vietnam in 1965—to regain control of the initiative which had been lost to the Communist-supported insurgent forces of the Viet Cong.

The combined capabilities of strategic superiority and a flexible response also make evident to an aggressor that escalation on his part would place him at an increasing disadvantage. The unprecedented state of readiness of U.S. military forces during the 1962 Cuban crisis made this point readily apparent to the Soviet Union.

Thus, modern warfare requires forces with the ability to defeat aggression at a selected level of conflict while simultaneously retaining the option to escalate because of obvious superiority at the highest levels of conflict. To meet this requirement, aerospace forces possess certain characteristics that enhance their capability to function efficiently and effectively in modern conflict.

The prime characteristic of aerospace forces is flexibility. More than the sum of operational capabilities, it is the inherent potential to perform a wide variety of missions under varying operating conditions. The other characteristics include range, mobility, responsiveness, and tactical versatility. The first of these, range, is enhanced by the very nature of the aerospace medium. Unhampered by natural barriers—ocean, rivers, mountains, and great land masses—aerospace forces have direct access to enemy rear areas and crisis zones anywhere on the globe. Mobility enables aerospace forces to make required shifts of operations to reconcentrate forces and exploit maneuverable weapon-launching platforms. Aerospace forces are also inherently responsive. They can react quickly to crisis anywhere in the world with selectivity and with surprise in the timing and location of attack. The last of the characteristics, tactical versatility, is achieved through a wide variety of speeds and related variations in attack altitudes and maneuvers, to meet the demands of any mission requirement. These characteristics give aerospace forces a vast potential for application; however, the complexities of modern warfare demand additional considerations if our capabilities are to be employed effectively to achieve national objectives.

Advising the Leadership

The actions of the political and military instruments must be closely integrated to achieve specific goals. Although the civilian leaders of the U.S. Government must make the ultimate decision to oppose aggression, the military has the responsibility of influencing these decisions through professional advice and providing a variety of options from which decision-makers can select appropriate courses of action. To assist the decision-making process, there are several broad categories of operations to guide the employment of aerospace forces in both peace and war. These include general-war operations, limited nuclear operations, conventional operations, and peacetime and counterinsurgency operations. Within each of these categories there are many options to provide a controlled and a selective response to any aggressive act. It is important to recognize that these classifications of aerospace operations are not intended to infer mutual exclusiveness, in the sense that only one type of operation could be conducted during any one conflict. On the contrary, these operations can be conducted simultaneously as well as individually. For example, conventional conflict could be transformed into some form of nuclear warfare, but conventional munitions probably would still be employed for many of the operations. Also, in certain situations, long-range strategic systems might perform tactical missions, and conversely, tactical systems might be employed against major strategic targets. U.S. air operations in Southeast Asia during 1965 provided a perfect illustration of this flexibility. B-52 bombers performed strikes in support of ground operations, while tactical fighters struck several targets in North Vietnam that might be identified as strategic—the Haiphong power plant, for example.

General-War Operations

In the interest of self-preservation, opposing forces may recognize certain restrictions when employing nuclear weapons in general-war operations. It follows that there are a number of forms in which general war could occur, depending on the numbers and types of weapons employed and the targeting options pursued. In general, these possibilities may be categorized as countervalue operations, in which urban-industrial centers are primary targets, and counterforce operations, in which the primary targets are military.

Countervalue operations are designed to inflict such extensive damage and casualties on an enemy that the survival of the nation is jeopardized. Primary target areas would include population and industrial centers. Although such warfare is improbable when both sides have the capability to wage it, an assured countervalue capability is essential since it can deter a rational enemy from making direct attacks on United States urban-industrial areas. However, a general-war force with only a countervalue purpose possesses very limited ability to prevent warfare in the lower intensities of conflict. This may be attributed to the inability to limit damage to one's own nation, with a resultant decrease in national resolve.

In counterforce operations, aerospace forces are used to destroy or neutralize the military capabilities of an enemy, thus limiting damage to our nation while coercing the enemy into ending a conflict before it reaches countervalue proportions. To achieve counterforce objectives we must assure an opponent that we intend to leave intact the vital economic and political framework of his society, if he exercises similar restraints. We can make our intentions clear to the enemy by communicating directly with him and, indirectly, by intentionally avoiding attack on nonmilitary targets and by carefully limiting collateral damage during counterforce strikes. Such action, of course, requires controllable weapon systems capable of conducting precise strikes against selected targets. If the enemy prefers the terms we offer through negotiations to loss of his urban-industrial centers and if our use of force is limited to the specific objectives we seek, it may be possible to achieve conflict termination before reaching countervalue proportions.

Offensive counterforce strikes can complement the mission of our defensive forces in limiting damage to our nation. By maintaining a quick-reaction posture, offensive forces can be launched in response to an attack on our nation, destroying enemy residual forces and his ability to regenerate those forces recovered from his initial strike. This second-strike capability is essential, when we consider that a portion of the enemy forces may be withheld for bargaining purposes. These forces, combined with an ability to relaunch successive strikes, could determine the outcome; therefore, our ability to inflict unacceptable punishment on an aggressor, even if he launches a pre-emptive attack, becomes an integral part of deterrence. We must also recognize that regardless of how well our strategic offensive forces perform, a significant portion of the enemy's forces can survive either a first-strike or second-strike situation. This possibility requires that a high priority be placed on the capabilities of our defensive forces.

National resolve to deter aggression depends to a great extent on our ability to limit damage to our own nation. This requires strategic and tactical warning systems to alert our general-war forces to an impending attack. Strategic warning may be obtained from intelligence sources. Tactical warning is achieved through the ballistic missile early warning system (BMEWS), the space detection and tracking system (SPADATS), and various air defense nets. The guiding principle in aerospace defense is to engage the enemy offensive forces as far out as possible and increase the pressure as he nears the target. In modern conflict, this kind of engagement requires systems with the range, speed, and controllability to provide defense against air, surface, and subsurface launched missiles; the airbreathing threat; and hostile satellites.

Passive defense measures also enhance our capability and resolve to oppose aggressive acts with whatever force required. Civil defense measures, including fallout shelters, can greatly increase the percentages of survivability. The location of military installations away from urban areas gives further protection to the population and makes counterforce operations more credible. Other passive defense measures are camouflage, mobility and dispersal of forces, and hardening of certain facilities—for example control centers and missile sites.

Survivable offensive and defensive forces are essential elements of strategic superiority and provide a credible general-war deterrent. Diversified offensive forces can provide numerous general-war options as well as contribute to the damage-limiting mission of our defensive forces. By demonstrating both the will and the capability to wage general war, even after we are attacked, we make our military posture credible and thereby enhance deterrence.

Limited Nuclear Operations

In attempting to achieve favorable resolution of conflicts below the level of general war or in its lower extremities, the United States may find it necessary to employ nuclear operations on a limited scale. The ultimate scope and intensity of these operations will, of course, depend on political considerations, along with such factors as the nature of the enemy forces and their nuclear capabilities, geographic factors, target characteristics, and probable collateral damage associated with particular actions.

There are a number of means to control the effects of nuclear weapons in limited operations, including selectivity in the character of targets, the size of weapon yields, the numbers and type of weapons, the height of burst, and delivery methods. In addition, decision-makers may employ limited strategic nuclear operations against highly selective enemy heartland targets or use tactical nuclear operations to carry out tactical tasks within a limited battle area.

It is essential that limited strategic nuclear operations be conducted in a manner to clearly indicate to the enemy that his national survival is not in jeopardy. Such operations demonstrate our resolve to raise the ante in a given situation. In this way, they offer a useful alternative to high-intensity general war or to protracted conventional conflict against massive enemy forces.

To illustrate how limited strategic nuclear operations can be effectively employed, we should consider illustrations representative of current conflict possibilities. In the first example, assume that a determined thrust has been made by an aggressor with the objective of overrunning a region occupied by our Allies—Western Europe, for example. In this case a decision to engage in large-scale conventional or localized nuclear warfare could be unacceptable to our Allies. Either of these alternatives, while representing a limited conflict to the United States, could jeopardize the national survival of those countries within the conflict arena. In a second situation, we could find the United States faced with the undesirable prospect of fighting a long, conventional conflict with a numerically superior enemy—Communist China, for example. Obviously, such an engagement would place a severe strain on our manpower, economy, and other resources. The situation could become intolerable in view of our other world-wide commitments and the necessity to maintain a credible general-war posture to counter the Soviet threat.

In both of the above examples, limited strategic nuclear operations, carefully tailored to fit the situation, offer an attractive alternative to end the conflict favorably. Precision attacks on certain high-value targets—hydroelectric facilities, oil refineries, or nuclear plants—might be carried out without significant reprisal, if the attacking nation possessed superior overall strategic power and if the use of force were keyed to the issues at stake. There are also a number of alternatives against an aggressor's military forces: a single sortie against a single target; a limited number of sorties against several diversified targets; attacks on targets of a particular type—bomber bases, antiballistic missile defenses, or submarine pens, among others. Each of these restrained operations is designed to convince the enemy that negotiations would be preferable to further escalation of the conflict, because of our obvious strategic superiority at the higher intensities.

Naturally, the risk of escalation to general war would be greater when conducting such operations against a highly capable nuclear enemy than when opposing a clearly inferior one. However, limited strategic nuclear operations do offer alternatives to high-intensity warfare and, therefore, represent potentially useful options against all opponents regardless of their capabilities.

Tactical Nuclear Operations

Tactical nuclear operations can provide additional courses of action to permit resolution of conflict below the general-war level. Restricting the use of nuclear weapons to a limited battle zone has the added advantage of avoiding risks associated with heartland attacks. In addition to demonstrating capability and resolve, tactical nuclear operations provide a means to regain the initiative against overwhelming forces, combat an enemy who employs similar operations, and in certain situations, accomplish a given objective more efficiently than conventional methods with a resultant savings in lives and material.

For example, let us consider a crisis in which the enemy threatens to introduce massive conventional forces into a low-order conflict. Our intelligence sources have identified large troop concentrations massed along a border adjacent to the combat zone, and our national authorities have evaluated the activities of these forces as preparatory to entering the conflict. The demonstrative detonation of a single tactical nuclear weapon, in an unoccupied area that is in full view of the enemy forces, could influence the aggressor to re-evaluate the consequences of his planned intervention.

In a similar situation, where topography restricts enemy movements, tactical nuclear weapons could be used to seal off a mountain pass, thus denying access, as well as demonstrating resolve. If these measures do not succeed in deterring aggression, then tactical nuclear operations could be directly employed against conventionally deployed forces to gain or regain the advantage. A credible tactical nuclear capability, backed by obvious superiority, to conduct high-intensity warfare could also deter the employment of similar operations by a nuclear-armed opponent. In the event an aggressor initiates tactical nuclear operations, our ability to successfully counter such action could influence conflict termination at a level below general war. On the other hand, if we initiate tactical nuclear operations against a nuclear opponent who is conventionally deployed, he will probably withdraw, because of his vulnerable position, or escalate to maximum use of nuclear weapons in the battle zone. For this reason, effective survivability measures for friendly forces are of primary importance. Alert and dispersal techniques can provide added protection. These include mobility, concealment, effective command and control capabilities, ground-to-air defense, and a large number of possible locations for each aircraft and missile. Mutual recognition of sanctuaries by the combatants can provide added survivability to both sides but also increases the problem of gaining control of the conflict, since the operating bases may not be subject to attack.

It may be necessary to employ a combination of conventional and nuclear weapons in accomplishing tactical tasks—for example, in supporting ground forces in close contact with the enemy or in destroying certain types of targets.

Conventional Air Operations

The attempts of our nation to achieve limited objectives at the lowest possible level of conflict and the increased Communist pressures in lower intensity warfare may well be attributed to a mutual interest in avoiding nuclear conflict. The increasing likelihood of conventional conflicts has generated increased emphasis on improving our conventional capabilities and strategies.

Conventional warfare, like nuclear warfare, can occur in a wide range of intensities. Similarly, its operations are designed to oppose an aggressor's military capabilities. However, conventional conflicts are normally viewed in terms of lengthy wars of maneuver and attrition, as compared to the short, decisive character of nuclear engagements. For this reason, the adversary possessing the greatest staying power in terms of national resolve, manpower, resources, productive capacity, and economic potential will most probably prevail. An in-being conventional military capability must also be recognized as an important factor. Germany's victorious three-week air and *Panzer* assault on Poland in 1939 readily illustrates a need for this requirement.

In conventional warfare, heartland industrial complexes may emerge as lucrative targets because of the necessity to deplete the enemy's national capacity to endure a long-term engagement. Therefore, such conflicts could develop into high-intensity warfare in terms of property destruction and casualties. On the other hand, there can be a mutual interest in keeping the conflict limited. This may lead to the recognition of sanctuaries or safe zones, which would have a significant effect on the nature of military operations. Rear supply areas, controlling headquarters, and supporting air bases may be located within the safe zones. The nature of such restraints would deny airpower access, in varying degrees, to enemy resources located in the sterile areas. This can cause a corresponding degradation in the overall effectiveness of the air campaign.

Air Superiority

Of all the tactical tasks, counterair must be given the highest priority, until air superiority is achieved. This is not to imply that the other strike tasks of close air support and interdiction are not important. However, they cannot be fully effective until control of air space is achieved. Once air superiority is established, a considerable amount of the air effort used in this role may be diverted to increase the magnitude of interdiction and close air support operations. The inherent flexibility in tactical air power permits this shift from one task to another with little or no decrease in efficiency.

To achieve air superiority it may be necessary to strike missile sites, selected command and control elements, and air bases, in addition to air-to-air engagement of enemy offensive and defensive forces. If sanctuary is permitted near the battle zone, then air superiority can be difficult to achieve and maintain, since enemy operating bases may be excluded from attack. Even if air superiority is achieved, a permissive environment in the battle area may not exist because of the presence of surface-to-air missiles and other enemy ground-to-air capabilities.

In supporting friendly troops, it is essential that air operations be responsive to close support requests, since the outcome of the battle may depend on how quickly strike aircraft can reach the target area. After arriving in the battle zone, aircraft must be able to deliver accurate and concentrated firepower, often in close proximity to friendly troops. This requires a high degree of coordination with the fire and maneuver of the ground forces, and is achieved through an integrated tactical air control system. Air Force forward air controllers, either airborne or accompanying ground forces, direct attacks by communicating directly with the strike aircraft. In South Vietnam, the accuracy and effectiveness of this system has been demonstrated many times. Friendly forces in close contact with the enemy have attested to its accuracy by stating that they could feel the heat and blast effects of ordnance dropped on the hostile forces.

Interdiction

Interdiction operations also support ground forces by restricting the moment of enemy forces into, from, or within the land-battle areas. Strikes against troop and supply concentration points may extend from the immediate area of the battle zone to deep missions within enemy territory, as required. The flow of men and matériel along the enemy lines of communication can be disrupted by destroying bridges, marshaling yards, and other targets facilitating resupply. The effects of an interdiction program will be difficult to determine in the initial stages, and successful operations will require concentrated effort over an extended period. Attacks against war-supporting strategic targets can also reduce the flow of matériel and thus complement the interdiction program. Sanctuaries, which contain these strategic targets and important lines of communication, will have an adverse effect on the interdiction effort. However, a concentrated effort in the strike zones that are not under constraint can still have a reasonable degree of success. Another influencing factor is the nature of the land battle. If friendly forces are able to actively engage the enemy continuously, his rate of logistical consumption will increase and combined with the air efforts, can deplete his reserves or reduce them to a critical level.

Air Reconnaissance and Airlift

To provide information concerning the structure, strength, movement, disposition, capability, and location of enemy forces, it is essential to have an efficient air reconnaissance capability. This intelligence data is essential to ground and air commanders and must be provided on a timely basis to permit rapid response to enemy tactics and strategy. Aerial surveillance of contiguous or sanctuary areas can reveal enemy activities on which to base future decisions. It also deprives the enemy of the opportunity for surprise in any escalation attempt.

In view of its world-wide commitments, it is essential that the United States be able to rapidly deploy large numbers of troops and matériel to any potential crisis zone. Strategic airlift is designed to accomplish this deployment and to provide subsequent resupply to the theater area. Strategic airlift may also augment tactical airlift's primary intratheater mission, as required. The primary objective of all airlift forces is the rapid, secure, and economical delivery to the final user with a minimum of aerial transshipments. This may require landings on hastily prepared, rough airstrips in forward areas. Alternate delivery methods include air-drop or ground-extraction techniques (in the latter method, the aircraft is flown to within a few feet of the terrain and a ground-extraction device pulls the payload out of a rear opening in the fuselage). Aerial resupply, under the most primitive conditions, is a vital element of the coordinated effort of air and ground forces.

Command and Control

To ensure the maximum effectiveness of conventional air operations, it is essential that command and/or service interests not divide aerospace forces among different controlling interests. Control must be centralized at levels high enough to ensure the coordinated application of air power in response to the varying demands of the composite combat zone. At the same time the control systems must be flexible enough to permit decentralization of authority during actual execution.

It is also important to recognize the interrelation of strategic and tactical systems during conventional operations. The heaviest requirement will normally be placed on tactical forces since their flexibility, range, and firepower permit them to perform multiple tasks throughout the battle zone. However, it may be necessary to use strategic forces on conventional missions requiring concentration of firepower and ranges that may be impracticable or uneconomical with tactical systems. In any case, a credible nuclear-deterrent posture must be preserved and continue to receive the highest priority in determining the extent of the role of strategic forces in conventional operations.

Peacetime and Counterinsurgency Operations

Aerospace forces can enhance deterrence and national prestige by conducting peacetime operations to demonstrate military and technological capabilities to other nations. For example, space achievements, weapons demonstrations, record flights, and similar operations reflect the potential of national power. In times of crisis, national will and intentions may be communicated through increased alert, shows of force, deployments, and prehostility surveillance. These methods have been successfully employed in a number of crises—for instance, Lebanon in 1958, Berlin in 1961, and Thailand and Cuba in 1962—to achieve limited objectives. National influence can also be exerted through direct assistance to other countries by conducting humanitarian missions, providing advice and aid to the air forces of friendly nations, and assisting in civic actions.

The latter activities come under the category of special air warfare operations and are required to deal with guerrilla or insurgency activities. There is really nothing unique about guerrilla warfare. In fact, the term "guerrilla," meaning "little war," was used during Napoleon's Peninsular Campaign in Spain. The difference between the older term "guerrilla warfare" and the newer term "insurgency" is in deliberately planned exploitation by Communist powers for purposes of subversion and eventual world conquest.

COIN

Insurgency is normally defined as a condition resulting from a revolt or insurrection against a duly organized government—but falling short of civil war. Insurgency movements seek to develop local support and external aid for subversive action against the organized government with the objective of supplanting it. Special air warfare actions to combat insurgency are called counterinsurgency (COIN) operations. They include those military, paramilitary, political, economic, psychological, and civic actions taken by a government to defeat subversive insurgency. Insurgency movements that are Communist-inspired or manipulated are identified by the U.S.S.R. and Red China as "wars of liberation" or "people's revolutions." The Communists have chosen this method as a means of exporting their ideology because of our deterrent capability in the higher levels of conflict. Also, many of the emerging nations of the world offer ideal conditions for insurgency, which the Communists can exploit to further their own goals. Factors that make certain nations ripe for Communist exploitation include an agricultural society with little or no industry, political instability, substandard social conditions, and a shortage of technical skills and facilities. The Communists exploit these conditions by fomenting dissatisfaction with the slow processes of economic and social progress and by organizing a "revolutionary" force within the target nation.

Counterinsurgency operations are designed to provide aid to assistance-seeking nations through a dual-purpose program. First, nation-building activities are designed to improve the political, economic, and social structure of the nation. Air power can contribute by improving transportation and communications to remote areas, expanding public health and educational services, training the populace in technical and manual skills, and eliminating distrust among population segments and between the people and the military. Second, through military-oriented activities we can provide training, advice, and aid to indigenous forces to increase internal security against insurgent elements. It may be necessary to actively assist in fighting insurgency that has developed to the organized stages. The active engagement of regular forces in support of, and in opposition to, insurgent groups can raise the level of intensity to a lower form of conventional warfare. The objective of military-oriented COIN activities is to provide an environment that will permit the accelerated progress of nation-building efforts.

The guilding principle in pursuing national objectives is to limit military force to those systems and intensities appropriate for the specific issues at stake. Military forces must be used in a manner that denies the aggressor his objectives—through persuasion or by destroying only those forces necessary to achieve satisfactory war termination. In some instances, it may be necessary to increase the intensity of conflict to signal our national resolve to prevent the success of an act of or a threat of aggression. This build-up requires superior, usable capabilities to provide the graduated escalation necessary to convince an enemy that each escalatory step moves him toward an increasingly critical disadvantage. In sum, we must have controllable forces which can provide a flexible response to any level of aggression, supported by strategic superiority at the highest level of conflict, if we are to ensure a credible deterrent posture for the future.

Appendix I

WAR DEPARTMENT
Office of the Chief Signal Officer
Washington

August 1, 1907

OFFICE MEMORANDUM NO. 6

An Aeronautical Division of this office is hereby established, to take effect this date.

This division will have charge of all matters pertaining to military ballooning, air machines, and all kindred subjects. All data on hand will be carefully classified and plans perfected for future tests and experiments. The operations of this division are strictly confidential, and no information will be given out by any party except through the Chief Signal Officer of the Army or his authorized representative.

Captain Charles DeF. Chandler, Signal Corps, is detailed in charge of this division, and Corporal Edward Ward and First-Class Private Joseph E. Barrett will report to Captain Chandler for duty in this division under his immediate direction.

> J. ALLEN,
> *Brigadier General,*
> *Chief Signal Officer of the Army.*

Appendix II

USAF Active Major Installations

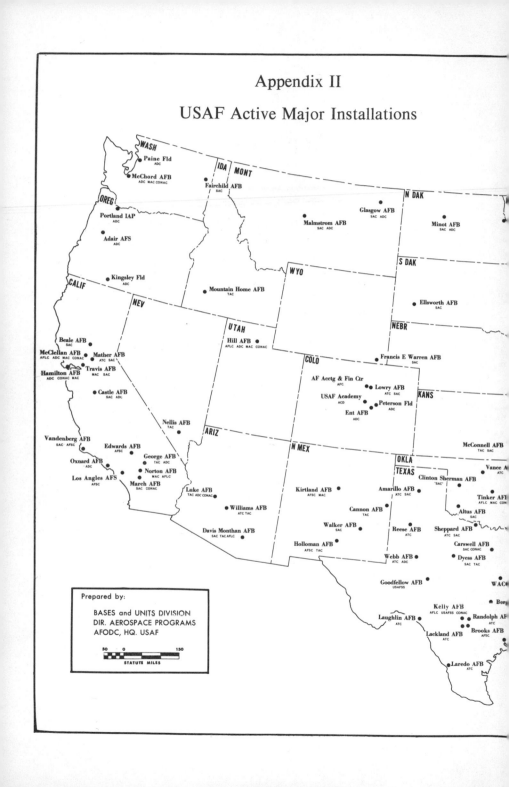

Prepared by:

BASES and UNITS DIVISION
DIR. AEROSPACE PROGRAMS
AFODC, HQ. USAF

50   0   150

STATUTE MILES

Appendix III

USAF Major Installations Outside Continental U.S.

NORTH - CENTRAL AMERICA - ATLANTIC

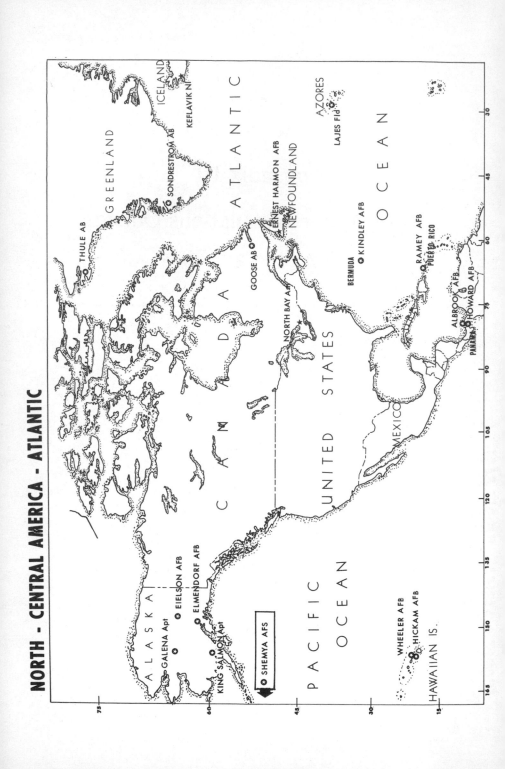

EUROPE - AFRICA - MIDDLE EAST

UNION OF SOVIET SOCIALIST REPUBLICS

ESTONIA
LATVIA
LITHUANIA
POLAND
CZECHOSLOVAKIA
AUSTRIA
HUNGARY
RUMANIA
BULGARIA
YUGOSLAVIA
ALBANIA
GREECE
TURKEY
SYRIA
IRAQ
LEBANON
ISRAEL
JORDAN
U.A.R.
LIBYA
ALGERIA
MOROCCO
SPAIN
PORTUGAL
FRANCE
ITALY
SICILY
SARDINIA
TUNISIA
CRETE
CYPRUS

BALTIC SEA
BLACK SEA
MEDITERRANEAN SEA

U. K.

ANKARA ASN
INCIRLIK AB
CIGLI AB
ATHENAI Apt
AVIANO AB
WHEELUS AB
SABINA
TORREJON AB
MORON AB
ZARAGOZA AB
CHATEAUROUX Asn
CHAUMONT AB
DREUX AB
EVREUX FAUVILLE AB
LAON AB
ETAIN AB
CHAMBLEY AB
TOUL ROSIERES AB
PHALSBOURG AB
RAMSTEIN AB
SEMBACH AB
RHEIN MAIN AB
WIESBADEN AB
LINDSEY Apt
HAHN AB
BITBURG AB
SPANGDAHLEM AB
NEW AMSTERDAM AB
CP
TEMPLEHOF Apt
WOODBRIDGE RAF
WETHERSFIELD RAF
BENTWATERS RAF
MILDENHALL RAF
LAKENHEATH RAF
RUISLIP Asn
So.
ALCONBURY RAF
UPPER HEYFORD RAF
PRESTWICK Afd

30
15
0
50
35

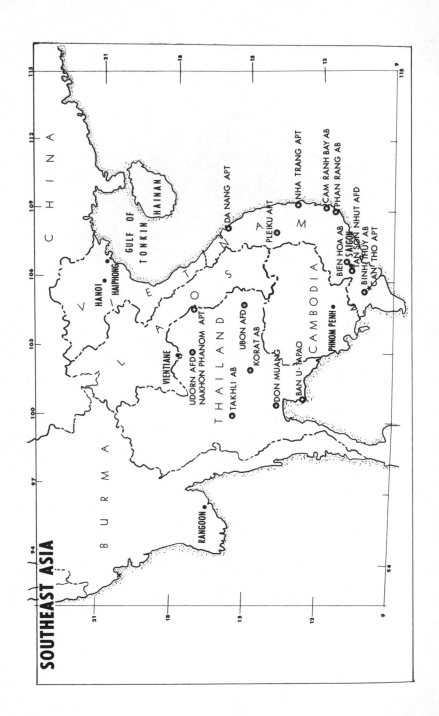

SOUTHEAST ASIA

PACIFIC AREA

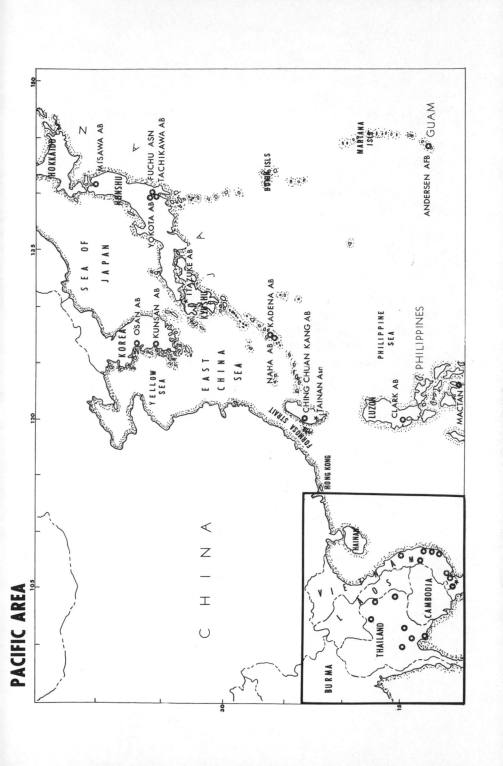

Appendix IV

Paths to Leadership in the United States Air Force

As a general rule, pilots and navigators must be awarded commissions before they reach the age of twenty-six and one-half years. For other categories, the age is usually thirty. The several ways young men (and various experienced specialists) can obtain commissions in the United States Air Force are as follows:

OFFICER TRAINING SCHOOL (OTS) Lackland Air Force Base, Texas

Airman Education and Commissioning Program

Enlisted airmen who at the time of enlistment hold degrees from accredited institutions of higher learning may apply for the three-month OTS program at Lackland, which leads to award of reserve second lieutenancies. *Enlisted airmen* who at time of enlistment have approximately two years of college credit may be sent to civilian colleges and universities at government expense for completion of their degree requirements. After receiving degrees, they may be sent to OTS for the three-month OTS course and award of reserve second lieutenancies.

UNITED STATES AIR FORCE
ACADEMY
Colorado Springs, Colorado

Unmarried high school graduates, 17–22 years old, may apply for admission by congressional or presidential appointment to the Air Force Academy at Colorado Springs, Colorado, where they receive at government expense four years of military/ academic training. Upon graduation they receive a B.S. degree and are appointed second lieutenants (regular commission) in the United States Air Force.

AIR FORCE RESERVE OFFICER
TRAINING CORPS (AFROTC)

College and university students who complete Air Force Reserve Officer Training Corps programs at participating institutions around the country receive appointments as reserve second lieutenants.*

COMMISSIONS FOR OUTSTANDING
RESERVE AIRMEN

A limited number of *airmen who have completed active-duty* tours as enlisted men and join reserve units may be recommended by their reserve unit commanders for award of reserve commissions as second lieutenants, first lieutenants, and captains, depending on age and experience.

DIRECT COMMISSIONS
FOR SPECIALISTS

Direct reserve commissions are awarded to members of *various professional specialties* such as physicians, lawyers, male and female nurses, dentists, dietitians, and physiotherapists.*

* In addition to reserve commissions, a limited number of regular Air Force commissions are awarded to AFROTC officers who have been classified as distinguished graduates and, in a few cases, to members of professional specialties receiving direct commissions. For specific details on latest Air Force policies, readers should inquire at U.S. Air Force recruiting offices in their localities or obtain information from campus AFROTC officials.

Bibliography

The following books are of particular interest to the student wishing to read more about the U.S. Air Force:

The American Heritage History of Flight. New York: American Heritage Publishing Co., 1962. Flying—from ancient dreams to modern realities.

ARNOLD, H. H. *Global Mission*. New York: Harper & Bros., 1949. An operational memoir by the commander of the Army Air Forces in World War II.

BONNEY, WALTER T. *The Heritage of Kitty Hawk*. New York: W. W. Norton & Co., 1962. Aviation from the Wright brothers through World War I.

CLARKE, ARTHUR C. *The Exploration of Space*. Rev. ed. New York: Harper & Row, 1959. Highly readable layman's guide to the space age.

CRAVEN, WESLEY F., and CATE, JAMES L. (eds.). *The Army Air Forces in World War II*. 7 vols. Chicago: University of Chicago Press, 1958. The official history.

DORNBERGER, WALTER. *V-2*. New York: Viking Press, 1954. An account by the director of Germany's World War II rocket program of the research and development that led to deployment of the first modern military missiles.

DOWNS, LIEUTENANT COLONEL ELDON W. *The U.S. Air Force in Space*. New York: Frederick A. Praeger, 1966. Authoritative account of present Air Force space programs and support of NASA efforts.

EMME, EUGENE M. (ed.). *The Impact of Air Power.* Princeton, N.J.: D. Van Nostrand Co., 1959. An anthology on various aspects of aviation and its influence on military affairs.

FUTRELL, ROBERT F. *The United States Air Force in Korea, 1950–1953.* New York: Duell, Sloan and Pearce, 1961.

GLINES, CARROLL V. *The Compact History of the United States Air Force.* New York: Hawthorne Books, 1963. An informally told story of the Air Force, with illustrative sketches.

GOLDBERG, ALFRED. *A History of the United States Air Force. 1907–1957.* Princteon, N.J.: D. Van Nostrand Co., 1957. A well-docu mented account of the U.S. Air Force and its predecessor se vices.

LEMAY, CURTIS E., and KANTOR, MACKINLAY. *Mission with LeMay: My Story.* New York: Doubleday & Co., 1965.

LEVINE, ISAAC DON. *Mitchell, Pioneer of Air Power.* New York: Duell, Sloan and Pearce, 1943. The story of the controversial General "Billy" Mitchell and his fight for recognition of air power.

LOOSBROCK, JOHN F., and SKINNER, RICHARD M. (eds.). *The Wild Blue: The Story of American ᵼ irpower.* New York: G. P. Putnam's Sons, 1961. An anthology of pieces from *Air Force Magazine* by contributors ranging from Orville Wright to MacKinlay Kantor.

ROSEBERRY, C. R. *The Challenging Skies.* New York. Doubleday & Co., 1966. Illustrated account of aviation's exciting years between World Wars I and II.

SCHWIEBERT, ERNEST G. *The History of the U.S.A.F. Ballistic Missiles.* New York: Frederick A. Praeger, 1964.

SKINNER, RICHARD M., and LEAVITT, WILLIAM (eds.). *Air Force and Space Digest. Speaking of Space.* Boston: Little, Brown and Co., 1962. An anthology presenting the views of scholars and officials on the impact of the space age.

For specialized information about the role of bombing in World War II, the U. S. *Strategic Bombing Survey* documents are available at most large libraries.

Index